Golden Frog Poison a Game of Twins Thriller

**A Thriller By
Tom Ranseen**

A note from the author

This book is a work of fiction. Names, characters, businesses, locales, events, and incidents are either the products of the author's imagination or used in a fictitious manner. Any resemblance to actual persons, living or dead, or actual events or locales is entirely coincidental.

Version 2- Sept 2024; the original ebook version was published in December 2023; the paperback version is also available. *Golden Frog Poison – Game of Twins* is the third novel in my thriller series, *Game of Twins,* and occurs in present time. This is the sequel to *Game of Twins* and *Game of Twins - Kidnapped.* In addition, there is a prequel to the series, *Game of Twins – The Special Agent*, that occurs in the 20th century.

For more information, please go to www.gameoftwins.com

Golden Frog Poison © Copyright by Tom Ranseen

Paperback ISBN-1-7324120-8-8

Table of Contents

A note from the author i
Author bio 268
Preface iv
PART I 1
Chapter 1 – The Game's Not Over 2
Chapter 2 – The Deadliest Poison 8
Chapter 3 – Lazlo 13
Chapter 4 – Oh, The Lies 18
Chapter 5 – Gary 27
Chapter 6 – Her Twins 35
Chapter 7 – Suzy & Lazlo 43
Chapter 8 – Kip Returns 52
Chapter 9 – Sinaloa 62
Chapter 10 – Dr. Jill 66
Chapter 11 – Sting 74
PART II 87
Chapter 12 – The Three 88
Chapter 13 – Kings & Queens 99
Chapter 14 – The Next Victim 101
Chapter 15 – Mary Jo 104
Chapter 16 – The Rainforest Hunter 111
Chapter 17 – The Journey to Durham 119
Chapter 18 – On The Run 128
Chapter 19 -- The Backup 134
Chapter 20 -- The Only Way to Fly 136

Episode 21 -- Dinner on Patricia..141

Chapter 22 -- The Detective..148

Chapter 23 – The Warrior..159

Chapter 24 – Suzanne the Assassin 168

Chapter 25 – The Man with the Midas Touch..........................175

PART III 181

Chapter 26 – Gary Redux 182

Chapter 27 – Missing..188

Chapter 28 - Ted Bundy...193

Chapter 29 – The Objective..200

Chapter 30 – James Bond 204

Chapter 31 – The Bait..209

Chapter 32 -The Freezer Killer..215

PART IV..231

Chapter 33 – Spain...232

Chapter 34 – Las Ventas..245

Chapter 35 - The Bullfights 256

Chapter 36 - A Deal With the Devil 260

Epilogue 266

Preface

a poison thriller that's anything but cozy...

Of course, the unrivaled Queen of Crime mysteries and Queen of Poisons is Agatha Christie, who killed off three dozen characters in 66 books with lots of poisons like Arsenic, Strychnine, Thallium, Ricin, Cyanide, Digitalis, Atropine, Belladonna, etc. Her books are whodunit, cozy mystery masterpieces – many laced with deaths by poison.

Like the three books*** before it, this a fast-paced, fun thriller mystery with lots of action, suspense, violence, and intrigue—with some occult, supernatural, and sex sprinkled in. It's not exactly a "cozy" mystery.

The dark *Game of Twins* backdrop is a story of revenge and an epic struggle between Good and Evil born of an event that happened four centuries ago, mushroomed in the era of J. Edgar Hoover, and then revved up again in the twenty-first century. And here we are with *Golden Frog Poison* – a *Game of Twins* story.

It's the 4th book in my *Game of Twins* series, but it reads great as a standalone and includes enough info from the earlier books to add plot context. Deadly golden frog poison plays a small role in two previous novels but is promoted to the star-of-the-show in this one.

Perhaps Agatha knew of golden frog poison – or perhaps not? Though, milliliter per milliliter, it is deadlier than any of her poisons by a factor of more than a hundred. If she did know of it, it's so rare, that it might not have fit well with her plots. While her poisons can be relatively easily tested for, it takes Gas or Liquid Chromatography-Mass Spectrometry to identify the active neurotoxin, batrachotoxin, in golden frog poison.

But I don't want to get too far ahead. Read on for much more about the deadliest animal poison there is. To my knowledge, golden frog poison has never played any role in any work of fiction. So, I figured it was about time that it did.

Enjoy!

Tom Ranseen

****Game of Twins - The Special Agent, Game of Twins, Game of Twins – Kidnapped, and Golden Frog Poison – Game of Twins are all available as eBooks on Amazon and other platforms.*

I took only a few minutes of hit-and-miss looks throughout the book copy, which seems okay, but your work on this book so far is pretty sloppy and worries me. I will do another review of the copy tomorrow.

GOLDEN FROG POISON A GAME OF TWINS THRILLER

PART I

TOM RANSEEN

Chapter 1 – The Game's Not Over

Her Galaxy alarm on the nightstand went off at 6:15 AM. A clip of her favorite muse, Eva Cassidy. Her beautiful *Fields of Gold* verse: "Will you stay with me; will you be my love...upon the fields of barley." Kip loved it, too.

Next to her, Kip was sound asleep. The bed was cozy, but she was playing golf today and had an 8:30 AM tee time in Eastlake's Women's Club Championship. Last night, she'd told her husband she'd drop their Welsh Terrier, Lilly, at the groomers on her way south. She leaned down to kiss him, reminding him, "Get Lilly by noon."

He mumbled, "Yes, mam. I'm getting up in a few minutes. Good luck, babe. Love you."

Suzanne suited up to do battle on the best golf course she'd ever played – something she'd never taken for granted. She was proud to be a member -- thanks to her father's legacy as a black Atlanta police officer who rose to second in command at APD. By the 1970s, Eastlake had fallen into severe disrepair, but by 1990, the once grand course where golfing icon Bobby Jones honed his skills had been rescued – after millions of dollars of renovations. The club, which now costs $300,00 to join (with a long waiting list if you're lucky enough to have a sponsor), is home to one of golf's premier events, the FedEx Championship, with its whopping $18 million first prize.

But better—much better – the prestigious tournament and the PGA helped raise enough money to establish a phenomenal free private school for underprivileged kids in South Atlanta. Their competitive girls' and boys' golf teams are always welcome at Eastlake. After all that happened a few years back, Suzanne was invited to speak at last year's school commencement. She knew she'd start with tears, but after wiping them away, she gathered herself and got a standing ovation. Looking at the young black and brown faces, her message was: "Life is good. All of you deserve a chance. Don't ever be afraid to take that next step."

Dressed in a hot pink sleeveless top and matching short shorts, she checked herself out in the full-length mirror. Statuesque at just under six feet tall and curves in all the right places. Flowing, pitch-black hair and caramel-colored, flawless skin from her Black father and Chinese mother. Not bad, she said. Her twin stepdaughters encouraged her to show it when you got it. You're hot. Go for it. Three years ago, at the age of forty-four, she'd been named *Atlanta Magazine's* most beautiful female across all age groups and ethnicities. Not an honor she'd sought but hard not to enjoy. After years of being Atlanta Police Department's top homicide cop, her star had shown even brighter when she solved the century of twins murders; she barely survived a deadly attack from Pamela Loncart's brother and cousin; she rescued her stepdaughter twins who'd been kidnapped; she killed her nemesis in a battle royale on the Salt Flats of Bonneville in Utah. It all seemed like a lifetime ago.

She bent over and gave her slumbering hubby another peck on his forehead. She smiled. She knew she was the luckiest woman on the planet. Her husband of five years and her intelligent, lovely stepdaughters gave her countless reasons for living.

She made a quick cup of Starbucks Pike Place and grabbed a banana to eat. She felt a little nervous and smiled. A positive sign that she was engaged. She'd played in a few big amateur women's tournaments when she was young, but these days, she was going up against some girls whose parents were members. They were frighteningly skilled and played way beyond her best.

But God, she loved to compete.

****

While Suzanne Delacroix was playing the 3rd hole at Eastlake, her husband, Kip Davies, was in the lower level of their home examining the agates he'd recently found in his favorite spot north of Gainesville.

He picked a couple to break open with his rock hammer and chisel. He loved the surprise. The first had spectacular swirls of orange, yellow, white, and rust. He secured it and cut eighth-of-an-inch slices with his diamond saw. Gorgeous! Later, he'd polish the agate slices to bring out even more of their beauty.

Kip was taking the day off to relax and putter around. Kip's law firm had done better than he could have imagined five years ago. For many years, considered the top criminal attorney in Atlanta, Kip had left his father's esteemed firm and attracted a crew of brilliant young attorneys who bought into his mantra: only clients we believe are innocent, and we can go to bat for. No drugs or cartel stuff. He turned down 80% of people desperate to be represented. He politely explained they could get their legal counsel elsewhere and gave many referrals to lawyers he knew were drooling for such cases.

While admiring one of his agate slices, the front doorbell rang. A bell dinged on all levels. Not bothering to wipe the rock dust off his hands, he bounded upstairs. He looked through the peephole. There stood a twenty-something dark-haired, well-groomed guy.

Kip told him, "Hit the button to talk."

"Yes, sir, I have a package for Suzanne Delacroix. Is she here?"

"No, but I'm her husband."

"Could you sign?"

"Sure."

"Perfect," the guy said.

Kip hit the 4-digit code to turn off the alarm code. He opened the door and stood in the doorway. The courier had a clipboard in hand. Kip thought, not very high-tech, probably a mom-and-pop. The courier extended his clipboard and then took a pen from his shirt pocket. But instead of handing it to him, he jammed the tiny, sharp point into the back of Kip's hand.

"What the fuck!" Kip yelled as the guy shoved him back from the doorway and shut the door. Kip tried to push back, but his legs buckled. He collapsed to the floor. He tried to move but couldn't.

The courier took surgical gloves from his pocket and pulled them on. From his other pocket, he removed a small box. Carefully, he extracted a small figurine from the box and placed it on the floor next to Davies. Thirty seconds later, his nondescript white van was gone from the driveway.

****

After a decent first round and lunch, Suzanne walked into the posh Eastlake Women's locker room and put her golf shoes in her locker. She'd take a shower when she got home. She called Kip to remind him again to pick up Lilly.

No answer. She left a short message. "Good news – Played well; shot 74. Bad news – I'm now five shots behind three hot-shot college girls. I'm leaving. Please text or call that you got Lilly. Thanks, S. Heading back north, through the guts of the increasingly congested city, the groomer called. "Ms. Delacroix, I'm sorry. I tried your husband but got no answer. We close at 3:00."

"Sorry. I'll be there in ten minutes."

Suzanne grew more annoyed as she drove to the groomer on the north side of Buckhead. Upon arrival, Lilly wore a cute pink bow and greeted her with kisses –and smelled great. Suzanne apologized profusely and left a 30% gratuity.

Before leaving the groomers, she tried Kip again. She tried to chill, but after only getting his voicemail, she was on the edge of going ballistic about her husband. She left a short message, "I just got Lilly. Better have a good excuse for not picking her up."

****

Suzanne Delacroix and Kip had plenty of money from her inheritance, book royalties, and Kip's legal work – which they tried not to flaunt. Except for their cars, including the cherry red Tesla Model 4 he bought for her last birthday. The most fun ride ever. Lilly always rode shotgun in any car, but the Tesla was her favorite.

More smoke billowed from her ears while she and her dog rocketed soundlessly northwest toward their condo. She was loaded for bear when she hit the garage remote. She was surprised to see that Kip's black BMW M8 was parked with his two "fun" antiques: his 1976 Porsche 911e and 1955 Chevrolet Convertible.

Lilly jumped out and sped up the stairs, barking louder than she'd ever heard.

Something wasn't right. A Glock and clips were in her Tesla's "frunk" (a Tesla front-end trunk). She grabbed the gun and slid a clip in. With two hands on the Glock, she ascended. She could tell by the pad on the wall that the security system was off. Puzzling. She eased open the door to the kitchen. There was no stopping her little terrier as she shot through. Then Lilly's barking became wailing.

She yelled, "Kip, you home?" Nothing.

"Kip?"

Lilly was in the foyer, standing over Kip and licking his face.

Her husband was on his back on the floor.

Suzanne shrieked, "Kip! Kip! God, please, No!"

She bent down to get a closer look. Unfortunately, she'd seen enough bodies to know he was dead. He was in the first stages of rigor with his face taught. No reason to check vitals. She knelt and kissed his cold lips. She picked up his right hand, covered with dust from his rock cutting and polishing. There was a tiny rivulet of dried blood on the back of his hand.

She saw no trauma. He'd been in perfect health. An MI? Maybe he was a ticking time bomb and blew his left main? A couple of friends of theirs who they played golf with - the guy ten years younger than Kip had a heart attack a few weeks ago. Or maybe he'd had a stroke? Lilly sat beside her, and Suzanne hugged her little dog harder than ever.

She wept; her dead husband lying before her. Nothing would change that. No reason to call 911 yet. She finally stood and, through her tears, noticed a small shiny figurine on the other side of his body. She sat down next to it.

A miniature replica, no more than an inch long.

Of the most toxic animal on the planet.

The golden poison frog. AKA the golden poison dart frog.

The word "revenge" blistered her brain. That's what the *Game* had always been about...

Chapter 2 - The Deadliest Poison

3 Years ago

On the Salt Flats of Bonneville outside Salt Lake City, with her dying breaths, Pamela Loncart admitted it was golden frog poison -- in the tiny, sharp-tipped cylinder she'd dropped during their epic mano-a-mano battle. Suzanne had no idea what she was grabbing and wasn't even sure she'd grazed Pamela's neck with the ampoule intended for her. But she did, and her nemesis was dead in less than a minute. Suzanne was glad about that - and that she hadn't touched the tip of the sharp glass object. Pamela's last words were strange: " golden frog poison. Mary Jo."

Suzanne told her heroic rescue bunch only that it was maybe a poison without being specific about the type. Any evidence was snatched up with Pamela Loncart's body and whisked away with her teenage boys on a private jet back to Mexico, where her longtime narco partner operated from—and where the former DEA agent had been living the past five years.

****

Suzanne had never heard of golden frog poison until Pamela Loncart said the words. After retrieving her stepdaughters, she had been curious about golden poison frogs and their potent toxin. The frogs are legendary and only live in forty square miles of the Pacific Coast Choco Rain Forest of Columbia, one of the wettest and most biodiverse areas on the planet, where the tiny frogs eat poisonous ants and insects that make them so deadly in the wild. Their brilliant colors vary by habitat and can be gold, yellow, copper, red, green, blue, or black. Deliberately flashy to warn—and ward off—potential predators, a tactic called "aposematic coloration."

GOLDEN FROG POISON A GAME OF TWINS THRILLER

The cute little frog emotes to a potential jungle predator, "Okay, I'm a little guy here wearing a bright color. I dare you. Go for it. Because there's something else if you try to touch or lick or, god forbid, eat me. Deadly poison."

Golden frog (Phyllobates terribilis) poison has been used for centuries on the tips of darts and shot from blowguns to kill animals of all types. One dart can stop a giant monkey – or, for that matter, a human, in its tracks. Hence, they are also called golden poison dart frogs.

Extracting poison from the frog's skin is a dangerous task at best. Indigenous people developed their time-tested, complex procedures. A captured frog must be handled with extreme care. Typically, it is stressed to emit toxin from its skin by touching it with a stick or introducing hot water. The toxin is carefully captured and put in a container. Then, it is used on the tip of hunting darts. Well stored, it can remain lethal for years.

The frog's extremely rare poison is a nerve agent called batrachotoxin, which causes paralysis and then cardiac arrest. It's off the toxicity charts. Nothing else in the animal kingdom is comparable. One of the little frog's skin is estimated to contain a dose that could kill twenty humans – or two African bull elephants. And it is sixty times more deadly than the same amount of cyanide or strychnine. There's no antidote.

In the wild, golden frogs can regenerate their toxin, but not in captivity, where they can't ingest indigenous poison ants and insects that, in turn, make their skins toxic. Harmless in captivity, golden frogs make unusual pets for amateur frog aficionados, and you can buy one for less than a hundred bucks.

Golden poison frogs are endangered – due to climate factors that have impacted their primary nourishment; their popularity for research (into nerve-related pain inhibitors); and collectors of rare frogs worldwide. Serious collectors who want the real poisonous version (versus a frog raised in captivity—that is not poisonous) pay $10,000 or more per frog.

****

Suzanne wanted to touch it and put the small golden figurine in her hand to examine it more closely. Then, fling it against a wall or crush it under her foot. She reached for it, but something told her to stop. Could the figurine be coated with the golden frog poison? She'd read the poison could remain deadly on any surface for many months. A double murder in the foyer of her own home? Kill Kip and make her suffer – then kill her with the same toxin. It felt like she was back in the *Game of Twins* that had been driven by revenge since the late 1600s – a game that had escalated beyond the periodic sacrificing of female twins.

She raced back down to the garage and got surgical gloves from the first aid kit in the trunk of her Tesla. Then ran up to her bedroom to get a jewelry box. The shimmering star sapphire ring didn't need it—and she put it aside.

She snapped a few pictures of the figurine beside Kip with her phone. She put the golden frog into the jewelry box with her gloves on. She'd investigated dozens of sneaky places where people hid things they wanted to keep private. Heck, this wasn't even a murder investigation for APD, and she intended to keep it that way. She could have gotten sneakier but buried the jewelry box in the sugar canister on her kitchen counter. She didn't stop there.

She surmised the tiny blood spot on Kip's hand was where the murderer had pricked him with a sharp object covered with poison. With a paper towel, she gently dabbed the coagulated blood drip from his hand. She looked closely and could barely see the spot since his hand was covered by rock dust.

Suzanne knew she'd already interfered with a murder crime scene – something she'd never done as an APD detective. However, that illegality had crossed her mind more than a few times to catch a bad guy. Her thoughts swirled. Her internal chatterbox revved on hyperdrive. Her precious husband had been murdered. No question. And her usually calm brain was careening off the rails.

She'd bet her house that the figurine was coated with poison, but she needed to find out. Would Raoul Menendez be surprised or disappointed that she wasn't already dead? Atlanta's well-regarded M.E. wouldn't be able to identify the rare animal poison that killed Kip using any standard or high-level tox screens. She'd think it was some cardiac event or other underlying health problem that killed Kip – unless Suzanne gave her a heads-up on what she knew to be true. If the poison had been found and Suzanne had been the only person in the house, that might not have played well if it were determined he was murdered around the time she'd left for golf. But she didn't give a damn about that right now.

****

Kip's death would make local, regional, and national news sooner than later. He was a well-known top criminal attorney in Atlanta. But more importantly, unfortunately, the hoopla would be because of her celebrity. She knew that her risqué modeling photos and photos of her stepdaughters after being captured in Mexico would resurface on millions of screens. The stories of Suzanne's hunt to find the murderers of twin teenagers over a century and the subsequent tale of rescuing her kidnapped stepdaughters—written by Atlanta investigative reporter Bobby Price – fascinated millions and were still on the *New York Times Nonfiction Best-Seller List.* Netflix and Amazon wanted to buy the rights to dramatize her stories; the offers to each had risen to eight figures. She and Bobby hadn't made decisions on that. Regardless, a portion of the royalties paid by Penguin Random House kept flowing in. If any of those big companies saw the potential for another sequel, the money could skyrocket. The thought of profiting from her husband's death almost made her vomit.

There would be plenty of publicity, regardless. Still, if it were known that Kip had been murdered using golden frog poison, the brouhaha would be deafening – especially for her twin stepdaughters. If this next installment of the *Game of Twins* started with her husband's murder, she realized there would be no way to escape the glare of worldwide publicity – which might last for a long time.

She sat on her living room sofa and did a couple of minutes of relaxation meditation. As she arose, her thoughts grew clearer. If Kip's murder came to light, there would never be direct proof to catch the person who ordered it even the figurine would be a valuable clue if it were smeared with golden frog toxin. The narco-murderer was so rich and powerful as to be untouchable.

Now what?

She wasn't sure.

Chapter 3 – Lazlo

Deputy Chief of Robbery Homicide, Lazlo Kianian, was in his office at the Atlanta Police Department headquarters cussing out a serial, civil rights-abuser homicide detective who had screwed up a good case yet again; the idiot broke into a home in an upscale predominantly black neighborhood without a search warrant. Lazlo was so loud that his admin, Molly, opened his door – a sign he needed to chill. The detective cowered out, and Molly shut the door.

To say that Lazlo was a good-looking guy was a serious understatement. His dad was a striking, dark-haired Jew whose parents moved to the U.S. from Israel, and his mom a drop-dead American blonde. He stood six-three and had muted but hawk-like features and a mildly dark complexion. Broad shoulders, slender waist, well-muscled. But not only that, he also had his mother's gorgeous blonde hair. Girls had been chasing him since he was four years old. Girls and guys since he was a teenager. As an only child in the Atlanta burbs, Lazlo had a happy childhood but hated getting bounced between his mom's hoity-toity Baptist church and his dad's synagogue He considered compromising and converting to Judaism but quickly nixed that after hearing about brit milah.

He graduated at the top of his senior high school class and then went to Georgia Tech. He graduated summa cum laude with a major in Biomedical Engineering. Upon graduation, he had more than a dozen job offers, several in the six figures to start. He also had full-ride graduate school offers from Cal Tech, Carnegie Melon, and MIT – and was a Rhodes finalist. At Tech he was a good lacrosse player who was comfortable with jocks and nerds alike. At age twenty-one, the world was his oyster. But a week after his cap-and-gown ceremony at Bobby Dodd Stadium, he got dealt a new hand when his dad was gunned down in a convenience store on his way back from a Braves game. Lazlo often attended games with his dad, but that night he was at a raucous Tech post-graduation party a couple of miles from Piedmont Hospital, where his dad died.

TOM RANSEEN

To the shock and dismay of family and friends, he entered the Atlanta Police Academy and became a cop. And ranked first in everything. He made himself a promise to solve the cold case murder of his dad and get justice his own way. A year after becoming a cop, and not yet a detective yet, he made good on that promise.

He made detective at age 26, joining his mentor Dusty Rayfield, and Dusty's mentor, Suzanne Delacroix, as the youngest detectives in the history of the Atlanta Police Department. When Dusty was assassinated in front of Suzanne in the mountains of north Georgia, Lazlo was all in on her audacious plan to bring his killer to justice and help rescue her kidnapped stepdaughters. Brilliantly, Suzanne accomplished that mission with him and four others – which he realized could end his career. They'd not only bent but also broken several laws. But Suzanne had figured out how to get them all off the hook. Instead of losing his job, Lazlo got promoted to the post held by his mentor and years ago by Suzanne's father, Hollis.

At age thirty-seven, Lazlo Kianian wasn't married and never had been. At a hoity-toity benefit auction at the High Museum of Art last year, the bidding for Atlanta's most eligible bachelor went bananas. He was purchased for $85,000 for a one-evening date. Lazlo liked females and had enjoyed more than his share of beautiful women. A couple he even imagined marrying. But couldn't pull the trigger. That reticence got much worse after he and Suzanne were in life-and-death situations in Nashville and then in Utah, where they recovered her twins.

Lazlo had been tempted a few times but had never slept with a married woman. It was a line he'd never cross. Suzanne was a decade older but was more astoundingly desirable than any woman of any age he'd ever met. She was the smartest and bravest and most empathetic and humble person of either sex he'd ever encountered. They became friends. Her husband, Kip, was a great guy, and her twin stepdaughters were delights. He'd visited their home several times, including many during the holidays. He and Suzanne occasionally had lunch or coffee under the pretense that he wanted to pick her brain about a homicide case. But mainly, he just wanted to see her.

Kept in his drawer, Lazlo's secondary cell rang. A number few had. He saw the caller ID and answered immediately. "Suzy?"

"Laz, Kip got murdered in our house while I was playing golf. I found him a few minutes ago. On the floor in our foyer."

"What happened!"

She chose her words carefully.

"Laz, you were the only one I told about what Pamela Loncart said while she was dying. Do you remember?"

"Golden frog poison, but I wasn't sure if she was bullshitting you."

"Trust me, she wasn't. Her narco-boyfriend had Kip killed today with that poison, and he was hoping to kill me, too."

"Jesus, Suzy, I'll be there with the cavalry. We're on it."

"No, that's exactly what I don't want to happen."

"Excuse me?"

"When we hang up, I'm going to call Jill Treece, who I'm sure will get the right folks here – even though it isn't an emergency. I want this to be a normal cause of death investigation. Probably, it will look like a myocardial event or stroke. I want Kip to die a normal death. Not by homicide."

"Suzy, are you out of your mind? What am I missing?"

"Laz, even Jill won't find the cause of death unless she has a roadmap to follow. The toxin is too rare. Maybe if she were looking specifically for it."

"Suzy, this makes no sense. How do you know it was this golden frog poison? And if you do, why wouldn't you tell Jill?"

She dodged his questions. "I'll text you later after the inevitable crowd disperses. Why don't you come over; door code 6544. I promise to tell you more later. I knew something like this could happen, but after three years, I hoped their dark *Game of Twins* was over. It's not."

"Please let me help. Whatever you need."

"I appreciate that, but it's probably best that Atlanta's top homicide cop doesn't show up at my doorstep right now. Jill has her own APD investigator specializing in unknown, unexpected, or unexplained deaths. She may bring him along."

"Suzy, I know who you're talking about, Gary Popov. Technically, he reports to me but is delegated full-time to Jill. He is a major dick but smarter than you might think from his appearance. If a death might be a homicide, he coordinates with us, and we take over."

"Got it."

She fetched food and water for Lilly and parked her in the laundry room. Her dog wasn't happy, but too bad, too sad today. She and Dr. Jill Treece, a forensic pathologist and head of the Fulton County Medical Examiner's Office, had worked dozens of cases together while Suzanne was a homicide detective. Jill was now in her mid-50s. Her silver hair was always perfectly coiffed; she wore stylish clothes; she was trim from a lot of working out. An elegant look that belied her work dealing with the messy, smelly, dead bodies daily. Straight-shooter, super-dedicated, and smart as a whip. Suzanne had the utmost respect for her.

Jill was genuinely distressed by her news, which Suzanne kept to a minimum. She had lost her husband a decade ago to a teenage hit-and-run driver. "Oh, Suzanne, I can't begin to tell you..."

"Thanks, Jill. It would be great if you could get the 911 stuff going."

"Done. I'll put it in motion. My investigator, Gary Popov, will likely get there before me. Don't let his demeanor fool you. He has an amazing sniffer and is bright. I'll also send a CSI to do photos."

Jill asked, "Suzanne, you don't think there was foul play, do you?"

Suzanne told her first whopper lie of the day. "No, and I didn't see any trauma. He was healthy as heck. Had a perfect check-up a couple of months ago."

"We'll figure it out. I should be there in the next hour or so."

Suzanne was exhausted and had no idea how she'd survive the rest of the day. Real tears would not come again as she sat down next to Kip's body. "My sweetheart, this was my fault, all my fault. Neither you nor your twins should have been part of this sick *Game*. There's no way to make things right. He won't get away with this, I promise."

She held his clammy hand and heard the emergency circus begin. Why did emergency vehicles arrive so quickly and loudly when someone was already dead?

In his office, Lazlo Kianian didn't know how to feel. He took a bottle of GlenAllachie from his desk drawer and poured a couple of fingers. The news was horrible; he felt so sorry for Suzanne and her daughters. Bubbling up, though, came a thought that made him gulp down his fine Scotch. My God, maybe now I have a chance with her. He shook his head in shame and poured two more fingers.

Chapter 4 – Oh, The Lies

They came in hot with sirens and lights blazing. A superfluous psychedelic light show with shrill, loud noises and pulsating lights – destroying the peace of her neighborhood. She opened the front door. An EMS unit, the two Fulton County police cars, and a fire engine, so far.

She met the EMTs at the door and ushered them in. "This is how I found him. I used to be a cop. He was dead when I got home."

The female EMT looked her in the eyes and said, "You're the APD investigator, the one in the books about the twins' murders."

"I am."

A male cop said, "We want to thank you for your service and are sorry for your loss."

She and others nodded in acknowledgment. "Can we get some basic information before the M.E. gets here?

"Sure, whatever you need."

She went to the kitchen to make a pot of coffee for anyone who wanted it and laid some pets on Lilly, who had sad eyes – before sequestering her again.

After announcing, "Help yourself to coffee," she answered several fundamental questions about Kip, herself, and when she found his body.

The next to arrive, without his boss, was Gary Popov. He was about 5'7" and at least two hundred twenty pounds, but stouter than fat; he looked strong as an ox. He wore an ill-fitted brown suit, a white shirt, and an ugly brown and black tie – no way to button any button on his coat. His scuffed brown shoes perfectly matched the rest of his outfit. He'd brought along a tiny, bespectacled blonde woman who carried a big camera and satchel. He ordered her, "Take pictures from every angle."

He was the Atlanta M.E.'s own investigator – not technically a CSI--but assigned by the M.E. when the cause of death was not readily apparent, unexpected, or suspicious. Autopsies were required in homicides, fire, body disfigurement, and in public health cases. Next of kin could request peace of mind. Gary would advise if death was sufficiently suspicious; Jill would then get involved and order an autopsy—or not. But she usually took his advice.

Gary had yet to introduce himself, so Suzanne did. He quickly glanced at the body, then, in his weird mix of Eastern European accent and southern twang, said, "I'm Detective Popov. That your husband on the floor?"

"Yes, Kip Davies. We have different last names."

He glanced again at the body, "Mizz Delqua, you got a more private place where we can chat?"

"Sure, let's go into the living room. Follow me."

On her way through the kitchen, he shouted, "Stop!"

Startled, she stopped in her tracks.

"I need you to slowly use two fingers of your right hand and remove the gun stuck in the back of your shorts."

She exclaimed, "I forgot it was there. I'm so sorry."

She did as he requested. He grabbed it, ejected the clip, and put it on the granite counter.

"You wanna tell me why you got a Glock in your cute little shorts?"

"Oh, sorry. I forgot it was there." She realized she was wearing short pink shorts and a clingy matching top.

"You got a permit?"

"Of course. You know I was an APD homicide cop, right?"

She was taken aback when he said, "And that should make a freak'n difference? Okay, now I'm following you without your goddamn gun."

She sat on a sofa. The thick, short cop plunked down on a chair opposite.

"Let's talk about your husband first. When did you last see him alive?"

"By about 7:00 AM, I was dressed and reminded him to pick up our dog Lilly at the groomer. I dropped her off on my way to the golf course."

"Where's the mutt?"

"She's in the laundry room. And she's not a mutt. You wanna meet her?"

"I hate dogs. And they hate me. Go on."

"Kip was taking the day off. He said he might work on his rock collection and do some reading. He's got a workroom downstairs."

"Rock collection?" he said derisively.

She pointed to the end table, "The top is made of agates Kip found and polished. I noticed some rock powder on his hands, so he must have been down there working on his agates."

Gruffly Popov replied, "Rock stuff ain't work. He go out after you left?"

"I don't know. I wasn't there. When I finished my round, I called to remind Kip about Lilly. Went to voicemail. On my way out, I called him again. Voicemail again. Then, the groomer called to say Lilly was there, and they were closing at 3:00 PM. I was pissed and decided to pick her up myself, which I did shortly before ."

"How much do one of them doggy haircuts cost? I'm bett'n more than my salary today."

She ignored his question and glared.

"So, ya drove home pissed off at your hubby?"

"Regretfully, yes."

"Which is why you had your gun on you when you got home?"

"What! No."

She already wanted to kick him in the teeth.

"Tell me why you had a gun on you, Mizz Delqua."

"I got my gun after Lilly ran up the stairs and whined like I'd never heard. She sensed something was wrong, and so did I. I hadn't heard from Kip. As a precaution, I grabbed the gun from my frunk."

He interrupted, "Your what?"

"Teslas have front storage called a frunk instead of a trunk."

"That's ridiculous, but go on."

"The alarm was off. It's unusual, but sometimes we don't have it on. I unlocked the door with my key. Lilly shot through. I yelled Kip's name a couple of times. No answer. Lilly was whining louder; I followed the sound toward the front door. Kip was lying on his back. She was licking his face. I screamed. I checked vitals but could see he was gone."

"That's when you put your gun in your shorts"?

"I guess. I don't remember. I was going to check out the whole house, but I didn't see any trauma."

"What was you thinking then?"

"How could this happen? He was such a healthy guy, no health problems at all; maybe a heart attack or stroke or something."

"Maybe. Or maybe something else?" With a half-smile, Popov let his question linger.

"He do drugs?"

If a look could kill, she just killed him.

"You know, like, opioids: coke, heroin, meth, weed, and the like?"

"No."

"Doc prescriptions?"

"Nothing regularly. Only Prilosec OTC."

"Ah, tums for the upper class. He never talked about suicide or dy'n?"

"Never."

"Do you have firearms in your house other than the weapon I took?"

"Yes, locked up in our bedroom."

"I'll need to check that out."

Suzanne had been on the asking-questions-end of investigations for years – and only once on the answering end of a bogus Internal Affairs investigation. She reminded herself that this wasn't an investigation of a murder. She tried to remain calm, but her patience was running on empty.

"You call anyone other than your hubby and my boss this afternoon?"

She may have waited too long before answering a curt "No." *Another lie already, but to say she talked to the Deputy Chief of Police would open another big can of worms.*

"You sure?"

"Yes, but I must call my twins as soon as possible."

He ignored her comment. "Saw you got a couple of cameras in front. Others?"

She told him, "Cameras haven't been working for a couple of weeks. The repair guy was supposed to come out this week."

Gary smiled. "Ain't that convenient."

"Pardon me?"

"I'm just saying..."

Suzanne lost it, "What the fuck are you saying?"

"Lose the attitude Mizz Delqa," he barked back and almost added, bitch. "I ain't say'n noth'n yet, at least till we nail down the time of death. I need to get your timeline. Out the door around 7:15 AM after reminding your hubby to take your mutt to the barber; you were at the golf course playing in your tournament? You any good, by the way? I can't play that game worth a damn."

She took a deep breath. "Pretty good; after my round, I ate lunch at the club and called Kip again to ensure he'd picked up Lilly."

"You didn't get a response, called him again, and headed back around 2:30, but the pet barber called that your mutt was there, and they'd be closing at 3:00. I'm sure she'll confirm your alibi about picking the dog up. By the time you got home, you were ballistic that he'd messed up. Were you going to scream at him or shoot him or what?"

She lost it again and said, "Go fuck yourself."

In walked Dr. Jill Treece, wearing a thousand-dollar beige suit with perfectly matching heels. Her beautiful snow-white hair was coiffed like a queen—missing only the tiara. She was the opposite of her investigator in looks and temperament.

"Gary, I overheard the exchange. You're treading on thin ice."

"Okay, boss. Lemme ask her one more question since she used to be such a hotshot APD homicide detective."

Dr. Jill closed her eyes and said, "Ask her. Then that's it."

"Yes, mam."

"Anyway, your hubby could have been murdered?"

Suzanne took a few moments to answer. "I don't see how that could be possible." *Another lie.*

The stubby, obnoxious guy picked up his portfolio and stood. Unlike when he entered, he stuck out his hand to Suzanne. She didn't shake it. He tossed a card on the end table and started to walk out. Then turned, "Another thing, Mizz Delqua, I'm curious, you gonna bury or burn him?"

In disgust, Dr. Jill shook her head and said, "Can you give me a minute, Suzanne?"

She took Gary by his elbow like a teacher would take a disorderly elementary student out of a classroom and marched him into the kitchen. Then, she waved her hand, telling a couple of others to vamoose.

They stood face to face.

"Gary, what the hell are you doing? You made her day much worse for no good reason. Go type up your interview notes and send them to me."

"Boss, I'm doing my job. I'm telling you something fishy is going on here. I don't know what it is. Yet."

Dr Jill took a deep breath and almost slapped him. With a smirk on his face, he walked out. Gary was an asshole. But he was her asshole – and she sometimes hated to admit it -- was rarely wrong in his advice on what constituted a suspicious death.

She returned to the living room and extended her arms to Suzanne, "Let me give you a big hug."

Suzanne broke down and cried on her shoulder.

"Suzy, I'll help you get through this. Do you want to see Kip again?"

"No, I want to remember him when he was alive."

"I'll take another look here, and we'll all be out shortly. At first glance, I'd say it's something cardiac and will put that down as the cause of death. Do you want an autopsy? It's not required and wouldn't necessarily give you an answer."

"I'd like to know what happened to him. *Lying again, hoping Jill would not find the cause of death.* "How long will that take?"

"Tell you what, I'll take a thorough but abbreviated look at his heart, liver, and brain and get a stat tox panel done. Assuming there's nothing unusual, we should have it done by tomorrow afternoon. I'll call you with our findings. In most of our homicide investigations, there's something nefarious. But in most other non-suspicious-death autopsies, we Medical Examiners often don't have the answer. And there may not be one for Kip.

"I hope there is." *Yet another in her string of lies.*

"And he wanted to be cremated."

Dr. Jill nodded and said, "You and Kip are well-known persons. You may want to get a PR firm to handle communications with the media."

"Yes, you're probably right. You won't announce his death today?"

"No, I'll wait for you. My office will say nothing until then, I promise."

"I gotta call my twins and talk to a few other folks before they hear it online."

"I understand."

Chapter 5 – Gary

After returning to the Medical Examiner's office on Pryor Street to do the Kip Davies write-up for his boss, Gary Popov drove home to the other side of the city. Jill was an Incredible bitch, but she gave him a long leash. He'd spruce up his report when he got home. Halfway there, he got an idea that gave him an immediate hard-on, a simply Grinchy idea.

He grabbed a Coors Light from the frig, opened it, and went to his little study. He was organized and meticulous about most things, but he'd always dumped the business cards he'd accumulated over the last couple of years into the bottom drawer of his desk. He didn't know what the hell he'd ever use them for. There were at least a couple hundred. He piled them all onto his desk, took a brief look, and tossed most cards on the floor. He found a couple that might do the trick and set them aside.

One caught his eye. Amy Neyland.

****

She'd given him her card at a greet-and-meet last year for two groups often at odds: Atlanta law enforcement and the local media. Amy was an investigative reporter at the Atlanta City Paper, a biweekly rag hocked at street corners by the homeless and available outside grocery stores, restaurants, bars, and businesses across the city – a slot for donations appreciated.

She was a cute little twenty-something, curvy brunette with vivacious eyes. Their interaction had been brief. Gary had introduced himself while she was getting a drink. She told him, "If you ever hear of a juicy crime story, I'd really appreciate a call. She winked, gave him her card, and then disappeared into the crowd. Why didn't he give her his card? She doubted he'd ever call him.

But never say never.

Gary's Grinch-like excitement, though, quickly dissipated. He wanted to invite her over to his place and talk --and take it from there. But she'd be driving, likely with GPS tracking of her car that could be accessed by savvy law enforcement. And her phone likely had Google/GPS tracking. These facts made any scenario that depended on her coming to his place – nearly impossible. This opportunity had presented itself without him devising a plan, which is what he prided himself on. He wished his tech skills were more sophisticated, but he knew a few things.

First, he knew that hurrying could mean the end of him in his favorite vocation. He sat down with another Coors Light. There might be a way.

He could take his phone and hers out of the equation. He left his iPhone at home and extracted from his desk one of a half dozen burners he'd bought over the past year with cash at a couple of convenience stores outside the city that didn't ask for ID. He jumped in his car and drove a mile back toward the town, then turned the burner on and called her number. He was surprised, she answered. "Amy, not sure you remember me, Gary Popov with the Atlanta Medical Examiner's office."

She was good with names. "Gary, how have you been?"

As if she cared, he said, "Hang'n in there. What's up?"

So much for the small talk, God, she hoped he hadn't called to ask her out. Her impression was that he was a dweeb, an ugly one at that.

"Amy, I'm working on the beginning of a potentially big Atlanta crime investigation – that no one else knows about, and I thought of you."

He got her attention.

"This has gotta be off the record for now."

"Sure, sure. What kind of story, Gary?

"You familiar with Suzanne Delacroix?"

"Never met her, but I read all the local print, and I read the two novels by Bobby Price. Pretty amazing lady."

"Yeah, right. And her husband, Kip Davies?"

"He's a hotshot criminal defense attorney."

"No, he *was* a hotshot criminal attorney."

Amy stood up from the chair in her apartment, "What are you saying?"

"Davies died in his home today. His wife found him on the floor after getting home from playing golf—or at least that's what she says."

"I haven't heard that on the news. How'd he die?"

Gary decided to lead with shock and awe. "I'm an expert about this stuff, and I'm pretty sure he got murdered."

Amy took a slug of the Johnny Walker Black in front of her. "No kidding?"

He continued, "Good look'n 50ish guy. No visible trauma. Dead on the entrance floor of their condo. I came from the scene. Supposedly, he was healthy as a horse."

"But you say he got murdered. By whom? His wife?"

"I interviewed her. I know she was hiding something."

"Wow, Interesting."

"Perhaps you and I can collaborate. You can win a Pulitzer and make a ton of money – and maybe one day I can arrest a bad girl and get a big promotion before I retire."

"Sounds good." She was already thinking about selling the story to the *Constitution*. No way it would go in her paper or online.

He was enjoying their banter. "Amy, I'd prefer not to discuss this on the phone. You've gotta promise not to tell your roommate about this."

"No problem, and I don't have a roommate."

A valuable, unsolicited piece of information.

"What area of town do you live in? I'll pick you up, and we can get a bite to eat or drink."

He could sense her hesitate and said, "I promise you'll get the whole story."

"My condo building is in the Old Fourth Ward."

"Great area."

She gave him the address and said, "I'll meet you at the curb in front."

"Perfect. I'll be in a black Nissan in about thirty minutes or so. Will that work?"

"Sure."

He was closer than that but needed to bring up an APD security map that indicated City CCTV cameras. He scanned the area; no cameras within two blocks. He pulled up Google Maps and looked at views of her condo. There was one camera outside, but it wasn't pointing all the way down the sidewalk to the street. Most importantly, he'd turned off the police GPS before he'd left work. Big Brother wasn't going to be tracking him tonight. And he slapped on a temporary tag to cover his APD license plate.

****

When Gary called, Amy was in her workout clothes. She took a quick shower and threw a few outfits on her bed. Picked a hot one. No reason not to look good. She reapplied her makeup and pursed her lips together. She admired herself in the full-length mirror and thought, girl, this is your chance to jump to the big leagues.

When he arrived, he drove a lap around her block to verify what he'd seen on his screen. He'd already gotten a bit lucky and knew he couldn't always count on that. A blonde babe appeared on Gary's swing around the block and walked up the sidewalk. He did another lap. On his way back, Amy was walking down the sidewalk. He parked in front. Gary wore his best professional duds, but no one would rate him higher than a four or five on any ten scale.

Strangely, he'd conjured up an image of Ted Bundy, who sat beside him. Super good-looking, suave Ted grinned, "*You got this.*"

Gary took a deep breath. He beamed as he hopped out and opened the passenger door for her.

"You, my dear, look simply divine."

Gary knew Atlanta babes were considered among the most primo on the planet. Amy didn't disappoint. The brunette was smoking hot in a short black skirt, a tight pink blouse with no bra, and black heels. Her Chanel was fantastic. The perfect, slutty bitch.

Amy thought this guy was even grosser than she remembered. Short, thick, baldheaded with a face few mothers could love. She told herself, "*Okay, he's a disgusting toad. It's not like you've got to fuck him. You gotta find out everything about Kip Davies's death and write a great story.*"

He eyeballed the area in front of her condo building and the building opposite. No one. They settled in their seats. Gary pulled out his Atlanta Police Department wallet with his badge from his suit coat. "Amy, here are my APD credentials. I want you to feel comfortable about who I am."

Then, in one motion, as he leaned over to show her the badge in his left hand, he hit the carotid in her neck with a right-hand chop – knocking her out instantaneously. She slumped in the seat. He undid her seatbelt and pushed her to the floor. He found her iPhone in her purse, immediately turned it off, popped out the battery and SIM card, and snapped it in half. Sure, Apple and Google GPS could track her phone's last location. Right here, near her place. But then, no longer.

He'd checked out a nearby, quiet, dark street with no cameras. He stopped, got out, tore off the temporary tag, and put it in the trunk. Back in the driver's seat, he grabbed the small bottle of chloroform in his glove box, lifted her head, sprayed her face, and let her breathe the fumes. He got the blanket from his back seat and covered her on the floor. On the way home, he tossed the pieces of her iPhone over the hood of his car.

****

Amy woke up naked on an unfamiliar bed. No idea where she was. Her head banged from getting karate chopped in the neck and sprayed with chloroform. Gary was standing over her, but nothing was in focus. She tried to move but fell back on the bed.

"This is your exclusive story, Amy. No one else will ever tell it."

She moaned weakly as he kneeled on the bed next to her. He firmly grabbed her shaved crotch with one hand while his other hand went to her trachea. Her eyes evoked both surprise and fear. He pressed down until it snapped. She gurgled and was dead the next minute as he held her down.

He carried her nude body down to his basement. He wanted to remember each of his women precisely this way. He chuckled. Did she think that he was going to rape her first? He hoped so, but not a chance. He couldn't even remember the last time his dick got hard experiencing a woman. No, but it did get hard while he killed her.

He wrapped her body in transparent polycarbonate plastic. He lifted it into the horizontal cryogenic freezer in his basement using protective gloves and an eye shield. The freezer cost $90K and was twice as big as the cryogenic freezer in the Fulton County Medical

Examiner's lab. Other guys his age bought a Tesla or a motorboat or sailboat or whatever. It was his biggest-ever splurge, and he loved it.

Amy was the second. She went on top of cute little Lori Summers, who, three years ago, he picked up hitchhiking in Douglasville, outside of Atlanta, after flashing a badge and offering to take her wherever she'd like. There was plenty of room for a half dozen. His girls were unique and needed to be preserved. He didn't want pictures of them. He wanted to remember them in the flesh – whenever he felt the need. They belonged to him.

Next to Amy, he put her clothes and shoes in a clear bag. Even at the low cryogenic temperatures, it would take her body several hours to freeze completely. Maybe then he'd take both girls out and admire them on the rack he'd made, especially for his frozen gallery.

****

Gary had read every non-fiction book about serial killers. He saw himself above them and was only now getting warmed up. He made sure that whoever found his girls would know it was him. Gary didn't rape, torture, maim, or devour his victims – before killing them. Their deaths were quick and pure—their bodies not damaged—as with other barbarian killers. No, he was better than any of them. He'd never be caught.

But, despite his criticisms of them, he knew he belonged to their exclusive fraternity. He didn't believe in prayer but felt like Dahmer, Gacy, Bundy, Lopez, Jack the Ripper, and others were watching over him that evening. A lot could have gone wrong; something had guided him.

****

Gary walked back upstairs, put the finishing touches on his report, and emailed it to Dr. Treece. He advised her that Davies's death was suspicious and must be treated like that with a thorough autopsy – including a panel of thirty-six tox screens (usually only done in criminal investigations). However, he knew it would take extra time.

He closed his report with, "There's something Delacroix is not telling us."

He hit Send.

****

Gary got another idea while sitting at his kitchen table with a Coors Light longneck. There was a wet-behind-the-ears reporter he'd met at the greet-and-meet who worked at the *Constitution but* couldn't remember his name. He immediately pegged him as a fag which he thought were vermin of the earth. He found his card and called.

He heard, "This is Justin; please leave a message at the beep." He even sounded like a fag. Gary said, "Justin, you should find out what's happening at the coroner's office. Suzanne Delacroix's husband, Kip Davies, was found dead today in their house. She has no explanation for his death – and she is a person-of-interest."

He hung up, put the burner on the floor, and smashed it with his heel. A call that could never be tracked.

Chapter 6 – Her Twins

Justin Collier was low-man on the totem pole in the *Atlanta Journal and Constitution's* investigative reporting group. That was fine with him. Even before matriculating to Columbia, he knew it was his calling. But after graduation, getting to work with an icon like Bobby Price-- he was 100% positive. Now in his early 70s, Price had won two Pulitzer Prizes in the last five years for his investigative work on the *Game of Twins* murders and his two best-selling books. Making Bobby a multi-millionaire and surprising the hell out of everybody, including Bobby. Last year, Justin got his dream job.

That night, he worked late at the office. He was starving and stopped at Waffle House for a waffle, eggs over easy, and bacon. It was almost midnight when he got home and took a shower. He wasn't sure if he heard his cell ring in his bedroom. He finished drying off and checked his phone. There was a voicemail from a number he didn't recognize. He was curious who'd call him this late. The voicemail was more than a little provocative.

Justin had Bobby Price's cell number, which he'd never called. He doubted Price would pick up at this hour. He took a quarter from his pocket. Heads he'd call now. Tails, he'd wait until seeing him in the morning. It was heads. More than a bit crotchety during the day, Price answered in a sleepy, even more crotchety voice. "Mr. Collier, you better have a goddamn good reason to call at this hour."

"Sorry, sir. I got this anonymous call with no caller ID. I figured I better call you. I checked online and didn't see anything to verify it."

"It? What the hell are you talking about?"

****

Suzanne needed to prepare for the onslaught of media coverage whenever it started. She hoped the media glare would last only a short time. Regardless, she needed professional help.

Marsha Kaufman was a top-tier Atlanta PR pro whom Kip had hired in a few of his big criminal cases – sometimes to get the lay of the land. And she provided advice on communicating with the media and funneled as much media attention through her as possible. Kip had trusted her implicitly. Suzanne would do the same.

They'd met only once briefly at a charity gala. She was an attractive brunette, 40ish, with the perfect tinge of a southern accent and a killer smile. Kip said she was smart as a whip and worth every penny he paid her.

Suzanne found Marsha's contact info on Kip's laptop. Thank God she answered.

"Marsha, it's Suzanne Delacroix. Sorry about the hour. I need your help."

"Suzanne, what's going on?"

"Kip died this afternoon."

"Oh my God! What happened?"

Suzanne gave her a summary without any mention of the golden poison frog. At best, she *was fibbing by omission.*

Suzanne said, "I'm doubting we can wait to say something before the autopsy is done tomorrow afternoon. Why don't we touch base in the morning?"

"Sounds good. I'll draft a preliminary release for you to review. I'm so sorry, Suzanne."

"Thanks, Marsha."

Marsha knew she would earn her exorbitant fee in spades starting that minute.

****

Suzanne needed to do this, then take a bath. She climbed the stairs with her phone and tablet and sat at the small desk in her bedroom.

She was pretty tech-savvy, she thought, for her age, but setting up video calls with more than one person was a mystery to her. She used her notebook and texted her daughter, Sarah: "I need to talk to you, but I need to see both of you. Can you set that up? It's important."

Within a minute, she was on a Zoom call with her stepdaughters.

Saville said, "Hey, Mom, hi from our favorite cliff spot overlooking Santa Barbara beach and the beautiful blue Pacific." Luckily, Sarah and Saville were both together with their notebooks.

Suzanne stared at them on her screen but had no idea what to say. Her eyes roamed to one of the most breathtaking vistas she'd ever seen. The front door of UC Santa Barbara. She kept the small talk to a minimum but asked what they were doing.

Sarah said, "We're practicing our Chinese. Which, by the way, you need to learn. Heck, your mom was Chinese."

She closed her eyes for a few moments before responding. She was scared she couldn't handle this. This the woman who'd solved more homicides at APD than any detective; who'd solved the mystery of her own father's cold case murder; who, with her now deceased partner, Dusty, killed Thad Sutterland and his cousin who'd slaughtered twin teenagers in Cascade Heights; who'd exposed Pamela Loncart's occult family as serial murderers over a century; who'd rescued her stepdaughters held by the most powerful drug lord on the planet and flipped the tables by killing his DEA girlfriend, the diabolical Pamela Loncart; and who'd been able to stand up to the bright lights of public scrutiny on multiple occasions.

She stared at her screen.

"Mom, what's up?"

She finally said, "Girls, I have terrible news."

She breathed deeply and exhaled, "Your father is dead."

At first, there was a stunned silence, then, "No, that can't be. It can't. No! Shrieks and moaning from both. Then, "Mom, what happened to him? What happened!"

The twins already knew too much not to be transparent with them. She tried to speak but failed. Haltingly, she got started, "I left at 7:15 AM today to drop off Lilly to play in a golf tournament. Your dad wished me luck and went back to sleep. I got back home around 3:00 PM with Lilly. Your dad was supposed to pick her up, but I got no answer when I called him. She raced up the garage steps. The door wasn't locked. Lilly went bananas, barking her head off when I opened the door. I yelled a couple of times that I was home. Lilly was licking his face on the foyer floor. I knew he was gone. Next to him was a small gold figurine. A golden frog. Then I knew."

"Knew what?"

"Who had him killed. You know that after we traded her twins for you two, I fought Pamela Loncart. She had a small ampoule that fell from her hand. I had no idea what it was, but I grabbed it. I scraped it across her neck. She fell back, looked up at me, and smiled, "golden frog poison." Then, she died on the White Salt Flats, where we picked you two up. It's the deadliest poison in the animal kingdom. A tiny drop is lethal. The little frog figurine beside your dad was undoubtedly smeared with the toxin. We'll have that checked out. If I'd touched it, I'd probably be dead, too. Girls, I do not doubt that Raoul Menendez had your father murdered, but that won't be what you hear on the TV tomorrow or online."

Three thousand miles away, the silence was deafening.

"My precious girls, I have no words other than I feel your pain, too. I understand if you blame me for getting your dad murdered – and getting you two involved in this horrible *Game of Twins*. I will deal justice to Menendez in my own way."

Saville piped up sarcastically, "How will you do that, Mom? Raoul Menendez has hundreds of drug dealers and sicarios and a gazillion dollars and can do whatever he wants."

She had no idea but said, "I'll figure it out."

It would be totally understandable if they wanted to excoriate her for the rest of the night or longer. Pamela Loncart had them kidnapped and held in Raoul Menendez's mountain retreat, where they were forced to remove their fancy clothing and then were fondled by him and photographed. Now, their dad was dead at the hands of the same scumball.

"Try to get a flight back to Atlanta tomorrow. We'll do a small service in a few days, but I need your company. I love you both so much."

The screen went blank. Suzanne went upstairs to the master bedroom and her jacuzzi hot tub. She turned on the water and dropped her clothes on the floor. Sitting on the edge of the tub, she called Laz.

He picked up immediately, "How are you holding up?"

"Barely."

Before she could ask him if they could talk in person, he said, "You must be starving. How about I pick up some Chinese and drive up? Any preferences?

"Unlike my Chinese family, I love all American Chinese. You pick. About a half hour or so?"

"Give me an hour. I'm in the bath, trying to wash some of the bad stuff away. Text me when you arrive, and I'll let you in the front door."

"Sounds good."

****

2 Years Ago -- Santa Barbara, California,

Suzanne and Kip traveled to Santa Barbara with their twins, Sarah and Saville, in search of the right college for them. The two beautiful blondes were each over six feet tall – a tad taller than their stepmother, whom they called mom and who she always introduced as her daughters and not stepdaughters – even though her skin was a golden brown and her hair raven black. Suzanne's mom was a full-blooded Chinese woman, and her dad was dark as night. Her daughters had grown five inches since Suzanne first met them in middle school, then married their dad. She knew they loved her, and she loved them as much as any mom could. They were thrilled being taller than their statuesque mother – which Suzanne also got a kick out of. Father Kip was a measly 5 feet 11, and they all kidded him mercilessly about being the runt of the family.

The twins were the stars of their private school volleyball team, which won the Georgia State girls' championship. Several universities noticed them, and they were offered partial scholarships from ten. Money wasn't an issue, scholarships or not. Kip and Suzanne told the girls they could go wherever they wanted.

The twins spent a couple of weeks whittling their top choices down to three. First on the list was UC Santa Barbara. Suzanne and Kip were sure they'd eventually pick one of the others closer to Atlanta, but that was fine. None had been to Santa Barbara, about a hundred miles up the coast from LA. Driving up 101 from LAX, They were all a little gaga gazing out at the sapphire blue Pacific on the left and the Santa Ynez mountains on the right. The contrast was startlingly beautiful.

Arriving on campus, they were met by the volleyball coach, Marilyn Robinson, a tall, skinny, thirty-something blonde with a huge smile who said, "Let's take a walk to our cliffs."

Their parents stayed back, letting her converse with the twins. Arriving at the edge, the coach pointed west and announced, "The front door to UC Santa Barbara. They took a wooden walkway down the cliff to the beach. Both girls ripped off their Nikes and waded into the Pacific without a prompt. The coach told them, "It's a little cramped down here, but there are plenty of beaches where we play. Have you ever played on sand?" Coach Marilyn asked.

Saville said, "We watched the Olympics. Amazing, but we've only played a few times on sand when we were on vacation in South Carolina."

Marilyn said, "Different tactics with only two on a side, but it's great training. Four of my gals play pro. She told them names that they'd heard of. Then added, "Fun way to live, but not too lucrative except for a few women who play on the top circuit worldwide." Marilyn already thought if they played as good as they looked, it was possible.

The coach and the twins stopped and turned back, smiling. When they approached their parents, Saville said, "Dad, we've made up our minds; we want to be Gauchos!"

Gently, Kip took Marilyn aside by the arm and said, "Look, my wife and I are thrilled that our girls were offered scholarships to your university. But you need to give them to another couple of girls."

The Coach looked stunned, "You mean…?"

Kip smiled, "They're coming here, don't worry."

"You almost gave me a heart attack, Mr. Davies."

Kip hesitated, then said, "Promise us that you'll kick their asses if they ever slack off and that the scholarships will go to girls who need them."

Coach Marilyn smiled and said, "I promise. But I already know they aren't slackers. And thank you for being so generous."

She asked the twins if they wanted to stay in a dorm room and get local cuisine. Of course, they agreed. Later that evening, in a quaint ultra-expensive B&B overlooking the Pacific, Suzanne arrived in bed naked and lay next to him. Propped up on one elbow, she told him as they lay in bed. "You did good earlier, Mr. Davies."

"Me? he chuckled.

Suzanne continued, "After the girls graduate, we'll establish an annual scholarship for two women volleyball players who can't afford what we can."

'Yes, we will," Kip concurred. As she moved on top of him, he told her, "God, if I get to do it all over again, I'm going to UC Santa Barbara for college."

Chapter 7 – Suzy & Lazlo

This must have been a nightmare day for Suzy. Even though her husband had just died, Lazlo could only imagine her in the bath while driving to her place. He shook his head and chastised himself. Laz, you are a true degenerate. She met him in creamy silk pajamas and a matching robe at the door. He held a couple of bags of Chinese. She threw her arms around his neck.

"Thanks for coming, Laz. I greatly appreciate it."

Her abundant jet-black hair was dripping wet. She wore no makeup, was in bare feet, and had a long, voluptuous body that was comfortably warm. He'd never seen or felt a more gorgeous female. Ever.

But her beautiful face was painted with pain.

They watched each other eat spring rolls, Chinese dumplings, and sweet and sour pork with chopsticks. She'd opened a bottle of Turley Old Vines Zin that they both sipped. Across the table, he stared into her amazing amber eyes. "You wanna walk me through what happened today?"

Suzanne took a healthy gulp of wine and told him the whole story. Then she opened her phone picture gallery and walked around the table to show him pics with Kip dead on the floor and the little golden figurine nearby. It was impossible not to glance into her cleavage when she bent over.

"Laz, I came a hair's breadth from picking it up. If I had, I'd likely be dead on my floor."

"From touching it?"

"I'll email you a file about the golden poison frog. Its poison is among the deadliest. I handled it with gloves and put it in a small jewelry box."

"Where's the little critter now?"

"Follow me." She walked into the kitchen, opened the sugar canister on the counter, and pulled out the box. With a half-smile, she said, "Creative hiding place, don't you think?"

She carefully opened the box. The tiny gold frog was dazzling. Almost mesmerizing.

"You removed it from the crime scene and hid it. Why?"

"It was a calling card from Raoul Menendez. Only I would understand that and what it means. Telling me how Kip was killed and who ordered it – and why. The golden frog would prove nothing. Nothing would tie Menendez to Kip's murder. Even without a murder investigation, the press circus will begin tomorrow. I can only hope it won't last too long."

"Yep, It's going to be hard to keep a lid on this."

"I can handle it, and my twins can, too. There's a minute chance Dr. Treece will find the actual cause of death without being pointed in that direction. And if she doesn't, the volume of frenzy the twins will have to deal with will be minimized. If this becomes murder by golden frog poison, media interest will be immense, even internationally. Law enforcement will trip over their dicks and get no results. In so doing, they'd make it harder for me to do what needs to get done. Otherwise, my twins, friends, and family will live under constant threat. And that could include you."

"You're going to take him out, aren't you?"

"I'm going to give it my best effort. Before Menendez kills others."

Such a killing would fall under Lazlo's Code. Guys like him didn't deserve to be tried in any court, nor did they deserve to live in prison while running their lucrative operations, just to get released or break out to perpetrate more crimes. No, they must be wiped from the earth, the same as any evil pestilence. He understood where she was coming from, but going after Menendez would be dangerous at best.

He took a big sip of the Zin, "How is that going to happen?"

"Not sure. I'll figure something out."

"I'd be surprised if you didn't. Is there any way to talk you out of it?"

"Not likely. Laz, I'm toast. I gotta get some sleep. But I want to ask a favor. I don't want to be alone in my house tonight. Will you stay?"

"Be glad to." He was embarrassed that his dick lurched.

"There's a big guestroom next to mine. Plenty of toiletries, towels, and a couple of robes are in the bathroom. He followed her up the spiral staircase to the next floor. She showed him the guestroom. "Wow, Suzy, this room is bigger than my flat in Buckhead."

She smiled and gave him a breast hug. "Thank you so much. Please keep your door open. See you in the morning."

"Suzy, I hope tomorrow is a better day for you."

"Me too."

****

He took a quick shower, sat on the edge of his bed in a robe he found in the closet, and clicked on the news. Nothing interesting. He turned off the light and eased into bed. He scolded himself for his thoughts about the recent widow in the next room. Then fell dead asleep.

In deep REM, he could feel her touch. It was wonderful. Was he dreaming? Nope. He saw her standing at the side of the bed. Her silky robe, PJs bottoms, and top dropped to the floor. There was enough of a crack in the curtains that the moonlight exposed her spectacular naked, light brown body. His eyes widened as she asked, "Laz, will you hold me?"

He nodded yes. Her warm, curvy backside melded into him as he lay on his side behind her. He put his arms around her. His hands gravitated to her shapely, natural breasts. She cooed as he touched them. There was no way he could keep his erection from growing. She turned her head, smiled, and her tongue dove deep inside his mouth. He continued to grow.

Her cell phone on the nightstand rang.

"Dammit," she shouted. "Should've turned it off." She reached over and looked at the number. "Sorry, I gotta take this."

"No problem," Laz said, now alone with a raging hard-on.

When she got up and left the bedroom, he tried to get back to sleep but failed.

She came back about twenty minutes later. He asked, "Is everything okay?"

"No, Laz, it's not."

I'm returning to my bedroom to try and get some sleep." Before he could say anything else, she was gone.

To say this was a bizarre circumstance would be an understatement; the gorgeous married woman he'd long lusted for and now a widow for less than 24 hours had been in bed naked with him, and he knew she wanted what he wanted. He had no idea how he'd get back to sleep.

****

The caller was Bobby Price. "Suzanne, "How are you doing?"

"In a word, shitty."

"Is it true?"

"Is what true?"

"That Kip is dead."

"How'd you hear that!" she exclaimed.

"A kid who works with me got an anonymous call ten minutes ago."

"Jesus H. Christ, Bobby, I haven't even notified all the next of kin. There's an autopsy scheduled for tomorrow. Sometime after that, we were going to do a release to all news outlets. We'll have to do that earlier than planned. I've retained Marsha Kaufman."

"That's good. Suzanne, I can't tell you how sorry I am."

"Thanks, Bobby." She gave him a barebones synopsis. Leaving out the golden frog poison.

"The anonymous caller said you are a person-of-interest in your husband's death. I know that's total baloney."

"It is. No doubt it's the Medical Examiner investigator, Popov."

"Who?"

"Oh, never mind; he was here earlier. We didn't exactly hit it off. He works for Judy Treece – and is a piece of work – well, no, he's a piece of shit.

Bobby Price cogitated. He respected Suzanne more than anyone he knew, and they were making a lot of money together, which now seemed irrelevant.

But he had to ask, "Suzanne, off the record, is this the next part of the *Game*?"

He could hear her take a deep breath.

"No doubt. Kip was murdered, and I know how and by whom. No amount of proof, though, would make a difference, and trust me, there is none anyway. The autopsy will show nothing. Hell, I'm lucky to be talking with you. He was trying to kill me as well."

"Let me take a wild guess." Which he did.

Saying nothing, she confirmed his guess.

"There's only one way out of the *Game* now, Bobby. You'll have to trust me. There will be another part of the story – and I hope the last -- if I live to tell it."

"Suzanne, how was Kip murdered?"

She decided to come clean. "Golden frog poison."

"What the hell is that?"

"Deadliest animal poison on the planet that comes from a small South American frog. It's what Pamela Loncart tried to kill me within Utah, but I was lucky enough to turn the tables on her."

He chuckled, "Ah, I left that part of the story a little fuzzy because you didn't provide those details."

"I'm sorry that the *Game* continues."

"All off the record, I promise. Let me know if I can help in any way."

"Will do."

"Stay safe, Suzy. May God walk with you."

Suzanne was surprised by his goodbye and teared up after she hung up. Writing the three *Game of Twins* books from Suzanne's perspective – although Bobby Price never faced what she did – he could often feel the Evil she did. Evil with a capital E. He had more of a sense of what this remarkable woman had endured – and knew she'd need to bear much more.

After seventy years, the cranky left-wing agnostic had gotten some religion and regularly attended a nondenominal Atlanta church. Maybe it wasn't too late for him to have Everlasting Peace. But there would be no forgiveness for the Evil that Suzanne was crusading against. He would pray for her strength, peace, and direction to battle as a Person-of-Light against the Darkness.

****

Suzanne called Marsha. "I'm sorry to bother you again."

"No bother at all."

"It's already hit the fan."

It had been tucked away in her mind for three years that Pamela Loncart's death would be avenged. She'd hoped against hope the *Game of Twins* had withered on the vine.

Until today.

She knew that the biggest narco on the planet could strike back at her, her family, and others – at anyone he wanted. No amount of security protection, even at the Secret Service level, could ever ensure her safety or theirs 24/7. The only alternative was being alert and living their lives. But now her husband was dead, and Menendez was also taking a shot at her with the same poison that killed Pamela. What would he do next after discovering she was alive? She had no idea – other than he wasn't done yet.

****

In Santa Barbara, the Davies twins shared a dorm room on campus. It was late, a typical time for a snack. But they were neither hungry nor thirsty. Laying on their backs on their beds dressed, Saville said, "You know, if Dad hadn't married her, we wouldn't have been kidnapped. And he would be alive. It's the cold, hard truth, and you know it."

Her sister hesitated, "I know, but she made Dad light up like we'd never seen. She's a ten times better mom than Sandra. Suzanne loves us more than anything."

"Yes, you're right, and we love her."

"The love of her life is dead at the hands of pure Evil. I can still feel his disgusting hands on me.

"Me too."

They fell silent.

Sarah asked her twin sister, "What will she do now?"

Saville said, "She'll give herself only one choice."

"I know, but getting to Raoul in his mountain hideout in Mexico will be impossible. It would be suicide. Do you think he'll come after her?"

"I don't know. I don't know if Mom knows."

"Do you think we're in danger again?"

"I don't know if Mom knows that, either."

Sarah nodded. They both fell asleep in their gym shorts and sleeveless tops, hoping tomorrow would be a better day.

****

Back in her bedroom, Suzanne was asleep in minutes. *But then she was wrestling with Pamela Loncart on the Salt Flats of Bonneville. A gargantuan golden frog was hopping toward her. Pamela laughed. Kip slammed into the frog before she could warn him. He collapsed.* Suzanne shrieked. Loud enough for Lazlo to hear. Lazlo jumped out of bed and was in her bedroom in seconds.

"Suzy, what's the matter?"

"It was a nightmare, a terrible one. Will you hold me again?"

He climbed in next to her. She prayed the golden frog would not return to her dreams but was dubious about that. Years ago, after she'd been assaulted at knifepoint by Thad Sutterland, Pamela's cousin, she had recurring nightmares for two decades about the knife he threatened her with. They only ended when she drove a knife into his evil heart six years ago.

The dread was real again.

GOLDEN FROG POISON A GAME OF TWINS THRILLER

But Lazlo Kianian was lying next to her.

Chapter 8 – Kip Returns

When Lazlo woke the following day, his first thought was, "Did I dream that?" He leaned over to the pillow next to him. Someone had put an indentation on it and left a slight hint of a dreamy perfume. He stood up naked and exclaimed "Jeez!" as Suzanne, dressed to the nines, walked into the bedroom with a mug of coffee and threw him a robe.

"Suzy, about last night..."

She smiled, "Let's leave that be for now, okay."

"No problem," he mumbled.

She sat on the bed and gave him a summary of her conversation with Bobby Price.

"The asshole who talked with Bobby's reporter was Gary Popov, who you know. No doubt there are other media he's told that I am a person-of-interest."

Lazlo said, "Yup, technically, he reports to Robbery Homicide but is assigned full-time to the M.E. He's one weird dude."

"Hard to dispute that. At best, Gary seems "off" somehow. I'll touch base with Judy and see what she knows. Laz, I gotta make a couple of calls. She walked up to him and kissed him on the lips. "I'll talk to you later."

Her kiss made Lazlo beam. Today, he felt like the luckiest guy on the planet. That feeling, though, was tempered by the circumstances which could hardly be worse for her.

For any red-blooded heterosexual woman, you'd have to be deaf, dumb, and blind to ignore his presence: sort of Cary Grant-ish, super suave without effort, friendly, bright – with a face chiseled of stone from his Mesopotamian ancestors, and an athlete's body. And that wavy blonde hair from his Nordic mother. He was impossibly good-looking.

Kip asked her once, "So if I weren't around anymore, would you fuck Laz?"

She'd grinned lasciviously at her hot husband. "You're going to be around a long time, mister."

Kip responded, "You know he's one of hundreds of guys in Atlanta that has a crush on you."

****

Gary Popov arose an hour earlier than usual. After a cup of coffee, he called Sylvia White at FOX. He didn't remember her – she must not have been a looker. He was glad she didn't answer so he could leave a short message, remarkably like the one he left with the *Atlanta Constitution* reporter last night. Whether someone would run with it, who knew? But why not stir the pot more?

****

Suzanne walked into Kip's downstairs office. She put her cell on the mammoth mahogany desk where he often worked and sat in his comfy, soft leather chair. She pulled up one of her favorite phone pics of Kip and touched his face on the screen. Out loud, she said, "I already miss you so much. I'll take good care of our twins, I promise. I also promise that Menendez will pay."

Suddenly, he appeared standing in front of the desk. Suzanne had experienced apparitions twice when the Monroe twins appeared to her in their house after their murders five years ago – and then in her "boardroom" study. She took a deep breath, "Kip, Is that you?"

He smiled, "It is my love."

"Can I hug you?"

"Unfortunately, that's not the way it works."

Standing and walking around the desk, she asked, "How does it work, Kip?"

He didn't answer that question but asked one. "Was it golden frog poison that the delivery guy got me with?"

"Yes, the same poison that killed Pamela Loncart. I'm so sorry, Kip. If not for me, you'd be here with me and our twins."

He smiled. "It's okay, Suzanne, and it certainly wasn't your fault."

On the verge of crying, she said, "I need help, Kip. Menendez may try to kill me, our daughters, and others."

"Suzanne, I can promise the twins will be safe. Menendez missed his chance with the twins; that chance is gone forever, and he knows it."

"What about others? Will you come back?"

"No, not physically, anyway."

"If I call for you, will you help?"

He smiled, "You can handle Menendez."

"But how?"

Then his apparition was gone.

She wailed, "Kip, don't leave me like this." She wondered if she'd ever see his apparition again.

She flopped back down into his big desk chair. She hemmed and hawed about the next call she needed to make. Might as well get it over with.

****

It was 8:00 AM and three hours earlier on the West Coast where Sandra, Kip's ex-wife-from-hell (his description of the twins' birth mom), was frolicking with her latest rich husband. Suzanne had to make the call before Kip's death was on every news station. Three years ago, after the twins were kidnapped, Kip had overlooked telling her immediately. Sandra heard about the kidnappings on TV and threatened Holy Hell if they were harmed in any way. Kip knew she was a blowhard and avoided pushing her buttons. There was no legal action after they were rescued.

Her twins hated Sandra Davies, as did Kip. They got their height, blonde locks, blue eyes, and beauty from her-- but thank goodness, their brains, and common sense from their dad. Their mom spent every cent Kip could make (which had been a lot) on jewelry, clothes, exotic "girls" trips, cocaine, and premium cases of booze and wine. She specialized in doing young pro instructors—golf, tennis, and skiing (and he'd heard recently, pickleball). After a trifecta of DUIs and multiple shoplifting adventures in some of Atlanta's toniest stores and a scene with her running around the house with a handgun threatening the girls, even her high-priced attorney couldn't make a case in front of one of Atlanta's top family court judges.

Suzanne could only imagine her reaction. But if she didn't call, it could get worse. She'd never talked to Sandra in the four years since Kip had gotten full custody of the twins, and they'd married. She didn't expect sympathy, but she would try to give some.

On the fifth ring, she groggily picked up.

"Sandra, this is Suzanne Delacroix."

"The bitch who's fucking Kip. Right? Who turned my girls against me. My girls, Goddammit. What do you want bitch? Do you know what the fuck time it is?"

It was all Suzanne could do not to light up her sorry ass. "Sandra, I'm sorry for the early call, but I have some sad news you need to hear."

"What, that he divorced you, too? Hell, that should be good news for you."

"Kip died yesterday."

A long pause. Then Sandra broke down and screamed. It sounded fake. Suzanne let her carry on for two minutes.

"I'm betting, bitch, that without you, he'd be alive." *If she only knew how true that was.*

"How did it happen?"

"Coroner thinks a heart attack." *But she knew that was another lie.*

"I'm sorry, Sandra. I'll text you information about his service when I have it."

Sandra replied, "I'll have my attorney check his Will."

She almost said, "Knock yourself out. He didn't leave you a penny after you sucked him dry for so many years. It all goes to Saville and Sarah." Instead, she hung up and prayed she'd never hear from her again or see her in person.

****

Suzanne hoped Sarah Baldwin (whom her stepdaughter was named after) wasn't in the middle of surgery when she called. Six years ago, Dr. Sarah Baldwin and her cousin Kip were like sister and brother again after a long hiatus. She was a well-respected vet surgeon in Roswell who lived with her husband, Tim, and son, David, now a superstar college lacrosse goalie and the same age as Sarah and Saville. They'd all become good friends and loved to go to Braves games together.

Sarah and her son had played key roles in the nasty *Game of Twins*. Articles and books subsequently made Suzanne out to be the ultimate *Game of Twins* heroine. In her mind, though, David Baldwin was the true hero. As a young teenager, he and his mom stood up to the DEA witch, Pamela Loncart, when no one else would.

Then, three years later, after his cousins, Saville and Sarah, were kidnapped, Suzanne realized the only way to get them back was to somehow kidnap Pamela's boys and make a trade. After having

Suzanne's longtime APD partner assassinated, Pamela gave her eleven days to rescue her daughters before they became sacrificial lambs in the dark *Game of Twins*.

Suzanne's theory was that the Loncart twin boys lived in the U.S. and played lacrosse under different names. Lacrosse in Mexico was pathetic at best. Pamela was all about lacrosse and seeing her twins become big stars. The challenge was finding them among the estimated 300,000 American high school lacrosse players.

A couple of highly sophisticated techie friends of Suzanne, Arnie and Sheila, combed through several hundred thousand data points, including info and photos of players online. They knew the Loncart boys' ages and had some middle school photos – realizing that they could have changed a lot physically, but with a professional sketch artist got a reasonable rendering – and a lacrosse fact that they were midfielders, AKA, middies. They were likely midfielders who would play on a good team in a competitive urban area. Unfortunately, most online photos of all lacrosse players were taken with their helmets on. But David Baldwin got a brainstorm. Instead of cradling the ball with their sticks, he knew the Loncart twins always show-boated and double-twirled their sticks in a unique manner frowned on by most coaches. The tech/data gurus reprioritized locations and schools and went after more videos found on school and recruiting websites. David located them twirling in two separate videos—playing at two different private schools in Nashville, Tennessee.

Then, the Herculean effort – to trade for her twins. Without David, she knew her twins would be dead. Suzanne thought of him as a son. He was critical, and others were a massive help in rescuing the twins. She couldn't help thinking, though, that she'd gotten help from someone behind the scenes. Something other than divine intervention. It remained a mystery to her.

****

She planned to tell Sarah the whole scoop. The Baldwins had a right to know. What she didn't want to do was scare the bejesus out of them. After discovering she was alive, Suzanne had no idea what Raoul Menendez would do next.

Dr. Baldwin had just finished operating on an Aussie injured in a hit-and-run. She had to remove one leg, her only choice, but she felt sure he'd learn to walk with his three good legs. Dogs were so much more resilient than most humans she knew.

Sarah saw her number pop up and said, "Hi, Suzanne." But before she could get a word in edgewise, Suzanne said, "I have bad news."

Sarah gulped and hoped it wasn't about David or the twins. "What is it?"

"Kip was murdered yesterday."

"Oh, my God."

"Sarah, it will likely be all over the news by noon – but nothing about his death being a homicide."

"Are you okay? What happened?"

"I'm hang'n in, Sarah; listen, you may hear some lies the media will tell, and I'm not sure how outlandish they could get. Let me walk you through what happened after I got home from playing in a golf tournament yesterday and found Kip dead on the floor."

Sarah listened to her story and asked, "So the Mexican narco guy had someone inject this golden frog poison into Kip?"

"Presumably. The stuff is deadly – with as little as a pinprick or simply touching bare skin. If I'd picked up the golden frog figurine without gloves, you and I wouldn't be talking now. Menendez may think I'm dead but will learn soon that I'm alive and kicking. He's playing his next iteration of the *Game of Twins*."

With concern in her voice, she asked, "Suzy, what happens now?"

"I have a PR gal getting out a preliminary short release in a few minutes. The Medical Examiner, who I know, said she should have the autopsy results later today. The poison is so rare that even the best M.E. will think it's something cardiac. The twins should be back tonight from California, late."

"Tim or I could pick them up."

"Thanks, but I'll have a car pick them up."

"I'm off work the next couple of days. I could bring dinner over?"

"Sure, that would be great. You can tell Tim and David what I told you, but they need not say anything about the frog poison, okay? If this were to become a big murder case and not a natural death, the hoopla caused by law enforcement and the media could be overwhelming. It will be hard enough as it is to go after Raoul Menendez."

"By yourself?"

"I'll need help. Sarah, I need to sit down and talk with my twins. After that, I may have a big ask of you."

"Okay, so do you think Menendez going after you again?"

"Maybe, but I honestly don't know."

"The twins?"

"They were meant to be sacrificed. I have a strange feeling he's giving them a pass. A hunch. *Only per what Kip's apparition told her.*

"David?"

"I don't believe so. But possible. Menendez waited three years to come after someone precious to me. I don't know how much pent-up revenge is driving him. He may see himself continuing the *Game* as Pamela would have -- or taking it in a new and maybe more deadly direction. That's why he must be wiped off the face of the earth. For now, you need to be ultra-cautious. Don't let anyone in your house or make a delivery of any type. Don't open any boxes in the mail if you don't know the sender. Don't accept anything from a stranger. And if you encounter a golden frog figurine, don't touch it. Call me. And tell David, who I assume is away at Duke, the same."

"Okay, let me know if there's anything I can do."

Sarah Baldwin felt horrible for Suzanne and her twins but didn't want her family to get dragged back into the deadly *Game of Twins*. Suzanne's heads-up she would take seriously, but a shiver, like an electric shock, shot down her spine. She knew how dangerous these people were. Her husband Tim wasn't going to be thrilled. He, too, had been involved in the nasty *Game of Twins* with her and their son.

****

It was 9:00 AM when Marsha emailed Suzanne a short release about Kip's passing for her approval. She emailed back, "Thanks for your help. I'll let you know about the autopsy when I hear something. Send it."

The release read:

Mrs. Suzanne Delacroix of Atlanta, Georgia, regrets to announce the tragic and unexpected death of her loving husband, Kip Davies. After being out of their house for several hours yesterday, she returned and found him unresponsive near the entry inside their home. He was not ill and had no apparent injuries. It appears he died of natural causes.

Mrs. Delacroix has requested that the Fulton County Medical Examiner perform an autopsy to better understand the cause of her husband's death. That should be completed by later today.

We would ask that you honor her privacy and not contact her directly. We may have more news later. Both have been longtime distinguished citizens of the Atlanta community. A fact sheet is attached to this press release if you are unfamiliar with the Davies-Delacroix's.

Marsha hit a few keys and blasted it out to more than two hundred media contacts in and around Atlanta and a bunch nationally. She knew there would be a lot of initial interest. Her job was not to let the story spiral out of control.

Chapter 9 – Sinaloa

El Nido de Augila Harpia in the Sierra Madre Occidental Mountains – Sinaloa, Northwestern Mexico

El Nido de Augila Harpia he named after the most vicious bird of prey in Mexico, the Harpy Eagle – and was a tribute to Adolf Hitler's *Kehlsteinhaus Eagle's Nest*. Built into the upper face of a 6,200-foot mountain, Harpia was accessible only via a steep, unpaved, well-hidden canyon and a pine and oak-lined road. Inside the mountain were two tunnels with multiple spokes, a pair of elevators, and two sets of interior staircases to the top. An underground garage held a dozen bullet-proofed black Mercedes sedans and Hummers. Nearby were two helipads with three Bell Viper Attack helicopters—well camouflaged. At the top was a four-inch-thick bulletproof window built underneath a natural granite overhang. Invisible even to the ever-searching, always-watching satellite eyes of the NSA. He owned dozens of places in Sinaloa and elsewhere – besides homes around the globe. Harpia was his favorite.

He sat with his brown caiman alligator boots propped on the edge of his Kingwood desk. He wore blue jeans, a belt studded with turquoise and opals, and a white linen shirt, looking like he walked out of a Calvin Klein ad. He could watch four large TV screens suspended from the ceiling while not interfering with his pristine view of the Sierra Madres. He controlled the screens, channels, and sound by voice command. Plus, perched on his desk were two Apple laptops where he monitored his stocks, bonds, gold, and cryptocurrency holdings.

****

That morning, Raoul was glued to the news on CNN, MSNBC, BBC, and FOX as diligently as he ever had. Watching CNN, he saw the *Breaking News* scroll across the bottom of the screen: "Suzanne Delacroix finds husband Kip Davies dead." That answered his first question. Raoul already knew her husband was poisoned and dead.

He'd rated the chances of Delacroix picking up the golden frog figurine smeared with golden frog poison at less than 50-50. He smiled. Touché. The *Game* was back.

For grins, he clicked on the audio for FOX. Ten minutes later, a leggy, big-tittied, blonde anchor took over the show and gave a short news update of what she called "the facts about Kip Davies's death." Raoul knew that FOX was often full of nonsense. But his ears perked when he heard the anchor say, "We have confirmed that Suzanne Delacroix is a person-of-interest in the death of her husband."

WTF? Menendez could scarcely believe his ears. He surfed to a few other sites on the nutty radical right. FOX had already gotten their attention. Now mushrooming online: a woman of color (an ex-cop) murdering her wealthy white husband – impossible to ignore. There were voices of reason from the major media players trying to remind the public that there was no evidence and there were no charges; it was unfounded speculation. Unfortunately for Suzanne, much of the damage was getting baked in, especially in the MAGA realm. He saw Twitter and Facebook already blowing up about "the nigger chink murdering her husband." Raoul beamed. Delacroix was being blamed for her husband's death. Priceless

Looking out at the surrounding mountains, lush vegetation, and cloudless blue sky, Raoul poured himself a double Código 1530. He was awash with calm. Delacroix survived the golden figurine—not a big surprise. It was hard not to be amused by the predicament that she found herself in. Not what he'd anticipated. But he remembered Pamela telling him the *Game* was neither totally controllable nor predictable.

****

Every time he looked at his beautiful girls, Raoul saw her. His almost four-year-old twins were turning into little Pamelas before his eyes. The identical twins had long, auburn locks, lovely cherub faces, and their mother's remarkable dark eyes. He wondered if they would become powerful witches like their mom. One day, he hoped the Dark

Lord would give each a kingdom to reign over. He knew his precious Pamela was in hers now.

Raoul had dozens of beautiful women over the years, but none comparable to her. Why her? The auburn-haired beauty was stunning and had seemed to get more beautiful with age, but she was so many more things: a sexual carnivore unlike he'd ever experienced; a person more intelligent than any he'd ever met, including himself; a woman who understood Machiavellian power and how it should be used (and never have a regret); and a female witch driven to seek more of everything that would gain the Dark Lord's approval.

Delacroix, a suspect in her husband's death. Indeed, she'd go public about the golden frog poison used in her husband's death, but then again maybe not? His Dark Lord was showering him with favor. He picked up the golden *Phyllobates Terribilis* figurine on his desk – custom made at four times the size of an actual frog – consisting of a dozen ounces of twenty-four-carat gold. He caressed the golden frog and laughed out loud. Then, one at a time, he picked up the miniature, real-size versions that he'd also had crafted. He lined up the six in pairs. He laughed and asked the golden figurines, "Where shall we hop to next?"

Presumably, only he and Delacroix knew about the golden frog poison that killed her husband, but how long could that last? He doubted a speedy autopsy and lab work would indicate the rare poison. She could start whining about him in the press, but he knew she'd never have an iota of proof linking him to her husband's murder. And regardless, good luck getting him out of Mexico.

Delacroix was screwed and probably knew it. Menendez would let the media carrion feast on her for a time; there was no big rush to eliminate the woman who had killed his Pamela. Besides, he hadn't decided yet how to kill her. It would be sadistic and merciless. After he and others wore her out, he would use the black double cross as the final instrument of her death -- as it had been used in twins murders for decades.

Right now, he was thinking more about others who'd aided and abetted the killing of his Pamela. There was no rush to kill Delacroix; he knew killing others would make her suffer that much more. This *Game of Twins* stuff could be so fun! In the meantime, he'd watch the Delacroix story unfold from on high.

****

Chapter 10 – Dr. Jill

The day after Kip's Murder

By 9:00 AM, Suzanne was antsy; she called Dr. Treece but only left a message: "Jill, I wasn't sure when you'd do the autopsy. We decided to blast out a short press release that reported Kip's death, that I'd approved of an autopsy, and that you were doing it. I emailed it to you. We did it preemptively because last night Bobby Price told me a guy who works for him got an anonymous phone message that Kip was dead and said that I'm a person-of-interest, implying, I guess, that I could have murdered him. I think it was Gary Popov. I imagine he'd called others in the media – which could quickly become a shitstorm."

By 10:00 AM, Dr. Jill was gowned up. She'd listened to Suzanne's voicemail and was pissed, but she wanted to get the autopsy done before she dealt with Gary and could give Suzanne some concrete news.

Lo and behold, the short, burly detective walked into the morgue and said, "Hey boss, stopping by to see if I could watch the Davies autopsy. I assume you got the report I emailed last night."

"Have a seat," she said brusquely. Gary sat down on the one metal chair. She towered over him and glowered, "Gary, you've done some good things here, and no one's perfect. I get that."

He smiled at her.

"But you crossed the line telling the press that Suzanne Delacroix was a person-of-interest in Kip's death."

"But I didn't..."

"Stop! Hell, it was pretty evident in the last line of the report you sent me. No one in the press even knew Kip was dead, much less that his widow was a supposed person-of-interest, which she isn't. You have no idea how your unauthorized leak to the press has harmed Suzanne and her family."

"Whoa, boss. I was trying to flesh out what was happening with Davies' death. His body temp showed he could have been murdered by his wife early in the morning before she left to play golf."

"Murdered? What the hell are you talking about?"

"I'm just say'n."

Jill Treece said, "Give me your badge."

Thankfully, he wasn't issued a gun, but she knew he carried his own.

Gary was stunned. He stood and unhooked the gold badge from the belt of his 44-inch waist. He handed it to her.

"You're on suspension until further notice. You will not mention Kip Davies or Suzanne Delacroix to the press or anyone else. Then maybe you'll get a shot at keeping your job. Is that clear?"

He nodded. Walking to the door, he turned and said, "I'm telling you -- he got murdered."

She despised Gary but, as the door shut, wondered if there might be a grain of truth in what he said.

Gary left angry but knew he'd need to toe the line, at least for a while. He had the discipline to do that. But he'd overplayed his hand, and to his credit, he knew it. To calm his anxiety, he hacked into APD's crime database that was uploaded daily to the FBI's NCIC database in D.C. He found a missing person's report on Amy; they didn't have dick on her disappearance, and it seemed they weren't treating it seriously. He grinned but knew that would change.

****

After painstaking planning and executing the murders of his parents and three siblings in Serbia at age sixteen, Ivan Surlov used the money he'd stolen from his family to buy a new identity, and five years later he became a U.S. citizen: Gary Popov, who lived in Atlanta. He decided to work from the inside versus outside of the law without becoming a doctor or lawyer. He graduated with honors from Georgia Tech and earned a scholarship to Boston University, where he got an M.A. in Criminal Justice. His thesis was on serial killer Ted Bundy.

In Atlanta, he'd reached an ultimate position unmatched by any other serial killer of note. Gary was charged with investigating suspicious and unexplained deaths, some that were homicides – in the crucible of violence that was Atlanta. The perfect laboratory to hone his craft. No one had found her body, much less knew Amy was dead, but he had to admit he'd been careless as he dissected his actions. It had been too tempting, but the hunger to kill Amy on a whim after a three-year hiatus since he'd kidnapped the teenage blonde cutie had clouded his judgment. Regardless, he knew he'd survive. He had a new target who might be the trickiest ever. The only way to make amends to further his mission in life: abduct and kill the bitch -- using new tactics. He was sure it would be fascinating and fun.

****

At 1:00 PM, Dr. Treece had a gown back on and walked back into the spacious autopsy room where she'd spent two hours examining the vital organs of Kip Davies. With instructions to keep his face covered, his body had been prepped by her top mortuary tech. She'd looked at his major organs. Nothing had gotten her attention from his brain to his gut. Zero. Her physical examination showed nothing unusual.

After the autopsy, Joshua cleaned and disinfected the room with industrial-strength chemicals that she'd always found unpleasant and barely tolerable. The smells of dead bodies were worse -- but were part of the job. Kip's body no longer smelled. His organs had been placed back into his body, which was now completely covered with a sheet, before being wheeled into a cadaver cold locker. She said, "Joshua, can you give me a few minutes alone here."

"Yes, mam."

****

Like Gary, Jill sensed something wasn't quite right. If so, she'd guessed it was due to the mark on Kip Davies's right hand. She lifted his hand and looked at the mark again. She bet Suzanne knew more about it. She also bet Suzanne wanted any potential investigation to go away. But why? She had to have a good reason. She was certain that if it was a murder, Suzanne didn't kill her husband. But she'd wager someone extremely dangerous did. Jill was way beyond needing kudos for her work from anyone. Asked by a stranger these days what she did for a living, she always responded, "I seek truth in death." She wanted to help get the prick who killed Kip.

She could handle a razor-sharp blade more precisely than her best tech or any knife murderer she'd helped put in prison. It took her two minutes to carefully take small slices of Davies's liver and heart; she put them into small polycarbonate containers and put her initials on each, then opened an empty compartment in her ultra cold (-80 degree Centigrade) freezer and slid the small containers in.

After she closed the flaps of Kip's chest and re-examined the top of his right hand again, she re-covered his body with a sterile white sheet and rolled him into a cold storage stall. His body would be at a crematorium tomorrow. So, she'd only have the frozen samples for any subsequent toxicology tests – to maybe understand what the hell happened yesterday at the Davies-Delacroix residence.

Back in her office, she pondered Kip's death more. She could only think that it might be a poison or toxin with which she was unfamiliar. She had to find out.

****

The M.E. of Fulton County called Suzanne from her office. "Suzanne, first, I want to apologize for Gary yesterday. Besides Gary treating you terribly, I'm 99% sure you're right that he was the one who leaked to the press that you were a person-of-interest in Kip's death. He's now on indefinite suspension. I assure you there is no person-of-interest in Kip's death, and there won't be one. That said, unfortunately, it's an unexplainable death. I'm sure that's not what you wanted to hear, but it is all too typical in non-suspicious deaths. I'll indicate it was likely something ischemic cardiac-related with questionable causality."

"Nothing more?"

"No, but I wanted your thoughts on one detail I found in the autopsy."

"Certainly."

"There was a small needle-like mark on the back of his right hand. And there was rock dust on both of his hands. Any ideas?"

Suzanne closed her eyes and gulped before saying, "Kip was an avid rock collector and loved to find, cut, and polish agates in his shop downstairs. My father had a similar passion. I'd suggested more than once that he wear gloves. He wouldn't have it. He had to be "at one" with his rocks and often nicked himself. *Would that fly as a believable lie?*

"Ah, that probably explains it. We did a basic panel of tox screens. He didn't do any illegal drugs?"

"No, of course not. Did your screens show something?"

Suzanne's heartbeat revved way beyond her normal seventy per minute. She was glad Jill couldn't see her body language.

"Nothing. Checking because the standard 12 panel doesn't cover everything, nor does a 24 panel, which I also had done. I'll email you my findings, which are only public if you want them to be. You use them how you see fit. And Suzanne, I can't tell you how sorry I am about Kip."

"Thanks, Jill, he wanted to be cremated. Can you email me a few places and what I should do next?"

"No problem, and call me anytime, Suzanne."

****

GOLDEN FROG POISON A GAME OF TWINS THRILLER

4:00 PM Press Conference - Ferst Center for the Arts Auditorium, Georgia Tech University

More than 500 people were seated, and more were piling in when she started. Now standing room only.

"Many of you know me, but if not, I am Marsha Kaufman of Marsha Kaufman Associates, an Atlanta P.R. firm. To my right is Dr. Jill Treece, head of the Fulton County Medical Examiner's office for the past ten years. Dr. Treece is a licensed forensic pathologist and a full professor of Pathology at Emory."

"We are doing this as a courtesy. Suzanne Delcroix and her husband, Kip Davies, have been distinguished citizens of Atlanta for a long time. We are deeply sorry to lose Kip. And we are sorry for his wife and daughters. There is no murder investigation since there was no murder. And let me get this out in the open. While most media are using good judgment about this tragedy, more than a few are stoking a big lie that somehow his wife was responsible for his death. And are painting her as a villainess. That kind of reporting is irresponsible, wrong, and frankly disgusting."

A redhead in the first row, a FOX reporter, stood and asked sarcastically, "Like, who do you mean?"

Marsha ignored the bitch. "Dr. Treece conducted the autopsy of Kip Davies herself. She will tell you what she knows and then take a few questions."

The large audience went silent, and Marsha was now glad she'd not let the TV crews in.

"Thanks, Marsha."

Dr. Jill immediately got going on what she knew – at least, what she was willing to share. "A summary of the facts I know right now. Mrs. Delacroix arrived home yesterday at about 3:00 PM after playing in a golf tournament. She tried to call and remind her husband to pick up their dog from the groomers; she got no response on his cell, so she picked up her dog and drove home."

"Upon her arrival, she found her husband unresponsive on the floor of their foyer. Being a former police officer, she checked vitals but knew he was dead. She contacted me as a professional acquaintance and asked me to call 911. I did and told her I could be at her place in an hour or so but would send my investigator to see if there was anything he could find to help determine the cause of death."

"Given that there were no apparent signs of injuries or external issues and with the knowledge that Mr. Davies had no health issues, I agreed, upon Mrs. Delacroix's request, to authorize an autopsy to attempt to determine his likely cause of death. I saw his body at his house. After a thorough physical examination at our morgue, we got the 24-panel toxicology results in the last couple of hours. All tox tests were negative. It was an all-too-typical, non-suspicious death. On the death certificate, I indicated it was likely something ischemic cardiac-related with questionable causality."

Before Marsha could entertain questions, a lady in the back barked, "Dr. Treece, you're saying you have no idea how Kip Davies died?"

"In the universe of autopsies that my office performs, maybe 33% are as the result of accidents, or injuries, or fires, or fatalities, or homicides tied to crimes. Fulton County and the State of Georgia require autopsies for those. Others are performed at the request of next-of-kin or if I deem the circumstances of the death suspicious, which I did not in this case. Where there is no known pattern of drug abuse or known illness and nothing material is found, those deaths fall into the unexplainable bucket. Always disappointing to us and loved ones, but that's where Kip Davies's death falls."

"How's Mrs. Delacroix doing?" asked an elderly male reporter.

"Okay, considering. Thank you for asking."

The next question wasn't so friendly. "You're saying that Suzanne Delacroix is not a-person-of-interest in her husband's death?"

Dr. Treece took a deep breath and said, "Correct, she is not. This isn't a criminal investigation."

"Dr. Treece, since the cause of death is uncertain, do you think it's possible someone murdered Kip Davies?"

She immediately lied, "No."

"Is it true that Suzanne Delacroix is a friend of yours?"

"I've known Ms. Delacroix as a professional acquaintance since she was an APD homicide detective, and I also knew her husband."

"So that was a yes?"

"Yes."

Chapter 11 – Sting

Suzanne's best-laid plans of *not* becoming a media centerpiece in the aftermath of her husband's death were unraveling, crashing, and burning. Minute by minute, the lies spiraled out of control. Social media amplified the lie that she was a part of her husband's death. Like Raoul Menendez 3000 miles away, though, Suzanne couldn't help watching the trainwreck – her trainwreck. Continually, she flipped channels of the major news networks to see what they were saying about Kip's murder. Mainstream outlets had only reported that the autopsy had indicated that Kip's death was natural and there was no investigation of his wife.

True to form, FOX doubled down on the lies that Gary Popov had fed them. Tucker Carlson told his MAGA audience in a Special FOX Report, "If you've read Bobby Price's supposedly non-fiction *Game of Twins* stories, it's now obvious they are nothing but outlandish fiction. We all got flimflammed. Suzanne Delacroix is a fake heroine at best, and she was likely involved in her husband's death."

FOX flashed up a photo of Kip in a suit; next to him, Suzanne in a bikini. Carlson closed with, "Can you say gold nigger? Oops, I meant gold digger. This is replacement theory squared. We are in trouble, America, when a Black-Oriental can kill her pillar-of-the-community white husband and get away with it. Yep, only in the lib's America."

The vitriol online was mind-boggling. She was the target of all flavors of right-wing loons spewing their white victimhood and hatred. One white supremacist group blogged a piece with her photos altered and deepfake darkened skin tone, nude, and fake photos of her twins, also naked. The caption on the TV screen: "Davies Twins? Do ya think? Not her twins! Not their mommy! Bitch killed him!"

On another site that was getting thousands of hits per minute was a disgusting, black & white, grainy, vintage video of a teenage black girl with her clothes being ripped off, then being mutilated with knives and sticks, then swinging from a tree limb with several dozen white men and boys watching. The caption: "This is what ornery black bitches deserve."

Other outrageous right wing online headlines included:

"Black foreigner slut murders white husband."

"Negro chink whore kills white husband for his money – his twins will get none of it."

"Will a former darky Atlanta homicide policewoman get away with murder?"

"Liberal ex-Atlanta cop about get her comeuppance?"

And on and on...

They dug up photos of her with Obama at an awards ceremony in Atlanta. The caption: "Look who Obama is schupping: the ex-cop, now a murdering nigger and whore."

And other photos of her at political rallies holding signs protesting Georgia's latest voter suppression attempts and more stringent regulations on a woman's right to choose.

The worst of the bombastic headlines: "The only good black cunt chink is a dead one."

****

Suzanne received several calls that afternoon and let them go to voicemail. Except one from Mia Gonzales, Special Agent in charge of the FBI Atlanta Field Office, a longtime friend who knew plenty about Suzanne's escapades in the *Game of Twins* –since she'd also played a role. A cute, feisty brunette Suzanne's age – who took no guff from anyone – was now happily married after two previous tries and with a daughter in law school.

"Suzy, how are you?"

"Truthfully, I'm a mess."

"I can only imagine. I'm so sorry. What can I do?"

"The girls are coming home late tonight from Santa Barbara, which will help."

"I can get them picked up for you."

"Thanks, I got that handled."

"What are you doing for dinner?"

"Hadn't thought about it."

"Pick any restaurant in the city, any food, and I'll have it delivered. What sounds good?"

"Mia, I don't know. Maybe ribs?"

"Done. Fat Mack's Rib Shack."

"That would be great."

"I can't come over tonight, but I'll have two agents watching your place for the foreseeable future. MAGA threat crap won't be tolerated. And you can call me anytime."

"Mia, you're the best."

"I wish I had a legal reason to get Tucker Carlson's pecker cut off.
"

Suzanne chuckled, "Yeah, that assumes Tucker even has one."

They both laughed. "Let's talk more next week. We'll have a small service. Mia, for now, this is off the record. Cross your heart?"

"Absolutely."

"Kip was murdered. I know the who, how, and why. But trust me on this: there's no evidence and never will be, and the who is untouchable."

Mia Gonzales didn't miss a beat. "Raoul Menendez. What a stinking piece of diarrhea dog shit. Maybe we can cut his pecker off instead of Tucker's."

Suzanne couldn't help laughing.

After they hung up, Mia said to herself, "She's going to try and take Menendez out. How's she going to do that?"

****

Most of the following week was a blur except for the remarkable service at the Ebenezer Baptist Church Chapel. Suzanne was happy to be with her twins. They saw the sadness in her amber eyes and volunteered to handle all the logistics of their dad's service. Intuitively, they knew she didn't want to speak, which was fine. They both told short, funny, heartfelt stories about their dad. And before the service, they'd told her she'd get the surprise of her life. She had no idea what it might mean.

Kip and Suzanne went to a UNICEF fundraiser at the High Museum of Art a year ago when he walked up to her and said, "Suzanne, you are more gorgeous than pictures I've seen of you and braver in the *Game of Twins* books than any woman I've ever heard of. It's a pleasure to meet you in person." He took her hand, bowed, and kissed it.

That afternoon, her daughter, Sarah, stood and told the small audience, "This was Dad's favorite song: *Fields of Gold*, which *he* wrote..."

Then "he" walked from the anteroom with his guitar and sat on a chair at the front of the small sanctuary.

Attendees gasped.

Dressed in a long-sleeve shirt, black jeans, and boots, Sting said, "I like Eva Cassidy's rendition better, but here's mine."

And with his guitar, he sang the haunting yet hopeful, romantic song, "Fields of Gold," that Kip and Suzanne loved. Within a minute, there wasn't a dry eye in the chapel:

"You'll remember me when the west wind moves

Upon the fields of barley

You'll forget the sun in his jealous sky

As we walk in fields of gold."

After his song, her face flooded with tears; Suzanne walked up and hugged him and whispered, "You are a person-of-light. Thank you."

He whispered back, "As are you. We need to stick together. If I can ever be of service, call me."

Spontaneously, they did an elbow and fist bump. Then he was gone.

After the service, Saville told her twin sister, "I hope this isn't catty, but it's too bad he's married."

****

Dark clouds raced across the sky. Thunder boomed as the guests arrived at Bernie's Pizzeria in Alpharetta for what was, in politically correct jargon, called a celebration-of-life. The Davies twins called it "Kip's Last Party." Bernie's had long been known as the best pizza place in Atlanta. The original proprietor was Bernie Scally. Three years ago, Bernie gave his restaurant to Tony Santucci, whom he'd adopted as a son in his late 20s. Tony was David Baldwin's lacrosse coach in middle school, then high school coach. Tony was named the national high school lacrosse coach of the year, and David Baldwin received the award for being the best high school lacrosse player in the U.S.

****

GOLDEN FROG POISON A GAME OF TWINS THRILLER

Tony greeted guests at the door and hugged Suzanne when she arrived. He told her that Bernie was on vacation in Belize and sends his regards. The tall, lanky thirty-year-old she viewed almost like a son. One of the nicest guys she'd ever met. When the guests arrived, a smorgasbord of antipasto and pizza was on the bar, along with several of the best Italian wines from Bernie's cellar.

Suzanne accepted condolences with thanks and grace. These were her loved ones and best friends. A couple of glasses of vino relaxed her. She was having a lovely time until she was struck by dread--and could scarcely catch her breath. She scanned the room; the evil *Game of Twins* had touched all of them – only because of her. Her guilt overwhelmed her. She walked outside and stood under the small veranda. She was filled with dread about how Raoul Menendez could harm any one of them if he so chose.

Saville opened the front door and asked, "Mom, are you okay?"

"I'm fine, Saville; I needed a few moments alone."

It was like a reunion of a battle-tested group of soldiers, but she knew there could be more battles to come. She walked back inside and found Lazlo Kianian in the kitchen. He looked terrific in a blue sports coat and jeans.

"Laz, I didn't see you sneak in. I'm glad you're here, but you missed Sting singing "Fields of Gold" in person.

"You've gotta be kidding!"

"Nope, it was pretty cool."

She smiled, her amber eyes sad, and said softly, "Laz, the girls are going back to California tomorrow afternoon. Could you maybe come over tomorrow night?"

She wore a short black dress and heels with her ubiquitous diamond and emerald platinum cross necklace – and looked phenomenal.

He winked, "Text me a time." and she continued to mix with the guests.

As she walked away, it was all he could do not to shout out a Hallelujah.

****

The following day, Suzanne got her twins up at 8:00 AM. "Rise and shine, sleepy heads. I have a surprise for you today before you leave town. Take quick showers. I'll have fresh donuts, bacon, and OJ on the dining room table."

She let them eat breakfast and then put the urn with their father's ashes on the kitchen table with a small cooler.

"Okay, here's what I thought we'd do this morning, which is undoubtedly frowned upon where we are going. We'll keep some in the urn to go in his columbarium when it's ready at the church."

The twins looked at each other. "Can we touch them, his ashes?" asked Sarah.

"Absolutely."

Each smudged a little on their fingers.

"Wow," they said in unison.

They were off after Suzanne poured the remainder into a small 6-pack cooler.

She and Kip belonged to two clubs in Atlanta, The Capital City Club, which had three superb golf courses. As an enthusiastic and skilled golfer, Kip played them for years, and after they married, she enjoyed them, too.

But the course they both loved the most was where she grew up playing with her dad, a former top Atlanta cop who was granted a membership long before it had its multi-million makeover. Eastlake was where Bobby Jones played most of his teenage golf in the early

20th century. It was now pristine and hosted the year-end Players FedEx Championship, where the best 32 men players from across the globe vied for a first prize of $18 million.

****

They drove down to Eastlake that beautiful, crisp, clear April morning. Suzanne often played a quick nine holes early before many people were on the course or late afternoon and could buzz around nine holes in less than an hour. When she arrived that morning, her golf bag was already on her cart. She carried her own small cooler.

"Thanks, Max. We're going to zoom around. My twins are spectating; we need another cart."

"Yes, Mam. And, mam, I was sorry to hear about your husband. A great guy."

She hugged the caddymaster whom she'd known for twenty years. "Thanks, Max."

He had another cart next to hers in two minutes.

"Enjoy your round, Ms. Delacroix."

****

Golf is the most social amateur sport wherein players at all levels can play and compete together. But she loved playing alone, too. The peace only interrupted off and on when she was smacking her golf ball. Suzanne said, "Girls after we drive down the first fairway, toss the ashes whenever and wherever you want."

Saville said, "Mom, this is pretty weird."

Her twin Sarah said, "Come on, it'll be fun."

Suzanne hit her first drive, and they zoomed off. She grinned as both girls took a handful of ashes and threw them up in the air. Suzanne hit a good second shot twenty feet from the hole. Despite being stellar athletes, the twins were not golfers, much to the chagrin of their dad and Suzanne. They gave her a big round of applause when her birdie putt dropped on the first hole.

Driving down the second fairway, she watched them toss more ashes and said, "Kip, honey, your twins are making you an eternal part of this beautiful place."

Then she entered a golf "zone" unlike any she'd ever experienced as her twins periodically tossed more ashes onto the carpet of perfect zoysia grass. Suzanne was a 4-handicap golfer; she'd grown up playing at Eastlake with her dad and had played many good rounds. But this was different. She was two under par after three holes. Something she'd only done once in hundreds of rounds. On the fourth tee, Kip appeared and said, "I love being part of the course! Thank you. Now play like you're a couple behind to win the U.S. Women's Open in the final round." And he was gone.

Many golfers at every level – but more common with pros and skilled amateurs – describe the "zone" in many ways. Something not to be analyzed. Only experienced. It was a Zen-like thing. Described by Junah Randulph in the story, *The Legend of Bagger Vance,* and Michael Murphy in his mystical golf masterpiece, *Golf in Our Kingdom.* It was personal. She'd experienced it before, but it was hard to bottle and lasted only briefly.

She was still in the zone as she birdied two of the following four holes and was four under par after seven holes. Something she'd never dreamed possible. Her twins periodically tossed out the rest of their dad's ashes and clapped when she hit a good shot. She made birdie putts on the eighth and ninth holes. She was six under par for the nine. She'd shot 29, which she guessed was the course record for the front nine for women. She was astonished. Her best front nine ever by four strokes. It was tempting to play the second nine and see if she could beat the women's 18-hole course record. But she smiled and decided not to press her luck. She knew any zone only lasted so long. After completing the nine, Kip reappeared as she dropped her putter into her bag. His apparition smiled and told her, "Great round, Suzy."

"Kip, please tell me who else may be in danger." But there was no answer. He was gone.

****

After a quick lunch with the girls and dropping them off at RDU, she already felt lonely when she got home. Driving in, she waved at the two FBI guys that Mia had promised. Inside, Lilly lapped her face on the couch.

She thought about her invitation to Lazlo to keep her company that night and frankly felt guilty as hell. She chose loneliness and not guilt. She composed a short text and sent it to Laz: L-sorry but I just can't do this evening. Raincheck?

Within two minutes, he sent back a sad smiley face and wrote, "OK - if you promise."

She sent back: "I promise."

Lazlo Kianian was disappointed as hell but knew whatever was going to happen between them wouldn't happen on his timeframe.

****

A few days later she got the courage to call Dr. Jill Treece. "Sorry you couldn't make it last week. I wanted to thank you in person for all you've done. If you're open for dinner tonight, I'll order it in. My place, say 7:00 PM?"

"I'd love to, Suzanne."

"Great, I'll text you my address."

****

Suzanne was wracked with guilt about not telling Jill all that she knew. She needed to make amends and ask for her help. The fashionable woman arrived in gorgeous tan silk slacks and blouse, heels, and a bottle of wine.

"Welcome," Suzanne took the wine, and Jill followed her. She'd never been inside the Davies-Delacroix place before. Not surprisingly, it was attractive, with a mix of colorful African and Chinese art accents and modern furniture – and no clutter.

"I hope you like pizza; I'm serving a special pie from my good friend's pizzeria where we had the wake for Kip."

"Sorry I couldn't make it last week."

"No problem."

They both felt uneasy as hell -- for the same reason. Suzanne opened the bottle of Caymus Cabernet and poured two glasses. The two beautiful, intelligent women walked to the great room and sat on the big leather sofa.

Suzanne needed a couple of sips to start. She looked Jill in the eyes and said, "I'm a liar, and I apologize."

Jill gave her a friendly smile. "Hey, we all sometimes fib with good intent. I fibbed to you. I could've made it last week. It didn't feel right."

Jill hesitated, "Kip was murdered, wasn't he?"

With a bemused smile, Suzanne said, "Not much gets past you, does it?"

Jill smiled, "Why don't you tell me the story."

As they sipped wine, Suzanne told it. All of it.

Jill nodded throughout and then, after Suzanne stopped, said, "I understand."

Suzanne teared up. The UberEATS delivery finally arrived with two of Bernie's pizzas and a note from Tony Santucci: "Anything you need from me or Bernie, just ask. Love Tony."

"Jill, I'm hungry."

"Me too."

Both women devoured pizza and drank the Zin. After her second piece, Jill asked, "What can I do? How can I help put this asshole away?"

Suzanne said, "Back in a minute."

She returned with a small jewelry box and a pair of medical gloves. She pulled them on and removed the figurine from the box:

"The golden poison frog. Menendez's calling card. Kip was already dead. But I think he was hoping to kill me too."

"You think the frog was dipped in the potent poison."

Suzanne nodded, "I do, but I must know for sure. I'm giving you the frog." She handed the box to Jill.

"Let me see what I can find out."

****

Jill Treece often longed for the touch of her late husband, but otherwise, her life was full of challenge and wonder. She couldn't remember being bored or depressed for one minute. Being able to help folks and provide some answers when she could about a deceased family member or friend was always rewarding. The best was helping the cops catch a murderer who would get maximum punishment. Jail seemed too good for Raoul Menendez.

Jill had learned to pace herself workwise over the years but was in a hurry the following day. She found him in her online contact files. A forensic pathologist, an expert in animal poisons/toxins at the University of Florida-Gainesville, she'd met Dr. Noah Kline at a conference two years ago. There was no answer, but she left a message and went about her business.

An hour later, Kline said happily, "Dr. Treece, so nice to hear from you."

Ten years ago, Kline's only son and his wife were killed by a drunk driver on their way home from Christmas shopping in Gainesville. Noah made good money from his university salary and consulting but lived frugally and never re-married. He was married to his research to improve the effectiveness of antidotes to help save more people from the deadliest snake bites – and make the antidotes more affordable -- for countries where snakes killed people in the thousands a year: India, Indonesia, Nigeria, Pakistan, Bangladesh, and others. A few years ago, he'd become interested in deadly toxins spewed by other animals and not only snakes.

"Noah, I need your help. I'm flying down to Gainesville with evidence in a murder case, probably involving golden frog poison. I need you to verify the poison on a couple of items. Can you get me picked up at the airport around 11:00 AM?"

"I'll pick you up myself."

"Thanks, Noah."

His brain swirled. He knew of the nerve toxin batrachotoxin from golden poison frogs but had never encountered it. It was deemed by many the most potent animal toxin on the planet. He'd need to do some quick research and went about setting up his lab for the necessary testing. Lord knows he'd lived a fascinating life but figuring this out and seeing Jill Treece again – it didn't get any better.

PART II

Chapter 12 – The Three

Five years ago, Suzanne was compelled to dive back into the evil *Game of Twins*. She and her former APD homicide partner, Dusty Rayfield, killed Pamela Loncart's brother and cousin who attacked Suzanne in her condo -- after Suzanne solved the recent twins' murders in Atlanta – and the murders of another half dozen twins – over a century.

Pamela was forced to flee with her teen twin boys, who'd played lacrosse with David Baldwin in middle school. She tried to cover her tracks by setting fire to her mansion in north Atlanta and escaping to Mexico to live with her longtime boyfriend, Raoul Menendez. She made it there with her twins and was placed on the FBI's and Interpol's most-wanted lists.

Suzanne had surmised that when a set of twins was born into their Atlanta Tribe coven, a sacrifice of teen girls was in order. Since the early twentieth century, six sets of twins had been murdered so far. Pamela wanted revenge for her brother and cousin; Suzanne's twin stepdaughters were perfect targets. And Pamela had recently given birth to twins via Menendez. She knew it was her Dark Lord's signal to do his bidding.

Pamela Suzanne's twins were kidnapped while starting to walk home in front of their Atlanta private high school. She brought them back to Mexico and treated them well--but also let Raoul have a little fun with them before the sacrifices would begin. Not 100% sure who the kidnappers were, Suzanne negotiated a ransom payment for her twins, but it was a ruse. Pamela's sniper assassinated her APD partner Dusty and left the $8 million they'd demanded next to Dusty's body. But then, in a so-called spirit of the *Game*, Pamela gave her eleven days to rescue her twins before they would be abused and killed like the twins before them.

With help from her friends, Suzanne did find and kidnap Pamela's twins and proposed a trade of twins which was set up on the Salt Flats of Bonneville, outside Salt Lake City. Raoul hadn't wanted her to go to Utah for the exchange. But Pamela had been adamant about getting her sons back and killing Suzanne in person. Besides, she told him she had an ace in the hole.

Things went sideways for Pamela on the Bonneville Salt Flats where the exchange took place. In their hand-to-hand combat, Suzanne wrested away the ampule that Pamela had attached to her sunglasses and (not knowing what it was) scratched her with it. She died. Only Suzanne knew Pamela's last words Suzanne: "Golden frog poison...Mary Jo." Her twin boys returned to Mexico and Suzanne took her twins back to Atlanta.

Raoul hated Delacroix but was impressed with her handling of her twins' kidnappings. There wasn't a single word about her and her compadres kidnapping and trading for Pamela's boys, which would have put them in legal jeopardy. It was ingenious, but Delacroix's string of good fortune was about to end. The golden frog poison had been a good idea for Pamela until it backfired. But now he was taking a page from her playbook – embracing this new iteration of the *Game of Twins* and the revenge gnawing at him.

****

An unlikely trio, they met in their usual Dark Web chat room promptly at 4:00 PM Central that Friday.

-Raoul Menendez, the Sinaloa drug lord who now controlled a third of all drug trafficking and distribution worldwide – that percentage was closer to 75% in the U.S.

-Mary Jo Cogburn, 7-term Republican Congresswoman from the tony burbs of north Atlanta; the current House Majority Whip and the odds-on favorite to be on the national ticket in two years as VP or President.

-Michael Abbott, unbeknownst to all but a few, the single wealthiest person on the planet. Michael's riches were currently valued at $7 trillion. He was a full Professor of Finance at Princeton and an acclaimed consultant and writer. Most recently, he authored the best-seller, *Laundering the Big Bucks*" His former name, which he changed many years ago, was Jeremy Sutterland of the infamous Atlanta Sutterland-Loncart family.

Their commonality: they were top members of the Atlanta Tribe, the wealthiest and most powerful modern-day coven, born of the Loncart coven in the late 1600s. The trio were arguably the most potent threesome anywhere. Mary Jo, who grew up with Michael and Pamela, became Chief of the coven after Pamela died. Raoul became a member years ago after being recruited by Pamela.

Their pet name for themselves: *"The Three."*

****

The agenda was always fluid, but *The Three* agreed that it was essential to communicate regularly. Mary Jo started, "Raoul, I'm guessing this "natural" death of Kip Davies was your doing. Why would you do that?"

"You know it is our way that twins must be sacrificed to please our Dark Lord after twin girls were born into our family. Besides, his wife killed my Pamela."

Mary Jo retorted, "Come on, Raoul, that was a while back after Pamela tried to kill her."

"I used the golden frog poison to kill her husband and had a shot at killing her, too."

"Obviously, that failed. I saw Delacroix on the news."

Michael asked, "Now what?"

Raoul said, "It's the *Game of Twins*. My revenge is done when I say it's done."

Wanting to put the drug kingpin in timeout, she noted, "You don't think Delacroix is coming for you, even now as we speak? I've read the two *Game of Twins* books. She's the most fearless, most resilient woman I've ever heard of."

Raoul said, "Of course, she knows it was me. I left a little golden frog covered with poison next to her dead husband. Gloating, he asked, "What could she do to me...to us?"

Michael interjected, "Raoul, Delacroix killed Pamela right in front of your freak'n nose."

Raoul hurled a flurry of Spanish expletives that neither Mary Lou nor Michael could decipher.

After a minute of silence, Mary Jo asked, "Are you done with your rant?"

She hesitated and stopped speaking. She needed to discuss an idea that was percolating with Michael. This was an opportunity that she and Michael had discussed among themselves. It was time.

"Raoul, we understand you are committed to the *Game* and your revenge for Pamela's death. But before you decide to eliminate anyone else, I'd like you to run it by me so that we, across the border, can at least have a heads-up to be mindful of any fallout. I ask this as your Chief."

Calmly, Michael added, "Let's be reasonable. In a few minutes, I'll show you my projections of your finances. You're on your way to a trillion dollars. You'll be pleased."

Seething at the idea of these gringos trying to control his revenge, Raoul said, "Yes, okay." He poured a Código.

Mary Jo moved to another subject. "Hey Raoul, are you attending your big bullfight in Spain this year? Isn't that coming up soon? I watched a documentary on Netflix about it. Fascinating."

"Yes, I plan to attend the Las Ventes bullfights in May. I own a nice place in Madrid."

After hearing stories of his youth, Pamela gave him the nickname Valiente Matador, Brave Matador. As a teenager, Raoul had trained to become the next Carolos Aruzza, El Ciclón ("The Cyclone"), the most renowned matador from decades ago. But his narco-father decided that bullfighting was too dangerous for his only son. His skills with banderillos and swords would come in handy but not for 2000-pound bulls; rather on enemies or traitors when his business was threatened or disrespected. His signature kill he saved for the most egregious offenders.

His father's side of the family included one of the most infamous Mexican witches from Catemaco, Esmerelda Gallardo Menendez. He grew up on stories his abuela had etched in his memory – when he first learned that men could be witches and brujas macho. She told him he had the makings to be a great one, especially after she'd realized that in person, no one could lie to him without him knowing it.

Their business meeting continued without fanfare. Mary Jo Cogburn could have been more attentive as Michael reviewed the financials with Raoul. But her mind was elsewhere.

****

Considered by many the savviest politician in D.C., Mary Jo Cogburn took her cue from what J. Edgar Hoover had made an art form decades ago. She was a big fan. But she was scarier than Hoover because she had more powers than the former Director of the FBI. She could discern any lie in proximity to anyone and read minds, too.

With her own band of private investigators (money was no issue), she continually collected mountains of dirt on her political enemies, friends, and others she didn't know personally. Those files, photos, audio clips, and videos were in an encrypted storage bin in the cloud. If the Majority Leader or Minority Leader knew what she knew about them, they'd piss in their pants, then have a heart attack or jump off a building. She could cut either off at their knees -- or balls whenever she wanted.

Often, it was best to play nice. But then again, it was best to play it like Hoover did.

In her powerful position, she was responsible for "whipping" her congressional colleagues to get solid vote counts on bills, especially when a tight vote was anticipated -- then help get the bill to the floor for a vote. Republicans, Democrats, and a few Independents were all over the map on this Banking Overhaul Bill, which would eliminate many of the regulations rammed through several years ago by Senator Elizabeth Warren.

The Senate was the problem now, and since the Senate Minority whip was a weenie, Mary Jo had to whip Senators as well. She was one, maybe two votes away. She considered Senator Lemuel Potts a decent target only after she attended a cocktail party hosted by the Majority Leader at his palace in Chevy Chase. She heard Potts wasn't a firm, yes. Unfortunately, she didn't have good dirt on the Senator from Kansas to sway him to her side.

She sidled up to the portly Senator, who had a vice-grip on his highball with a lime, a tad of tonic, and the rest, vodka. She wore a tight red dress with sumptuous cleavage and noticed that he noticed. She decided to be direct, "Senator, how about I take you to the Capital Grille tomorrow for lunch?"

Looking at her boobs, he asked, "Why the hell would ya want to do that? I ain't voting for the bill your party shoved through the House."

With her teasing smile, she said, "Well, ya never know, Senator. Maybe I could change your mind."

He started to fantasize about titty-fucking her and hesitated. Then said, "Oh, hell, why not."

"Great, I'll have a car pick you up outside of Russell. Say 12:30?

"Alright, he reiterated, "But I ain't vot'n for it."

"We'll have a nice lunch, Senator. I'm sure we'll find something to talk about."

Besides being a fat pig with a bulbous, red, pock-market nose, she surmised from his booze intake, he wasn't all that personable either. She decided to take a flyer. She got a drink and moved out of eyesight and earshot. She tuned into Lem Potts, conversing with two elderly Senator buds. It had taken her a couple of decades of practice to hone her occult powers to filter through many static thoughts and zero in on a specific person or persons, in this case, more than sixty feet away. She smiled when she overheard Lem say to them, "Guess who I'm having lunch with tomorrow, boys?"

"Who?" one asked.

Lem said, "She's here somewhere unless she already left. Mary Jo Cogburn. A serious piece of ass, especially for an older gal. Great tits."

The Senator from Kentucky remarked. "I hear she's not to be screwed with. A couple of boys say that under that pretty exterior, she's not merely a bitch but a witch. Takes no prisoners."

Lem said, "Yeah, yeah, okay. Hey, that reminds me. I gotta tell you what I did a few nights ago when the wife traveled home to visit relatives.'

He asked them, "What's the youngest gal you screwed since you've been Senators?"

The two looked at one another. "Hell, I don't know. I did one of my 16-year-old page gals a few times." The other said, "Yeah, maybe a couple of seventeen-year-olds."

"Boys, you ain't done nothing 'til you've fucked a couple of thirteen-year-olds – simultaneously."

"Come on, Lem, that's such bullcrap."

"Here, I'll show you on my phone." He made sure his back was to other folks and showed them a clip with the audio off. Their eyes got gigantic.

"Lordy, Lem, how in the world did you arrange that?"

"Well, let's just say that I know a guy who knows a guy. Grand apiece for the whole night. Worth every cent. Best sex of my life. You boys, lemme know if you're interested." He winked at them and walked to the bar.

Glancing around, he didn't see Mary Jo but thought lunch tomorrow might be fun.

****

The next day, Mary Jo had a limo pick up Senator Lemuel Potts outside the Russell Senate Office Building. It was a nice walk to the Capital Grille, especially in good weather, but she figured Lem wasn't much of a walker. She had a standing lunch reservation at a booth by the far window. The Matre'd said, "So nice to see you, Congresswoman. Your usual table?"

"Yes, thanks, Jeffrey."

"You must lunch here a lot." Potts said as they approached the table.

"Once a week or so. Nice place to talk politics or anything else."

She loved the ambiance of the restaurant. Lots of polished, dark wood, comfy leather booths and chairs, bronze railings, and accents. Not too light or dark for customers so the old boys could read their menus. Most of all, the Grille oozed power, her favorite thing.

They slid into opposite sides of the booth. A tight squeeze for fatty, Lem. She heard him think, "I need a drink."

"Lem, I'm going to order a vodka martini."

Their waiter arrived. She said, "The usual, thanks."

Lem didn't falter. "Dirty Stoli, three olives." A classic lush with a big gut, though covered by expensive threads, his nose glowed like Rudolph's – drooling for his first cocktail.

The drinks arrived. She sipped. He gulped. She mentioned the banking bill and the votes her party needed in the Senate. She gave him her best pitch and got no comment. But she heard him think that she would be big-time fun in the sack.

Lem downed his martini. Mary Jo signaled their waiter and pointed to his glass. He had a new martini in less time than he'd drunk the first one.

She asked, "Lem, can you tell me why you won't vote for the bill?"

"Okay. I'm a politician and want to be here another term. A reporter in my state ran a series of articles about how the bill screws consumers. Which you know it does. I've gotten tons of blowback and will get more if I vote for it. I told my big donors to deal with it."

Mary Jo was surprised by the metal the Senator was showing – for now. Lem ordered a sirloin rare with fries and added onion rings; she ordered a shrimp salad. Lem's martini glass was again empty. Mary Jo saw his eyes dive into her voluptuous cleavage. She heard him think, "Man, I'd like to stick my dick between those titties."

Lem wolfed down his lunch while she picked at her salad. He was feeling good and enjoying Mary Jo's boobs in between bites. When their waiter arrived back, she ordered coffee. Lem slurred, "Yeah, with Drambuie on the side."

After the coffee and liquor arrived, Mary Jo gave him her best smile and leaned over to give him a primo view of her cleavage. She asked, "Lem, what will it take to get your vote for the bill?"

Lem leaned back and said, "Sorry, it ain't happening." *He thought, unless I can cum on your tits.*

She wasn't surprised at his answer. She went with shock and awe. "Lem, I know you're fucking a couple of thirteen-year-old girls.

Mandatory sentences of ten years per girl. And you know what happens to pedophiles in prison."

He could barely mumble. "How could you possibly know that?"

Then, he realized that he verified his misdeeds.

She smiled. "You shouldn't keep kiddy-porn pictures on your phone."

Lem grabbed at his suit pocket to make sure his iPhone was there. Somehow, she'd hacked his phone? He'd get rid of it today but knew he was too late.

She sipped her coffee, "I know I'll have your vote on the banking bill and that you'll recruit two others. Maybe the two boys who also admitted to having sex with minors?"

His answer was quick, "Yes, mam."

"One more time, soldier," she said with the authority of a Marine drill sergeant.

"Yes, mam!"

"Louder."

"Yes, mam, I promise!"

"That's the right decision, Senator. You'll need to get your own transportation back."

After extricating himself from the tight booth, Senator Lemuel Potts rushed to the Men's Room. He barely made it before he tossed his sirloin, fries, and onions on the floor.

****

After *The Three* hung up, Mary Jo called Michael on another secure line. "I've got an idea."

"It wouldn't have anything to do with the bullfights in Madrid, would it?"

She cackled, "You're such a smart boy."

TOM RANSEEN

Chapter 13 - Kings & Queens

The irony of the situation was not lost on Mary Jo or Michael. Unbeknownst to Delacroix and Raoul, they had facilitated the complicated kidnapping (by Suzanne) of Pamela's twins and rescue of Suzanne's twins – with neither Suzanne nor Raoul being the wiser. Now, they were sure Raoul would take dead aim at Delacroix -- and equally sure she would go after him.

Three years ago, they'd conceded that Pamela wouldn't be helpful in Mexico -- or anywhere. She was a fixture on the FBI's and Interpol's top-ten-most-wanted lists, making travel difficult. However, she'd used fake IDs and disguises off and on to see her twin boys play lacrosse in Nashville (where they had fake names). Two decades ago, she'd been the Tribe's most prolific rainmaker when she brought Raoul into the Tribe, but her DEA and Homeland contacts were now toast. Besides, Mary Jo had always felt the Chief title should go to her (even if she wasn't a blood family member). Mary Jo had acted as Chief while Pamela was in Sinaloa, but she wanted the actual title. It was more important to her than her congressional seat.

****

Mary Jo and Jeremy were best friends and lovers as teens; having sex with coven family members was condoned and encouraged. Mary Jo only liked sex with her stepbrother Jeremy Sutterland (now Michael Abbott). After a couple of rounds of athletic banging, they would lay naked outdoors and talk about many things. Her favorite subject was about how one day they would become Queen and King, the two most powerful people on the planet, and pave the way for a new world order while doing the bidding of their Dark Lord. They agreed they could never have enough power, money, and sensual delights.

But there could be only one Queen and one King.

With Michael's blessing, Mary Jo had surreptitiously helped put Suzanne Delacroix in a position to take out Pamela. It was a long shot, but it worked. Delacroix performed admirably despite Pamela cheating and bringing golden frog poison to their showdown. Mary Jo believed the bitch got what she deserved.

But if Raoul ever found out how the two had conspired to help eliminate his longtime partner, the results for them would be unspeakable.

Delacroix did the heavy lifting, but how Mary Jo and Michael had helped was hardly insignificant. They had an FBI agent (who was a legacy member of the Tribe and reported to Pamela) killed because she'd guessed where the twins were -- before their plan was put in motion. They helped Suzanne and her people evade a bunch of Nashville cop cars racing out of the city with Pamela's twins. And they protected Suzanne from being murdered after she'd taken out Pamela on the Bonneville Salt Flats in Utah.

One queen was wiped off the board, but there were still two kings.

Chapter 14 – The Next Victim

Gary remembered that Jill Treece loved roses and tended her own garden. Every day for a week, he had a dozen roses – all different colors – delivered to her office. He was leaving it in her court. Three days after he'd stopped the deluge of flowers, she called his cell.

"Gary, thanks for all the roses. But I haven't gotten any the last couple of days."

Gary, who was missing a sense of humor, was stunned and said nothing.

"Gary, I'm kidding. Sweet of you. How about you come by my office at 8:30 tomorrow, and I'll get you re-instated."

"Thanks, boss!"

****

That was all good, but Gary couldn't focus on his next move. He drank a couple of Heinekens as a change of pace from his Coors Lights and did one line of blow. His thinking cleared. He needed more practice before his big kill. He used his white van to scout the popular nightclub spots on the city's edge for three nights to ensure he knew where the traffic cams and business CCTV were. He chose Armond's –a popular Gen Z spot on the fringe of town. He wasn't interested in low-life sluts walking the street in shady areas. The exception was his first kill, Lori. She was a hooker slut, but she was a pixy cutie, and he was itching to put his freezer to use. No, Gary's taste was classy, hot, young things, like Ted Bundy's. He parked on the other side of the street a half block down. Nothing much was happening at Armond's until 2:00 AM when some of the beautiful boys and girls were exiting.

After three nights of additional surveilling in his black Nissan Altima, he spotted his target. A willowy blonde, half stumbling onto the sidewalk in her heels and tapping her cell and maybe ordering an Uber? He quickly turned his car around in front of the nightclub. He put the passenger window down and asked. "Miss, do you need a ride somewhere?"

Veronica Perkins wobbled on her high heels as she tried to take a couple of steps toward his car. She was drunk and high as a skunk but sober enough to tell herself that an Uber could take a half hour to show up. But who was this guy?

Leaning toward the passenger side, Gary didn't miss a beat. "I'm a policeman." He stuck out his recently re-instated gold badge. She took a couple of steps closer and grabbed it.

While her eyes tried to focus on the badge, he said, "I was doing surveillance for a case but saw that you might be a damsel in distress who needed a ride. I'll drop you off wherever you'd like."

She handed it back.

"Okay, thanks, that would be great," she slurred.

Gary didn't want to leave his car but had no choice. He had to get the drunk girl inside ASAP. He dashed around his car, opened the door, gently took her elbow, and ushered her into the passenger seat. He shut the door and raced back to his driver's seat.

"Tell me where you need a ride to. What's your name?"

The leggy blonde looker mumbled, "Veronica," and said her address was in Virginia Highlands. She leaned back in her seat, utterly zonked on booze and whatever else. He perused her long legs and small breasts lacking a brassiere. He stopped a few streets away. He reached for his small bottle of chloroform and sprayed it into her nose and mouth. Her head jerked, but then she was still. He fetched her purse, which had her cell phone. He turned it off, popped out the SIM card and battery, snapped it in two, and tossed it in a bush. He covered her with a blanket from the back seat.

The drive to his place was only fifteen minutes in the light traffic. He raised the double garage door with his remote. After carrying her inside and removing her microskirt, top, and panties, he wrapped

Veronica in polycarbonate. He lifted her into his hyper-cold freezer with the others. By morning, she'd be hard as a rock. And the others would have company. He smiled.

But walking to his frig, Gary realized he'd screwed up. He hadn't turned off his car's APD GPS tracking. His brain somersaulted. He banged his head against his refrigerator so hard that he dented it. "You dumb ass!" he yelled at himself. But instead of completely tearing up his kitchen, he fetched a beer and sat at the kitchen table. He took a few deep breaths, then a few swigs. He was worrying about something that would only be consequential if they could ID his car. Unlikely since there were no cameras nearby. Or if they had a reason to suspect him and were interested in tracking his GPS. Even more unlikely. Satisfied that he was okay, Gary knocked two big gulps of Coors. But knew he needed to be even more careful in the future.

****

Chapter 15 – Mary Jo

Suzanne had no idea how she had her cell number, but her phone lit up and gave the caller's name.

"Suzanne, this is Congresswoman Mary Jo Cogburn." Suzanne was momentarily stunned and thought back to those last few words from Pamela Loncart. Then on Thanksgiving three years ago, she remembered being drawn to the TV screen with Mary Jo posturing at an Atlanta soup kitchen.

"I'm sorry for your loss and apologize for not calling sooner. You and your husband have been so valuable to our Atlanta community."

"Thank you, Congresswoman. I appreciate that."

"Please call me Mary Jo. I'm going to be in town on Thursday. If you're available, I'd like you to join me for lunch at my place in Buckhead. I've wanted to meet you in person and ask a favor."

"Okay..."

Before she could ask, Mary Jo said, "Great, I'll have my assistant get you lunch info. See you then."

Suzanne couldn't help but wonder about the real reason for the invitation.

****

Mary Jo's "place" was on the twentieth floor of the ritziest condo building in Buckhead, St. Regis, at the corner of Peachtree and West Paces. The Black valet, dressed in a crisp white shirt and bow tie, dark slacks, and spit-shined black shoes, opened her car door and refused the tip Suzanne had pulled out of her purse.

The security guard inside said, "Hello, Mrs. Delacroix."

"Jeez", she thought, *"and I've never been here."*

He pointed. "The elevator behind me will take you to Representative Cogburn's penthouse apartment on the twentieth floor."

On the way up, Suzanne wondered if all this was her tax dollars at work or if Mary Jo was filthy rich – but she knew people wondered about her own wealth.

Suzanne had Googled her and looked at several YouTube videos but didn't know what to expect. Mary Joanne "Jo" Cogburn was in her seventh congressional term representing Atlanta's most affluent and conservative district in the north burbs – where she also had an address in Roswell. Besides being Minority Whip, she was a member of the House Armed Services and House Budget Committees and was the ranking member of the House Permanent Select Committee on Intelligence and Banking.

If the former president decided not to run again in 2024, she was on the short list of vice presidential and presidential candidates. She was a Magna Cum Laude graduate and cheerleader at Georgia. She'd launched her political career as a reporter -- then anchor – at FOX News, which Suzanne never watched.

Congresswoman Cogburn met her at the door and, instead of a handshake, hugged her.

"Thank you for coming, Suzanne."

Suzanne followed her into a mega room with a 180-degree view of the sprawling metropolis of Atlanta, its twelve-county population now over five million.

"Wow, I've never seen the city this way."

"It is beautiful and impressive. It's not New York, but I like Atlanta better. A glass of champagne?"

"Absolutely."

As if on cue, an impeccably dressed, handsome, slim Black man appeared with a bottle of Louis Roederer Cristal Brut Champagne and two flutes.

Admiring the view few Atlantans would ever see, she tried to find Delmont in the heart of Buckhead, the street where she grew up – only a few blocks away. But hers and the other middle/upper middle class, small homes and quaint brick apartment buildings were gone, replaced with multi-million-dollar monstrosities. Progress? She wasn't so sure.

Suzanne was impressed by the décor in Mary Jo's expansive condo with its 13-foot ceilings. The main living area was at least two thousand square feet. It was adorned with tasteful, custom, modern furniture in shades of off-white, blue, and gray, several brilliantly colored pieces of art, and a few accent rugs on the blonde hardwood floor. A smattering of large plants were perfectly placed.

Sitting a couple of feet from each other on a twelve-foot buffalo leather sofa, the two attractive women in their late 40s checked each other out. The verdicts: Mary Jo wasn't sure she'd ever seen such an exotic, beautiful woman. Suzanne thought she was a lovely brunette who looked even better in person than on TV and the videos she'd pulled up.

Mary Jo commented on Suzanne's diamond and emerald platinum cross necklace. "Your necklace is spectacular." *Did she wear that cross necklace because of something she'd learned in the Game – that it blocked occult powers?*

"Thanks, my dad gave it to my mom many years ago. They're both deceased."

Mary Jo sipped her champagne and asked, "How are you getting on? And your daughters?"

Suzanne paused to gather a thought. "It's been hard at best. I love our twin daughters. Kip and I had been so happy for a few years. The twins won't admit it, but they're struggling."

"I cannot imagine. I'm so fortunate that my husband, Paul, takes care of our two teen girls almost full-time. I'm away so much. We have a nice home in Roswell. I'll be driving up there when we've finished here. The favor I wanted to ask you was about joining a small bipartisan committee. You know I'm a Republican, and I've researched you and know you are active in Democratic circles around Atlanta. Despite what the party line is, I want to re-institute Roe—but as a federal law and pass an assault weapons ban bill. The Supeme Court are most loons."

Suzanne was shocked," You're kidding, right?"

"No, I have enough political capital at this point to press those critical topics. I want to add three or four nonpoliticians to our group. Sane people."

They both giggled. "I know you were a homicide detective in Atlanta and still do some work with Interpol. Your reputation is impeccable. Will you think it over? I don't need an answer today."

"I'm flattered, but I have a few other things on my mind. I'll think about it."

"I understand."

Lunch arrived, and it was exquisite. Sliced lobster tails in a tasty but not too spicey Cajun sauce, fried green tomatoes, and melt-in-your-mouth puff pastry rolls. Followed by a crème Brule to die for. The conversation was pleasant, but Suzanne was getting a weird vibe; she decided to rattle her cage sooner rather than later.

She asked, "Mary Jo, I'm curious if you've read Bobby Price's *Game of Twins* books?"

"Compelling stories that would make a great TV serial."

"Maybe. Bobby and I are in negotiations with Netflix."

"That's wonderful. You are a woman to be reckoned with, Suzanne. If I remember, you were fighting to the death to get your twins back in the third book. You ended up scratching a woman with a needle meant for you, and she died."

"No doubt a poison, but the ampoule and her body were sent to Sinaloa. Pamela Loncart was a former DEA agent and longtime paramour of Raoul Menendez."

"Ah yes, the drug kingpin. His name has come up many times in my Congressional Committee hearings. An unbelievably bad guy. Said to be the wealthiest drug lord on any continent. And said to be untouchable by any government."

"No one is untouchable. Here's the thing, Mary Jo – and this is something not in Bobby Price's book."

She proceeded with the partial white lie, adding her last name, "The final words out of Pamela's mouth before she died were, "Mary Jo Cogburn."

Suzanne looked for a facial reaction. She was well-trained in body language. She saw the slightest twitch in Mary Jo's left eyebrow.

"How strange."

"Can you think of any reason she would have said your name?"

Mary Jo tried to think fast. She shook her head, "No, I have no idea. She probably lived in my district. How long ago has it been since you rescued your twins."

"Three years."

"Why mention it to me now?"

"Honestly, I only want to put this evil *Game of Twins* out of my mind. Until a couple of weeks ago when my husband Kip was murdered with the same type of poison that Pamela Loncart tried to kill me with."

Mary Jo frowned slightly. In Mary Jo's eyes, Suzanne saw a flicker of something, indicating she wasn't surprised.

"But I thought your husband died of natural causes."

Suzanne smiled, "You can't always believe everything you read in the papers or online."

"That's for sure."

Suzanne stood and said, "Thank you for lunch. I've taken up enough of your time, Mary Jo. It was a pleasure to meet you, and I will consider your invitation."

Mary Jo asked, "What are you going to do next?"

"Off the record, I'm going to make him pay."

"Him, who?"

Smiling but not answering, she turned and left.

Driving back home, Suzanne was 95% sure that Mary Jo Cogburn knew that "he" was Raoul Menendez. As a friend or foe? That, she wasn't sure about. But at least she had direct contact with the man she intended to kill.

Not much surprised Mary Jo Cogburn because of her ability to read minds. She was always a step or two ahead of any friend or foe. Acting as an occult barrier, though, Suzanne's cross necklace precluded that advantage, she didn't doubt Suzanne knew that. Mary Jo grabbed a bottle of her favorite single malt and a tumbler from her bar. As she sipped the smoky, smooth Scotch, she smiled and thought, *"This could turn out better than I'd imagined. She was now positive Delacroix was going after Raoul, but she guessed she'd need a ton of help to make that happen. The same as three years ago.*

****

Mary Jo gave Michael a summary of her meeting with Delacroix and told him she intended to go after Raoul. "It's perfect, don't you think?"

"A lot of planning is needed, but I like it. Maybe take out two birds with one stone?"

"Maybe."

Mary Jo beeped Menendez to talk in their secure chatroom on the Dark Web. Within a minute, he checked in with her and Michael.

"What's so important to get a high-priority message?" he asked.

Mary Jo said, "We have an idea to help take care of the person highest on your revenge list."

"I'm listening."

"I talked to her by phone and then met her in person."

Incredulous, he shouted, "You what?"

"I wanted to see who we were dealing with. A gorgeous and bright woman. And she said she's coming after you."

"Yeah, right. I'm going to enjoy the bitch and then kill her slowly and painfully."

****

Someone says, "All you need to do is kiss the frog. It will turn into a handsome prince."

The frog standing before her is her size. It puckers up.

"No, no, you can't make me."

"We'll see about that," the frog says. He turns colors – from green to bright golden. It lunges toward her.

Suzanne screams and wakes up shaking from her dream.

Chapter 16 – The Rainforest Hunter

After Raoul had Kip Davies poisoned but failed to kill his wife, his next target was David Baldwin. Going back several years, he'd heard about Baldwin and his family from Pamela and from her twins, who played lacrosse with Baldwin in middle school; some of it detailed in Price's *Game of Twins* books. If not for Baldwin (when Pamela was his middle school lacrosse club chairwoman), Pamela would be guiding guys and girls lacrosse programs at Eaglewood High School in Atlanta – and no doubt having fun with her favorite players of both sexes on the side.

She'd told him, "If it weren't for that pissant, Baldwin, Suzanne Delacroix would never have entered my life." Raoul knew her lacrosse-playing twins hated Baldwin, who was now a collegiate All-American lacrosse goalie – as they languished playing on a crummy Mexico City team – after being taken back to Sinaloa. Pamela would be doing DEA work as a senior consultant, helping him eliminate all narcos and thinking about challenging him. The downside was if the boy had not set it all in motion, she wouldn't have been living with him – maybe for some time or ever, and who knows if she'd have birthed his twin girls. But he was sure that without Baldwin, Pamela would be alive and masterminding the Atlanta Tribe and helping him dominate the worldwide drug trade via her DEA credentials and connections – and her occult powers many times stronger than his. It could – no, it should –have been her and him against the world – then owning and controlling it.

He also guessed that the intelligence of discovering where Pamela's teen twins were playing under false identities involved Baldwin. Yes, Baldwin started all this and helped mess up his life. Now, Raoul was going to get his revenge. He wasn't crazy about Pamela's older twin boys but figured that they'd get some satisfaction if he got Baldwin killed. He might even become friends with the spoiled assholes.

Raoul decided that shooting or knifing or blowing up Baldwin would be too pedestrian. It had to be golden frog poison. Raoul had already procured four milliliters of the precious, lethal poison from his contacts in Columbia – enough to kill a regiment. But this time, it wouldn't be a narco delivery guy popping Baldwin with a pen needle.

Raoul had been reading on Google about how for centuries the indigenous rainforest tribes had killed wild game of all sizes: jaguars, spectacled bears, deer, tapirs, peccaries, boar, giant anteaters, and others -- with blowgun darts, their tips dipped in the golden frog poison. He was amazed at how many people all over the globe liked the sport of shooting and hunting with a blowgun. He decided to go old school; it had the advantage of being lethal from fifty yards or more; it was soundless, and no one would expect it. And a blowgun could be easily imported to the U.S. – or purchased there. No weapons laws regulated anyone buying and or using a blowgun or darts.

He had two of his Tenientes send feelers to his contacts in Columbia: A reward of $100K to anyone who came up with a person in the next three days who didn't look too ethnic, spoke fluent English, but most importantly, was good with a blowgun...and was interested in making a lot of money.

Raoul wasn't sure such a person existed, but less than 24 hours later, Joaquin Ruiz, a top cocaine and meth producer, called him. "Patron, I found someone, but that someone is a female. She's a Columbian Rainforest hunting guide who uses a blowgun and poison darts. She goes to Javeriana University. Her name is Patricia Dias. I have yet to talk to her."

Raoul thought, Perfect. "Many thanks, Joaquin. Tell her I'm getting on my jet to Bogota to have dinner with her at Harry Sasson. I want to make her a business proposition, not involving drugs or sex but, instead, her skills with a blowgun – one shot with a blowgun. Regardless of her decision, I'll give her $100,000 if she shows up at dinner. If she agrees and is successful, I'll pay her an additional million. And you'll get the $100K finder's fee if you get her to the restaurant.

"Thank you, Patron."

****

Joaquin had no problem accessing her class schedule, dorm room number, and university photo by paying $100 to a secretary in the administrative office. The Patron had also asked him to check and see if she had a passport. That took another visit to the Aministracion of Passports. And this time, $200 to pay off a clerk. She did have a current passport. He knew the Patron would be pleased.

When a well-dressed man approached her as she walked to her dorm and said, "Miss Dias, we need a favor from you; I mean, Raoul Menendez needs a favor," she cringed. She'd heard the name. He quickly added, "Not drugs, not sex. Mr. Menendez needs your blowgun skills to make one shot. That's all I know. He's flying from Mexico to Bogota as we speak. If you agree to meet him for dinner at Harry Sasson this evening, he'll pay you $100,000 – even if you say no."

What a strange request, she thought. Unspoken, but she had no doubt Menendez would ask her to kill a person with a blowgun. Maybe another narco? A politician? Another important figure? Whatever he wanted, she knew it would be dangerous. But there was simply no way not to agree to meet with him. She decided to have dinner. The man beamed, "Thank you, Miss Dias. I will have a car to pick you up at 7:30."

Patricia Dias had no idea what to wear to the famous restaurant to meet the infamous drug lord. Maybe dress down in jeans, a nice top, and heels? Nope. She dispensed with her sweatshirt, jeans, and brassiere. She grabbed a few rarely-worn dresses from her closet and tossed them onto her bed. The first couple of options she viewed in the mirror. No, and no. Then, one she'd forgotten about. A teal number off the shoulders that showed some cleavage. Why the hell not?

A limousine was parked in front of her apartment building. The driver got out and opened the back passenger door. "Miss Dias, if you would like a cocktail, there is a bar in the back."

It was only a twenty-five-minute drive to Harry Sasson, a primo Bogota restaurant she'd heard of but had never been to. She felt like a princess when the driver opened her door and said, "Enjoy your evening, Miss Dias."

She nodded and thanked him.

Inside, the place was amazing. Like she'd entered a magical bubble whose height rose two stories and was crisscrossed with white, decorative supports zigzagging through the vast open space, she recognized dozens of large trees and plants from her time in the jungle. The artwork throughout was a panoply of colors and traditional Columbian designs.

The maître-de smiled and said, "Miss Dias, please follow me."

He stood at a private table for two that enabled a panoramic view of the restaurant. Raoul Menendez wore a black silk sports coat, a white silk shirt buttoned to the top, black jeans, and alligator boots. No jewelry. Instead of a handshake, he bowed, took her hand, and kissed it. A super-stud if she'd ever seen one and not what she'd expected.

"Thank you for coming, Miss Dias." He pulled out her chair for her to sit.

A waiter was already there. Raoul asked her, "A cocktail or glass of wine?"

"Yes, please, I'd like a glass of red wine."

"Almivera 2016," he told the waiter.

"Right away, Mr. Menendez."

He perused the college student. She was five foot four inches plus three more inches this evening in her heels. She sometimes wished she were taller, but she knew tall girls wished they had her 34c's and curvy body. When she wasn't tromping through the Rainforest, she kept in shape with daily exercise. And she knew her bronze-colored face ranked well on any scale.

Raoul asked, "No doubt a foolish question, Miss Dias, but tell me, are any other guides as beautiful as you?"

Her cheeks reddened. "Ah, well, I'm the only female guide I know of. And having some looks isn't necessarily a good thing in the big forest with a bunch of hyped-up, horny, white boy hunters ogling me.

He chuckled, "Ah, the bane of gorgeous women."

****

The wine arrived, and Raoul insisted on pouring it himself. He toasted, "To a new business relationship."

She had no idea what he meant but clinked her glass with his. He wanted to hear more about herself and how she became an expert with blowguns.

"I grew up in a small town on the edge of the Rainforest called Puerto Sandanter. It has become a decent place, but years ago, it had no running water, no sewage disposal, and no electricity. Many Rainforest villages still don't have those things. I knew I wanted more after seeing pictures of other places in magazines. A friend of my mother's knew English and taught me to speak, read, and write it. My father taught me the age-old skills of hunting with a blowgun. Even he was amazed at the animals I learned to shoot. I don't know how, but it came naturally to me. I became a hunting guide that white men, mostly Americans, paid good money for. It didn't matter if they personally killed the animals or not – if they could go home with a trophy they didn't have on their walls yet."

"I gave most of my money to my parents but wanted to save some to attend Javeriana University and study Rainforest sustainability. It would take at least four years to have enough money. Then, on a trip, a hot shot tech executive told me, "I want a jaguar; it's the only cat head I don't have on my animal wall in Jackson Hole. Supposedly, a few dozen roam around the West in the U.S., but I've never talked to anyone who'd seen one."

She told Raoul that Columbia's jaguar population has dwindled to a couple hundred. "I'm sure you know they are on the endangered species list. Right?"

"I've never seen one in the wild, though there may be a few in our northwest mountains."

She continued, "I love the big cat's puzzle-piece pattern of different black and brown oblongs on a white canvas. We're talking about a cat whose muscular body is around two meters long and can weigh 700 pounds. It can run at 50 miles per hour. And only eats other animals. Late one afternoon, I spied a male about 100 meters away. I whispered to my hunting group, "Don't try and shoot him, or he'll vanish."

The mega-rich tech guy said, "If you can bag that cat, I'll pay for four years at the university."

"I was shocked but tried to keep my focus."

I gently crept to within about 50 meters. The cat knew I was there and charged me at full speed. If I missed the shot, I'd be mauled. My blowgun dart hit his head from about 30 meters away. I quickly got another dart in my blowgun. He kept coming, but slowly, and then he collapsed. The tech guy made good on his promise. And he got the jaguar's coat, head, and paws."

"Was that a fair deal?" Raoul asked.

She said, "I guess. I don't know. Killing a jaguar is something I'll never do again." She did not tell him she vomited after kneeling to pet the magnificent dead animal."

He knew she wasn't lying and cut to the chase. "What if your prey was one person in the United States?"

Her eyebrows raised.

"Before you say anything, let me tell you more. This person is not a famous politician, businessman, or celebrity; he does not deal in drugs. You are only a couple of years older than him. We will provide any intelligence we can glean about him. I will share that he lives in Durham, North Carolina."

"Patricia, this is a matter of vengeance. Some of this saga has been told in two so-called nonfiction novels, but it's only part of the story and not all true. That said, one person who was instrumental in a plot to kill my Pamela culminated in her dying of golden frog poison. If not for this person, Pamela would be alive, helping me in my business endeavors and keeping me warm at night. It's something I must do."

"Golden frog poison, you're sure? Who is that person?"

"That will be revealed if you decide to board my jet tomorrow morning. He pointed to a leather purse on the floor. "It contains $100,00 and is yours regardless of your decision. Plus, another million dollars payable upon killing your target."

Patricia's eyes got wide. "A million dollars?"

"Yes, and trust me, your target is not nearly as majestic as a Rainforest Jaguar—and is much smaller and slower. If you're interested, pack a bag; bring your blowguns, darts, and passport. I'll give you the golden frog poison. We will ensure your safety to North Carolina and then back to Bogota. Sleep on it. A car will be outside your apartment at 8:30 AM. In the purse is also a burner; call the number taped on the back and say, Yes or No."

"But enough business, let's eat. Are there types of foods you don't like?"

"I'll eat almost anything."

The narco smiled, "Exellente."

He signaled their waiter. Tell the chef I'd like my usual and the same for the lady. And another bottle of wine."

He stared into her deep brown eyes, "Trust me, you'll like your dinner."

Chapter 17 – The Journey to Durham

The stretch limo arrived promptly outside her dorm at 8:30 AM

The short, husky, dark-complexioned driver was all business and took her bag. He unzipped it and slipped in a thick envelope. He didn't bother introducing himself.

The night before, thank goodness, her roommate was visiting her boyfriend. She'd opened the purse that Menendez had left at her feet at the restaurant and stared at the ten stacks of $100 bills on her bed. In her clothes in the bag, she'd buried the $100K – in case things went south, wherever she was going. She realized that flying internationally with that much cash could land her in deep trouble. Considering her options, though, she rolled the dice. She also put ten bills in her wallet.

Patricia had flown only a few times but had yet to fly on a private jet. Bogota was cloudy and gray as they took off from El Dorado International Airport in Menendez's Falcon 2000 EX, from Bogota to Hartsfield in Atlanta, and then to Raleigh Durham. On both legs, she was the only passenger with two pilots and one attractive blonde female flight attendant who told her she could have anything to drink. She also had choices of meals and snacks. *"So, this is how the wealthy folks live. Wow,"* she thought

She daydreamed about what she could do with a million dollars. Get out of Columbia and live anywhere she wanted to; buy a place in the U.S., Portugal, or Australia; or start an environmental business. But she'd always wanted to be an artist.

Then she thought back to two decades when her town in the Amazon was barely surviving. She'd been lucky things changed for her village, but it hadn't for dozens of villages she'd traveled through on her blowgun expeditions. Maybe she could help fund the basic infrastructure, healthcare, and school in another village or many villages – and do something good with all that money.

****

The landing at Raleigh Durham International was so smooth she hardly knew she was on the ground. It was like Customs was irrelevant. The pilot took care of everything. She assumed that meant paying one or more agents at each airport to look the other way. She hadn't been sure she could pack her favorite 2-piece 60-inch Venom blowgun and Predator darts in her bag, but there were no questions about her weapon or the money. She could see her bag on the ground. As she descended the stairs, one pilot behind her said, "Miss Dias, I wouldn't spend it all in one place. Welcome to Durham, North Carolina."

If the pilot knew, then Raoul knew that she'd taken her $100K to the United States. What would he think? Would he care? Maybe the money wasn't in her bag anymore.

A slender, well-dressed man met her after she de-planed and said politely, "Miss Dias, I'm Diego, your driver. Let me get that."

Wanting to maintain control of her bag and look inside, she acquiesced and followed him to a small parking lot, which she guessed was only for upscale clients. Another limo.

"We'll be at your hotel in a half hour or so. Relax and grab a drink if you'd like."

Worrying if the cash was still in her bag and what Menendez would think about her taking it to the U.S, she poured a healthy hit of bourbon into a short glass. Hoping it would take the edge off her anxiety. It didn't.

The sun was drooping behind the tall pines, allowing slivers of red and gold sky to shine through as she arrived at The Washington Duke Inn & Golf Club that sat atop a course that meandered through the pines and sand hills of Durham, North Carolina – with Duke University nearby.

When she walked to the back of the limo, she told him, "Thanks, Diego, I've got it from here."

She started to reach into her wallet to tip him, but he shook his head and said, "I hope you have a nice stay, Miss Dias."

Patricia was almost hyperventilating when she trudged in with her bag. Before checking in, she sat in a high-back chair in the lobby that faced away from the front desk. She tried to calm herself when she unzipped her long bag; her hands dove into her clothes to find the money. The stacks were there. She zipped up her bag and let out a big sigh. But she was sure Menendez knew she'd packed the $100,000.

She took a couple of deep breaths and walked to the front desk. She was greeted by a matronly black woman with a luminous smile.

"Hi, I'm Patricia Dias; I have a reservation."

The woman pecked at her computer keys. "Ah, Miss Dias, it looks like your reservation is paid for seven nights, and you also have a thousand dollars in your account to spend at the hotel or our club. Our pool and workout facilities are on the ground floor."

She handed Patricia a folder with her keycards and room number and told her, "There's room service 24 hours a day. Honey, you sure look like you could use a bite to eat."

Patricia asked, "What would you recommend?"

"Honestly, honey, the pork barbeque sandwich is as good as any in town, and there are a lotta good ones. With baked beans and fried okra. And our banana pudding is to die for."

Patricia smiled, "Sounds good, but I also need a beer. You choose, Ivey." Which was on her nametag.

Patricia extracted her wallet from a small purse. She pulled out a $100 bill and handed it to her. The woman from Columbia grinned and said, "Of course, I'm taking your word about the food." Then, I walked to the elevator.

Ivey Thomson had never heard of anyone who worked at the front desk who'd gotten a tip like that. Maybe once in a blue moon, a drunk Duke alumni tipped a valet that much. She couldn't remember the last time she'd gotten a ten-dollar tip. She watched the attractive brunette with a slight Spanish accent walk to the elevator. And said aloud, "Thank you, Lord Jesus."

On the seventh floor, Patricia slotted her keycard into the lock. Dead tired, it was all she could do to stumble inside with her bag. She flopped down on the big king bed. It was seductive, but she let it grab her only for about ten minutes. She arose and dumped all the contents of her bag on the bed.

Ten stacks of $100 bills first got her attention. She undid the paper wrapping around one stack. She let the bills spill onto her bed. There was also a thick envelope. On the outside, "Do not open until you arrive in N.C." In it, note, a USB drive, a thin black acrylic box, and a burner with a number taped on the back. The typed note said:

"Call the number once a day to give your progress. Minimal words. No names. Do your work and fly back here. A jet will be waiting after your last phone message."

She opened the box. Two ampoules in soft Styrofoam. The lethal golden frog poison. She knew how to handle them with care. A drop on her hand could kill her. A knock on the door startled her as she put the flash drive into her Apple notebook. Room service. She threw the bedspread over the money and opened the door.

She let the young Hispanic woman put her food and beer on the small table near the TV. She asked if Patricia needed anything else. Patricia read her nametag, and said, "Muchas gracias. Olivia." The young woman turned to leave. Patricia said, "Please wait." Olivia turned back as Patricia pulled a bill from her wallet. All she had were $100s. No matter, she handed her one. Olivia was incredulous, hugged her, and said much gracias repeatedly before leaving. Patricia told herself, maybe I did a couple of good things with the money today.

She gobbled down her southern fare in a few minutes. It was awesome.

She slotted the USB into her iPad. When she opened it, there were a few images and one Apple Pages file; the only words were David Baldwin and a Durham, NC, address. Her target. Menendez had already told her a little about him. As a young teenager, he'd caused Menendez's girlfriend, Pamela Loncart, a lot of grief. Patricia knew nothing else about him and immediately Googled his name. Hundreds of entries. Menendez had said he wasn't a famous person. That was a lie.

She looked at the images of Baldwin. In one old picture, he was painfully skinny and white as a ghost. But no longer. In other photos, he was a rangy, broad-shouldered, tan, blonde guy. Handsome by any measure. She Wikied him. His story was fascinating. She immediately ordered the two Amazon books, *Game of Twins* and *Game of Twins-Kidnapped,* and downloaded them. She skimmed until she got to the parts he appeared in the books. He was the one who stood up to Pamela Loncart in middle school and the reason Suzanne Delacroix got involved. No matter what Menendez had told her, there was no question Pamela was the bad girl – which led to Loncart getting killed by his aunt in Utah. How that happened was murky, but it sounded like the poison Loncart had brought to their showdown – backfired on her. No doubt, golden frog poison.

She was so riveted reading the books that she didn't realize it was 3:00 AM. She needed sleep. In her dream, the jaguar was coming at her. She panicked; she couldn't find a dart for her blowgun. She finally did and then fumbled and dropped it. The big cat would crash into her. She awoke covered with sweat.

*****

It seemed like Deja vu all over again. Being paid to kill the jaguar had made her vomit, and she swore she'd never do it again. But the jaguar had paid for her college.

And a million dollars was a lot of money.

She was nervous but remembered she was a professional hunter who stealthily tracked and killed game in the Rainforest. She could do this. For the next three days, she did reconnaissance on David Baldwin walking the area around his old but well-kept, two-story apartment complex off campus. She rented a cheap car and followed him. Like other top college athletes, he had a routine. He was disciplined. He got up at 7:00 AM and drove to campus, only five minutes away, attended classes, went to lacrosse practice, worked out, and drove back home. He sat on his small back porch with a Corona Light – and relaxed after his school and athletic activities, then went inside and did schoolwork or watched Netflix or whatever. Lights were out by 10:30 PM. He didn't go to bars; she'd seen no girls at his place and thought, what a waste. He was a stud.

That Thursday, she checked in on the burner and left a message. "Tomorrow, I hope, or it could be next week."

Her message was immediately relayed to Raoul Menendez. Sipping his Código 1503 Anejo, he smiled. Whether she took a shot or two, what happened in Durham tomorrow or in the next few days wasn't critical. He wanted to send Suzanne Delacroix the message that he'd be ready for her. The advice from Mary Jo and Michael was ingenious.

****

Patricia Dias had three outdoor options to shoot Baldwin with her blowgun: 1) In his parking lot in the morning when he was leaving or 2) late afternoon when he was getting home. Both were logistically problematic, especially with cars coming and going and the difficulty in getting a clean line of sight. Or option #3 was to shoot him on his little porch that backed up to the woods. Clearly, the best, even if it was a longer shot. After parking her car in the adjacent lot to his apartment building, she figured out the best way to walk unseen in the woods. She wore a black long-sleeve shirt and windbreaker and loose dark blue workout pants – under which she could easily hide her expandable blowgun by running it down her right leg and up under her windbreaker. She'd already dipped two darts in one of the golden frog poison vials and carefully put them in a plastic container that went in her windbreaker pocket.

The weather was cooperating. There was barely a breath of breeze – and a comfortable 75 degrees. The sun would set behind her in the next hour. No glare. Good, because she didn't like shooting with sunglasses. She knew a few things could make her abort today. But she guessed Baldwin would have a less predictable schedule Friday through Sunday.

She'd staked out a couple of positions in the pine forest. Sixty to seventy yards away. Both provided unfettered shots. She picked the further one with some elevation, looking into Baldwin's little patio. She put on thin gloves and firmly fit together the two pieces of her six-foot-long blowgun. It was 4:45 PM. She prayed that her creature of habit would remain one.

At 5:05, David Baldwin walked outside his back door with a can of Bud in hand and plopped down on a chair to the side of the one small table. He was bushed from a grueling practice. He sat sipping his beer in his long-sleeved Duke lacrosse practice jersey and shorts. He was already getting nervous about the big game on Saturday. Alone, looking out into the trees always calmed his mind.

****

It was time. She thought about all the money she'd have after the poison dart hit Baldwin. It would change her life forever. Easy shot. Piece of cake. She carefully slid the deadly dart into the blowgun. She held the long, thin cylinder with her right hand near the mouthpiece and left hand down the barrel. He was dead in her sight.

As she'd learned years ago and described to others, it wasn't a long, strong exhale but, instead, a short spitfire exhale. The dart would be traveling at four hundred feet per second, not as fast as a gunshot, but twice as fast as an arrow shot by an expert – and it only had to travel about two hundred feet.

At that instant, a jaguar flashed across her mind.

****

Chilling on his patio, David Baldwin felt something whir past his right ear. He then heard a thwack behind him. He hadn't heard a gunshot. Two seconds later, he felt the same whir past his left ear and another thwack. He hit the brick floor face down. What the fuck!

An athlete with world-class reactions who could anticipate a lacrosse ball fired point blank at him 120 miles per hour, David was at a loss for what to do. Stay down or make a run for it? He decided to stay prone. His mind said, "Son, you are screwed, blued, and tattooed." A minute passed. Then, a dark figure emerged from the woods in front of him.

A female voice with a Spanish accent said, "David Baldwin, please stay there. I'm not going to hurt you."

He peeked at her walking toward him. She was in dark clothes and carried a pole or something. Not a gun. As she got closer, the dark-haired woman shouted, "David, look at the darts stuck in the wall behind you."

He rolled over and looked up at two thin darts impaled in his brick wall. With a cell phone, she took a couple of photos of the darts sticking out of the brick, then kept advancing.

"Raoul Menendez hired me to kill you with a golden frog poison dart."

On advice from Aunt Suzanne, he'd already been warned to be on his toes. This wasn't as crazy as another sane person would think. He stood up. She walked closer and handed him her blowgun. She flipped off her dark ballcap, letting her long black hair spill out. She was beautiful. She extended her hand as he stood, "My name is Patricia Dias. I could have put both darts in the middle of your forehead."

David Baldwin smiled, "Jeez, thanks for not killing me. My coach would be pissed if I missed the game Saturday," he deadpanned. "But what am I holding?"

"A blowgun."

She smiled, "I'm not proud to say it, but I once shot a 700-pound jaguar coming 50 miles an hour at me with a poison dart blowgun. Jaguars are my favorite big cats. They're on the critically endangered list. He was dead in less than a minute. I did it for a huge amount of money. A rich American hunter paid my college tuition for the jaguar kill I did for him. I swore I'd never do that again. Raoul Menendez said he'd pay me a million dollars if I shot you with a golden frog poison dart. I tried to convince myself this was a different situation, but it was much worse."

"Wow. That's a lot of coin. Not sure I wouldn't have shot me."

The raven-haired beauty couldn't help but laugh.

David said, "My Aunt Suzy is going to love this story. You want a beer?"

Chapter 18 – On The Run

Suzanne saw her nephew's number pop up on her cell. "David, hi, so are you guys going to kick some Tar Heels butts on Saturday? I can't wait to watch. I'll drive down with your folks."

"Damn straight we are."

"What else is up with you?"

"Well, Raoul Menendez sent an assassin to kill me with that golden frog poison. Shot from a blowgun. Two shots zipped by my head a couple of minutes ago."

Suzanne was thunderstruck, "You're okay?"

"Yep, here let me introduce you by speakerphone to Patricia Dias, who is remarkably skilled in using her blowgun to kill animals in the Columbian Rainforest. Hired by Menendez. She's my assassin."

Both women were knocked off their axes from long distance.

"Mrs. Delacroix. It's true. I was recruited by one of Menendez's drug guys in Columbia. I was paid a hundred thousand dollars upfront, which is locked in my hotel room safe. He promised another a million dollars after I killed David."

"Call me Suzanne. And if you didn't kill him?"

"I don't know. I thought I could do it for the money. It took a lot of money to kill a beautiful jaguar a couple of years ago against our laws. But this would be horrible. I couldn't do it. Menendez told me to take my best two shots. Then send a message, and the plane would be ready the next morning to take me back."

"You missed on purpose?"

"Yes, or David would be dead. I thought I could do it until the last instant."

"How quickly will Menendez know if you killed David or not?"

"I didn't have an exact deadline. I check in daily in the evening and update my surveillance. I haven't done that yet today."

"Is there someone else backing you up? Someone who could verify your shots for Menendez?"

"I don't think so."

But it wouldn't surprise Suzanne if Menendez had someone tailing Patricia and that she didn't know about it. If so, he knew she'd missed. Purposely, since she wasn't high-tailing it out of there. Regardless, she'd bet the girl's phone was being monitored.

"Here's what I think. I'll bet it's better than 50-50 you're being followed. If so, Menendez already knows you missed intentionally. Doubt he'll be happy. Or if you missed unintentionally. Your only choice is to not get on the plane in the morning."

Patricia considered, "And Menendez knows I took the $100,000 with me."

"He could care less about the money. Likely sooner than later he'll know that you fucked with him. As soon as you accepted any money from Menendez and then agreed to do his bidding, he owned you. I'm not going to kid you – you aren't in a good spot."

Silence.

"Okay, what happens to me?" Patricia Dias almost dreaded to ask.

"Honestly. I'm not sure. My number one priority is my nephew."

The Columbian girl said, "I understand."

"David, take your phone off speaker and go inside. I need to talk to you alone."

****

In David's tiny kitchen, Suzanne asked, "So is she on the up and up?"

"Yes."

He sounded certain. Suzanne trusted him. He was smarter and more mature than any 20-year-old she'd ever met – including her twin daughters, who were good friends with him.

"Okay, I hope to be in Durham in about four hours, but I'll keep you posted on ETA."

David said, "Aunt Suzy, your Tesla won't make it here that fast."

She replied, "Who said I'm driving? In the meantime, here's what I want you to do..."

It was 5:15 in Durham as he listened to her instructions.

"David, you haven't called your parents yet, have you?"

"No."

"Good. Let me handle that. You can talk with them later. Okay?"

"Yes, mam."

"And David, what were the two things you once told me a good goalie does?"

"Head on a swivel and always look where the next shot is coming from."

"Please keep those things in mind. I'm being extra cautious, but I have no idea what Menendez might try next."

****

David walked back to his patio. "Patricia, here's the scoop per my aunt. She's coming down from Atlanta, hopefully in four hours or so. We need to get out of my place. I'll tour you around the campus, and we can hang out in the Student Union. You can leave your message when you normally do. Then, shut it off, and I'm going to use a sheet of aluminum to wrap it in. That should temporarily block phone tracking – in case. I'll call and get a reservation at nice restaurant downtown. My aunt says she'll pick up the tab."

"No way, I'll pay for dinner. She pulled out a wad of hundreds from her wallet.

He smiled, "That should cover it."

"David, I need to go to my hotel and get my stuff, including the rest of my money."

"You're checked in?"

"Yes, through Monday."

"Good, but Aunt Suzy also said to *not* go back there. She'll get your stuff after she arrives."

"Okay, but I could shop for clothes? Mine aren't right for going out."

She had plenty of money to do serious shopping damage. Then David thought shopping might be better than going on campus so he wouldn't run into anyone he knew. She looked hot in her sweatpants, hoody, and camo boots but knew she'd look even better in nice clothes.

"Yeah, that'll work. There are a bunch of stores at Southpoint Mall. We'll go there first but stop outside town, and you can leave your message; then we'll turn the phone off and wrap it. We'll tour around campus another day.

****

Her message was short and sweet, "Missed with 2. I'll be there in AM." Patricia knew there was no turning back now and that she might never see her family and friends again in Columbia

****

David Googled how many stores at the mall sold women's attire. Forty-eight. Oh boy. They hit a dozen or so. He could tell she was in seventh heaven. She gushed about the selections compared to malls in

Bogota. He tagged along. He was pleased she asked his opinion while she tried on garments. He liked her taste.

He'd always hated to go clothes shopping and let his mom pick out everything. But watching a hot Columbian girl shop for beautiful clothes wasn't all bad. She said she was only buying one outfit, so she was picky. She bought a short, tight, red skirt that looked like it was painted on, a sheer plunging white blouse that showed nice cleavage, black high heels that got her a little closer to his six feet, a black leather jacket, a new purse, and a wallet. Then there was dessert: lingerie at Victoria's Secret. She popped her head out of the dressing room, giving him more than a couple of mind-blowing peeks. She bought a black G-string, a black half bra, and a makeup kit.

It was almost closing time. She asked the cashier if she could change into her new clothes. The cashier was okay with it. She returned to the dressing room with the bags he'd been carrying for her. Five minutes later, maybe not a Cinderella moment, but close. He could only gawk.

She twirled and in her soft Spanish accent, "You like?"

"I like a lot."

She asked the clerk if she'd photograph them with David's phone. She took several. He was trying to remember seeing another woman around his age who looked that gorgeous.

Patricia Dias had a strange and stressful day. She was ready to enjoy herself. She had to admit she liked the guy she was supposed to kill. Before they got into his car, she walked up and kissed him; her tongue danced in his mouth. That, if David were honest, stiffened him.

A parking aisle away, Javier Rubio watched the two kiss and get in their car. The parking lot had been a possibility, but there were too many shoppers on their way out. He followed as they left.

****

Before leaving, David called and made a reservation at Plum Southern Kitchen & Bar downtown on Washington. A couple of buddies on the team had gone there with their folks and raved about it. Upscale southern fare and designer drinks.

Patricia asked, "Where are we going?"

"A surprise. You'll like it. You hungry?"

"I'm starving."

"Me too."

Chapter 19 -- The Backup

Javier Rubio was trained by the Mexican Special Forces Corps, *Cuerpo de Fuerzas Especiales*. Like most of his colleagues, he received a regular "stipend" (AKA kickback) in addition to his meager government salary. But that money hadn't impressed his to-die-for girlfriend. She needed more. He needed more. Then, three months ago, he'd been summoned by the Patron himself. Driving to meet him, he had to stop and vomit. What had he done? Would he be executed? Or his family? Instead, he was shocked that Menendez made him an offer to work full-time with money he'd never believed possible. Plenty of money—and even more depending on his performance – that was sure to gain favor with his girlfriend.

Rubio thought the mission was strange but knew that wasn't his call. He'd taken a commercial flight arriving in the Triangle area the evening after the Dias girl arrived. He'd read the intel that she was a professional guide in the Amazon – not just a cute piece of ass. Which was apparent in her photos. He liked the fact that he had to be on his toes. Track the tracker without being seen. He'd be ready.

****

After following her for three days, Rubio knew the blowgun girl had picked a good spot to kill Baldwin. He was forty yards further away and forty degrees to her left in the woods. Visibility wasn't great, but it would do. His disguise: a bird watcher with loose khakis, a plaid shirt, an outdoor vest, hiking boots, and a frumpy, green hat that, unless he was hunting in Mexico, he'd never be caught dead in. Plus, binoculars and a SAT phone in his vest pockets. Tucked into his waist at the back was his Glock 19, which he could shoot with deadly accuracy from up to forty yards.

He could see Baldwin sitting on his patio sipping a can of beer. To his right, he could partially see her put the blowgun to her mouth. A second later, Baldwin's head jerked left. A couple of seconds later, his head jerked again. He went prone to the floor. She got him!

But then she walked up to the apartment, holding her blowgun in the air and seeming to be saying something. Baldwin stood as she approached. He could see the darts stuck in the back wall from another angle. She'd missed. Baldwin went inside and then came out with beers for both. They talked for a couple of minutes, and then Baldwin went inside. She walked in about five minutes later.

The bitch had chickened out and missed on purpose. Rubio checked his phone. The app indicated her phone was in the apartment. Then, she was on the move with Baldwin. Rubio's rental car was parked a block from the small apartment building. He raced to the side of the building and saw Baldwin take off in his car. He followed for a few minutes. Baldwin was driving toward the city away from the main Duke campus, then stopped. Dias's GPS phone signal died. He smiled. She'd turned off her phone or otherwise blocked or destroyed it.

Good thing he'd also put a tracker on Baldwin's blue Nissan.

The blip on his phone was steady.

He called the Patron and filled him in. Menendez didn't seem surprised or upset even after he'd told Rubio that she'd left him a message that she missed two shots and would be at the airport tomorrow morning.

Rubio offered, "Patron, I could easily kill one or both almost anytime."

There was no reason for Menendez to let Javier Rubio know that the primary mission was already accomplished. He was sure he'd gotten Delacroix's attention. That he could kill anyone he wanted whenever he wanted and wherever he wanted --even in the U.S. Then he thought, what the hell, he might as well play on in Durham. After all, he was the maestro of the *Game of Twins* now. He loved American football and how the best quarterbacks could change tactics based on what they saw on the field. He gave his backup in Durham new instructions.

Chapter 20 -- The Only Way to Fly

Bernie Scally was one of Suzanne's dearest friends. They'd gone through what seemed like a lifetime of *Game of Twins* wars together. Bernie was a barrel-chested, 78-year-old with a wrinkled, tanned, swarthy complexion, prominent nose, abundant white hair combed back on the sides and top, and black eyepatch. Hard to miss him in a crowd. Super sexy for his age.

In a former life, Bernardo Conti Scalise was the top hitman for Carmine "Lilo" Galante of the Bonanno crime family. When the Five Families Commission put a hit on Galante, they put one on Scalise, too. He survived the hail of bullets that riddled his Cadillac in Newark. His wife and young son did not. He moved to Atlanta and started a pizzeria in Alpharetta that became the talk of the town. Seven years ago, when his protégé pizza pie maker (now his officially adopted son and David Baldwin's middle school, and then high school lacrosse coach), Tony Santucci, overheard the hanky-panky Pamela Loncart was enjoying with her lacrosse boys that included her sons, Tony was threatened and ordered to leave town. He escaped to Montana. It didn't matter where he went. Pamela Loncart wanted him dead. Bernie Scally called an old friend in Atlanta who owned a private jet and said he had urgent "work" to do in Montana. Outside a small resort near Gardiner, he cut down one of the top hitmen on the planet – and brought Tony home safely.

It was a lot to ask, but Suzanne made the call.

"Suzanne, how are you getting on? I'm sorry I didn't make Kip's service and get-together."

"I'm okay. No, I'm not. I need your help."

Bernie simply said, "What can I do?"

She got right to the point, one of the many things he liked about her. She took a deep breath. "Bernie, Menendez tried to have David Baldwin killed an hour ago in Durham. He's okay. There's a lot more to the story. This is a big ask. I need to get to Atlanta, pronto, and protect David the best I can."

He looked at his watch and didn't hesitate. "Be at Dekalb Peachtree by 6:45 PM. There will be a jet to meet us. I'm coming, too."

She had to fight back the tears, "Thanks, Bernardo."

She threw some clothes in a bag. She wasn't sure what the regulations were for an Interpol agent carrying a handgun on a private jet, but she threw in her Glock G43X.

The next call went to Lazlo. She'd finally accepted the raincheck and had invited him for dinner at her home that evening. He was going to be disappointed again.

"Laz, change in dinner plans. Be at DeKalb Peachtree ASAP. We're taking a private jet that Bernie has arranged to fly to Raleigh/Durham."

For an instant, he thought that could be an even hotter date. But then she said in her most serious voice, "Laz, Menendez sent an assassin to kill David with golden frog poison darts. The darts missed, but I gotta get there and will need help. Bernie's coming, too. I'll tell you more on the flight."

Like Bernie, he didn't hesitate. "Got it."

Lazlo Kianian never wore blues except at required ceremonies, and even then, grudgingly. His daily uniform was jeans, a button-down shirt, a sports coat, and Tony Lamas. His badge and gun holster were on his belt. He dropped in his Smith & Wesson M&P9. He always kept a small overnight bag with a few essentials in his office. His floor at APD headquarters was almost empty. He'd call his admin in the AM.

He'd never used the new high-tech blue light strip inside his Mustang. This time, he did. He screeched out of the APD garage and headed north on 85. A lot closer than Hartsfield, but traffic would be a bitch. He didn't give a rip how fast he'd be going.

****

Dekalb Peachtree Airport, Atlanta, Georgia

The pilot, copilot, and a flight attendant were already there when Bernie met them.

The female pilot said, "We can fly in fifteen. Approximately an hour fifteen to get to Horace Williams in Durham."

Bernie asked, "Can you get us there faster?"

She smiled, "Depending on headwinds, I'll do my best." She wondered who the distinguished old guy was.

Somehow, the luggage was all on, including the guns. Suzanne didn't ask. Bernie wore a black leather jacket, a white shirt, jeans, and Italian loafers. Laz, well, every time she'd seen him, he'd been striking in whatever he wore – and even better looking when he wore nothing.

She called David, who told her they were okay, and that Patricia shopped for clothes at the mall; they were heading downtown for dinner at the Plum Southern Kitchen & Bar downtown on Washington St. Suzanne said, "Great, see you in a couple of hours." She hoped and prayed they'd be fine in a public place.

Then, a call she didn't want to make.

Sarah Baldwin answered. "Suzanne, how are you doing?"

"I'm okay. Is Tim there, too?"

She must have heard something in her voice, "Suzanne, what's the matter? Lemme yell up to Tim. I think he's in his office."

Suzanne waited.

"Tim's here. I'll put it on speaker."

"I'm on a private jet with Laz and Bernie, and we're flying to Durham."

"Jesus, is this about David?"

There was no reason not to be transparent with her friends. "A woman with a blowgun shot two golden poison frog darts at David a couple of hours ago at his apartment. She admitted Menendez hired her to kill him. A million dollars if she succeeded. She is some kind of wunderkind blowgun hunter-tracker in the Colombian Rainforest. She intentionally missed with both darts. Said she couldn't bring herself to do it."

Their long-distance anxiety was palpable.

"I don't know what Menendez will do next. Maybe nothing. As a precaution, we're getting there ASAP. I gave David instructions to spend time in public places. They've been at the mall and are on their way to eat downtown. He and the girl are fine. I should arrive in Durham in about an hour or so and will get downtown in another half hour. The plan is for Laz and Bernie to stay with David. I know his big game is Saturday. We'll be here. I'll try to learn anything else I can get from the girl. I'm asking you both to wait to call David until we arrive; then, I will make sure he calls you. You've gotta trust me on this."

Haltingly, Sarah said, "Okay, Suzanne. Tell him we love him lots and to stay safe."

On the short flight, Suzanne ran through contingencies once they got to Durham. She dozed off for a few minutes. The shock of her dream woke her up. It was as if the plane hit some serious turbulence. Her seat belt was the only thing preventing her head from hitting the ceiling. She prayed she was wrong about Menendez having a backup following David. In her dream, she'd seen a big car speeding down the highway and gaining on David's car with a pulsing light.

She grabbed Laz's wrist. "Jeez, they could've put a GPS tracker on David's car. Laz, I don't get a good vibe on this."

He took her hand and winked, "The Tigress has got this." Lazlo Kianan was still a teenager when Suzanne Delacroix was a young Atlanta cop. Her mind flashed back. She hadn't told him the story firsthand, but the legend lived on.

****

Two decades ago

It was a gorgeous blue sky Sunday afternoon. She was the youngest ever black female Atlanta Police Department Detective. And there were only a handful of women of any age or color. She and her partner had been up all night after dragging in a familiar perp who'd shot and killed a tourist outside the Omni Hotel.

She told her partner to go home to his family. She walked into the seedy cop lounge to watch the last round at TPC Sawgrass in Jacksonville. None of the several Neandertals were watching the Braves baseball game on the ancient Sony. She turned the channel. Tiger Woods was staring down his birdie putt on the famous island hole. One cracker got up and turned the channel back to the ballgame then spit out, "Tiger's a pussy nigger chink."

His lineage was much like hers. She got in his face and kneed the roly-poly cop so hard in the balls that he could only moan after hitting the floor like a sack of flour. A bystander buddy laughed, "Never mess with the Tigress." After that, no one ever did, and that's when her legend as Atlanta's top homicide cop took off – without explicit help from her APD Deputy Chief dad, who didn't tolerate nepotism. Nothing made him prouder than his daughter.

Right now, though, she didn't feel like the Tigress.

****

Episode 21 -- Dinner on Patricia

David parked a block away. Patricia offered him her hand, and he gladly took it as they walked to the restaurant. The place was well-lit and airy, with tall ceilings; the furnishings were blonde wood and bronze. It had a funky, friendly feel. She said, "It's beautiful."

Rubio was waiting for the best opportunity. It could've been the mall parking lot while they sucked face, but there were too many people in their aisle and adjacent aisles who exited as the mall closed. No, he needed to keep following Baldwin's car. He had no idea where he was going.

Rubio arrived in time to see the two walk into the Plum Southern Kitchen & Bar holding hands. Then he parked.

****

The server took a long look at Patricia. His eyes said, "Amazing." Gay or straight, David couldn't tell. He had to smile. Patricia was a serious looker. He asked the server, "You going to card me?"

The well-groomed bearded guy smiled, "Nah, you're both good. What will it be?"

Patricia perused the menu and asked, "Agave in Autumn?"

"That's a good one. Tequila, Cointreau, Lime, Orange, Spiced Simple. Tasty and potent."

David ordered a Heineken. The waiter left.

"The menu looks yummy, lots of things I've never eaten or heard of."

"You and me both. Pick a couple of appetizers."

Their drinks arrived, and she asked their server, Joel, "Do you recommend the Cheddar Drop Biscuits or the Plum Deviled Eggs?"

"Can't go wrong with either."

David said, "We'll order both. We're in no hurry."

Once he left, David toasted: "To me, not getting killed by golden frog poison shot by a beautiful assassin."

It was dark humor, but hard for them not to chuckle. They clinked glasses.

****

Time flew. They chatted about this and that as they sipped their drinks. They were both only children, but her parents had been dead a couple of years from a rare jungle parasite. He told her about his parents, his mom, a veterinarian, and his dad, a business consultant. "They try to get to as many of my lacrosse games as possible. There's a big one on Saturday against our archrivals, North Carolina."

"I've heard of lacrosse but know nothing about it."

His face lit up. He explained, "It's the oldest game in North America. Native Americans in what is now northeastern America and Canada started playing a version of it four centuries ago. It has evolved a lot but, in many ways, is much the same. It's sort of a combination of soccer, basketball, and hockey – but played on a field that is 110 yards long and sixty yards wide. Ten players on a team. Each player has a stick with a large web to catch, pass, and block a small ball. Hard as a rock. The object of the game is to toss the ball into the opponent's goal, which is six feet by four feet high. There are three sets of three players: attackers, midfielders, and defensemen. My job is to guard our goal and keep the ball out. I play the goalkeeper position. Only one of those.

She smiled. "I'm thinking you're a good player?"

GOLDEN FROG POISON A GAME OF TWINS THRILLER

David rarely bragged about his lacrosse success but couldn't resist in the presence of this beautiful girl. "I play on the top-ranked college team in the U.S., and I made First-Team All-American."

"Meaning?"

"Meaning I was voted the best college lacrosse goalie in the country."

Her smile got bigger. "That doesn't surprise me, and I can tell you love to play."

"Depending on what happens, you can watch me play Saturday and meet my Aunt Suzy and my parents."

"That would be fantastic!" she beamed.

"David, do you have a girlfriend?"

"Nope, not right now."

"Would you like to have one?"

He smiled, "Yes, I would."

After an awkward silence, he begged her to tell him about blowguns.

"How far away were you when you shot at me?"

"About seventy yards or meters."

"And you could have easily hit me that far away?"

"Yes."

He knew she wasn't bragging.

"What kind of wildlife are hunted in your Rainforest?"

"Sloths, several monkey species, tapirs, peccaries, spectacled bears, deer, large tropical rodents such as agoutis, pacas, and capybaras. Lots of others. Unfortunately, now, there are few jaguars because of hunters. Did you know that jaguars are the third biggest cat anywhere? Only lions and leopards are larger. And unlike any other big cat, they like to swim."

"I didn't know that. Cool."

"I've been shooting darts for a dozen years and working as a guide since I was a teenager – taking rich white men into the jungle for them to shoot animals with their guns. Not easy with a gun. Less easy with a blowgun. Many were amazed I was a lot more accurate with a blowgun shooting poison-tipped darts – than their high-powered rifles. Most ended up never shooting their guns; rather, they watched me shoot. They got the animal parts and meat if they wanted. The good news is that our country is about to outlaw all jungle trophy hunting – and not only jaguars. I won't be leading any more hunting expeditions. Maybe sightseeing excursions to make some money."

"The golden frog poison you use is always deadly?"

"Yes. There are no antidotes. I must be cautious with the darts whose tips are dipped in the poison extracted from their skins. The frogs are now rare and live only in a small area in the Rainforest where they eat ants and insects that have, in turn, eaten toxic plants. In captivity, they aren't poisonous. I could get you one to keep as a pet," she giggled.

David shook his head, "Thanks, I don't think so. I'm mainly a dog person."

****

From a bag in the back seat of his rental, Rubio grabbed a pair of black-rimmed glasses, pressed on a short dark beard, sat, and readjusted them in his rear-view mirror. Waiting in the mall parking lot, he'd already changed out of his ridiculous bird-watcher costume. Now, he looked like a young executive. He walked into the Plum. He asked the first waiter to point out the restrooms down a long hallway from the open cooking area. Ladies and Gents both had open doorways, indicating there were likely multiple lockable stalls in both. He checked out the Gents, then came out and scanned the hallway both ways. No one. He didn't know who might be in the Ladies' room. As he poked his head in, a plump, well-dressed woman was preening in the big mirror. Her head swung toward the door,

"Sorry, mam, I wasn't paying attention to the signs," he lied.

She frowned as he left and returned to the Gents room, which was mostly a mirror image of the Ladies room, only in different colors. The Gents had two urinals blocked off by the two stalls. Everything was granite and tile. He walked to the bar and sat down. Rubio had a lot of quick thinking to do. He realized this could all be a waste of time, and he couldn't control the timing. A lot of variables. He'd have to be alert and ready.

From his bar seat, he didn't have an ideal view of their table, but he did have an unencumbered view of the path to the restrooms. He asked the bartender to choose a specialty drink.

"Smooth Texan. Texas blended whiskey, Benedictine, house peach and cocoa bitters with an orange twist."

"I'll give it a try."

"Coming right up."

He glanced over nonchalantly a few times at Baldwin and Dias, who were about thirty paces away at a table-for-two in the middle of the well-lit restaurant. They were deep in conversation.

****

A half-hour later, they were finishing an appetizer. It looked like Baldwin was ordering another round of drinks and maybe entrees. Rubio was sipping his second Texan. He saw her in his line of sight, walking toward the restrooms. Bingo.

A lot of stuff could still go wrong, but he slid off his bar stool and followed her down the hallway like he was going to the Gents room. He was a few steps behind as she turned the corner into the Ladies room. When she started to walk in, he was at the adjacent entrance to

Gents. No one in the hallway. He slipped into the Ladies room as silently as he could. No sign of anyone else.

Speed was critical. He startled her before she could open a stall. He was a big, strong guy. He grabbed her right arm and spun her around. Wearing high heels, she lost her balance. He grabbed her wrist and hit her hard enough in the solar plexus to knock the wind out of her before she could scream. She fell to the tile floor, unable to make a sound.

He kneeled and reached into his coat pocket. He pulled out what looked like a generic fountain pen. Carefully, he pulled off the top -- exposing a metal tip that had been dipped in the poison. He bent down and stuck her at the base of her neck. As he stood up, he put the top back on. He didn't bother to see if she was dead. He moved quickly back into the hallway. It all took less than forty-five seconds. But just then a skinny, red-haired lady started down the hallway. She would see Dias on the floor. He would have to kill her, too, or keep moving.

Rubio picked up his pace to the bar and put a hundred-dollar bill in front of the bartender, "Thanks, sorry I got called away. Keep the change."

He strolled to the front door but not too fast. When he was outside heading to his car he said a "Hail Mary." He knew how lucky he'd been. He would say more of them later.

****

The new drinks had arrived. But no Patricia. He knew that females, especially good-looking ones, could spend an eternity in a Ladies room before emerging. What they did in there, he had no clue. He kept sipping his Heineken. It seemed like Patricia had gone to the Ladies room more than five minutes ago. He walked to the bar intending to ask the bartender if he could send a female server to check the restroom. But then heard a loud shriek down the hallway to the right. More shrieks. A slender red-haired woman stumbled down the hallway and yelled, "Call 911."

David ran down the hallway into the Ladies room. She was on the tile floor. He knelt and could feel a faint pulse. "Patricia, what happened."

"Golden Frog Poison," she mumbled but then went slack. He began CPR, alternately pumping her chest and blowing air into her mouth. He prayed out loud, "Come on, Lord, she doesn't deserve this."

He stopped resuscitating and gave her one last kiss.

Emergency vehicles' sirens blared louder and louder as they approached the Plum. Four paramedics rushed in and went to work, but David knew she was dead.

He moved out of the way, then walked out the front door to gather himself.

He called his Aunt Suzy.

She immediately answered. "David, we're on the ground and should be at the restaurant in less than thirty minutes."

"She's dead. Golden fucking frog poison. We both know who killed her."

She shook her head in disgust and hesitated, "David, if the cops start asking you questions, don't mention the poison. Okay? Maybe just a simple, short story about meeting her this evening."

"Got it," he said, sadly.

"Hang in there. And believe me, I'll get Menendez."

****

TOM RANSEEN

Chapter 22 -- The Detective

Durham Detective Sam Rollins was a large Black man, 6'4" and about 260 pounds, but at age fifty-five, looked much like the college athlete he used to be. After dinner with friends in Chapel Hill, Sam was driving home through town when he heard the scanner: Code 10 -54, dead body, possible coroner's case at the Plum Southern Kitchen & Bar. He lit up his interior dash strobe and headed toward the Plum. Three cruisers were there with two EMS vehicles when he arrived. He entered, and the cops pointed him down the hallway. He told them to try and keep people and staff inside for now and see what they'd observed.

The body hadn't been moved from the Ladies'Room floor. The lead EMT said the woman was dead when she arrived. "A young guy, I'd guess his date, tried giving her CPR. Said her name was Patricia. He walked outside. I called in a CSI team."

Sam bent down and looked her over from head to toe. No violence that he could see. Interesting that she was face up. A beautiful, dark-haired, twenty-something girl who was dressed to the nines. He knew expensive clothes when he saw them; these were top-shelf. He stood up and considered: a young attractive woman drops dead on the little girl's room floor didn't compute. Maybe drugs? Maybe a natural cause? Maybe something else? He already wanted to know how she died. He was sure that Dr. Jacob Weintraub, the Durham County coroner, and a good guy he'd known for years, would give him that answer. He was probably on his way over.

A small, rectangular leather purse was a few feet away from her. "Did anyone pick up the purse?"

"No, sir," a couple EMTs said in unison.

"Good."

He got a pair of gloves from his coat jacket pocket and pulled them on. He took out his iPhone and snapped a few photos of the scene. He picked up the purse and opened it. One lipstick and a small makeup tube; a passport belonging to Patricia Dias, 25 years old who lived in Bogota, Columbia; a car key to a National rental; a Washington Duke Inn & Golf Club Hotel keycard. But the most intriguing item was a wad of rolled-up money. He removed the rubberband and counted eleven crisp $100 bills. He put the bills back in the purse. A CSI team arrived. He handed them the purse.

Rollins told the CSIs, "I need to talk to the guy she was with." He left and walked toward the restaurant's front entrance. The patrons looked restless while the cops were getting statements. Jamie O'Hara, manager of the restaurant, introduced himself and asked what he could do.

"For now, ply them with more drinks. The cops should be done talking to your guests shortly, but I'd like to keep them here a bit."

Jamie replied, "I can do that."

He asked Manny, one of the cops he knew well, what they'd found out.

"The bartender and others said she was eating dinner with a tall young blonde guy. He's outside. I told him a detective would come to talk to him. A couple of servers and a few patrons said they'd seen the two smiling, cocktailing, and eating – looking like they were having a fun time. The bartender remembered seeing her date sitting there alone for several minutes, then the shit hit the fan when a lady shouted "Call 911" from the hallway. "The young guy got up and ran toward the restrooms."

"Thanks. See if the lady who found her can tell you anything else. And see what else the bartender might remember. And if any cameras catch the entrance."

****

Sam walked onto the little front patio and introduced himself.

David stood and did the same.

Sam said, "David, I must have walked by you on my way in. Let's sit down. I hear you did CPR on Miss Dias."

"I tried, but she was gone."

"I'm sorry. Tell me about Patricia Dias."

"Well, I met her for the first time at the mall about 5:30 this evening. I was looking for a birthday gift for my mom but had no clue what to get. I don't know. She must have seen me shaking my head in frustration. She introduced herself as Patricia and said, "You look lost." I smiled and introduced myself and told her my predicament. She said, "Come with me. I've got clothes to buy. We'll find something nice for your mom, and you can help me choose a beautiful outfit. We started walking, and she took my hand. I was surprised but fine with it.

"So, she picked you up?"

"Ah, I guess you could say that. Shopping, which I hate, started to be incredibly fun. She bought a bunch of nice clothes and picked out a bracelet for my mom. It was expensive. She insisted on buying it. She used $100 bills to pay. I said, okay. Time flew. The mall closed at 7:00 PM. She changed into the outfit she bought at the last store we went into and put her other clothes in a shopping bag. I asked her to dinner. She insisted that I'd been a big help, and it would be her treat. I'd never been to the Plum but had heard good things."

"Sounds like a great start to the evening."

"That didn't end well."

"Yeah, that's too bad. I'm sorry. What did you two talk about at dinner?"

"She told me she lived in Bogota and attended a university there. Said she'd gotten a grant to attend a big environmental conference that started this weekend on the Duke campus and that she was majoring in Environmental Sciences. She grew up on the edge of the Amazon. Said her folks had died of some rare disease, and she had no family to speak of. She made enough money as a hunting guide to pay for school."

"A hunting guide. What kind of hunting?"

"All sorts of wild animals in the jungle, but she said many are now endangered. She only uses a blowgun and could hit an animal from seventy yards away."

"A blowgun? You're serious?"

"Yep, she uses poison-tipped darts like the indigenous population has used for hundreds of years."

"Interesting. Anything else?"

"No. I told her some about my family and going to Duke and that I played lacrosse, which she'd heard about but had never seen. I'd invited her to the game Saturday."

Sam said, "Ah, that David Baldwin. I recognized your name from reading the sports pages. You're a 1st Team All-American. Congratulations. Lacrosse is a great sport."

"Thanks."

"David, did you have any suspicions about her?"

"Like what?"

"Like her being from Columbia and like her carrying a bunch of cash?"

"No, sir."

"Did she offer you any drugs."

"No."

"She wasn't high on drugs."

"No way."

"Okay. Can you walk me to your car and give me the clothes she changed out of?"

"Sure, only a block away."

They walked silently, and David fetched the shopping bag she'd used to put her clothes in; he gave it to the Detective.

"Thanks, I appreciate it."

As David and the detective returned to the front entrance, his Aunt Suzy met and hugged him, "David, you all right?"

"Yeah, I guess."

David shook hands with Lazlo and Bernie.

Next to him stood Sam, wondering who all the people were. He introduced himself as Homicide Detective Sam Rollins of the Durham Police Department and said he'd been talking to David about the deceased woman, Patricia Dias.

Suzy did first-name introductions and mentioned that they flew down from Atlanta to watch the lacrosse game Sunday and stroll around campus tomorrow.

She asked, "You think it was a homicide, Detective?"

"Nothing to indicate that, but it's an unexplained death, so we'll investigate. We've got a top-notch coroner. He'll be able to figure it out." *Suzanne thought yeah, in his next lifetime. I'll bet you any amount that he won't figure it out. But no need for anyone in Durham to know the dead girl was murdered with golden frog poison. And no need to mention that Lazlo was Deputy Chief of Atlanta PD Deputy Chief of Robbery and Homicide.*

"David, unless you've got anything else to tell the Detective now, why don't we get you back to your apartment. Detective, he told me what happened on the phone. Tough evening for anybody." *And wondered if the Detective knew that David had survived an assassination attempt, what he'd think.*

She pulled a generic card from her purse and gave it to Rollins. "If you have more questions, Detective, don't hesitate to call me."

"Thanks, mam, you all have a good evening."

Detective Sam Rollins bore a striking resemblance to her father, who was Deputy Chief of Atlanta Robbery Homicide before he was killed by Pamela Loncart's family nearly two decades ago. She was already outraged that Menendez had her husband killed and had gone after her nephew. Thinking back about her dad being a victim of Raoul's former DEA paramour's witch family made her blood boil more.

****

Rollins couldn't help staring as they walked away. He said to himself, wow, that is one good-looking lady. He returned to the restaurant to tell the cops to let the patrons and staff leave – and to see if the CSIs had found anything interesting.

"Sam, you need to talk to the bartender. He remembered something else."

Sam introduced himself to Brian, the bartender. "What did you remember before all hell broke loose?"

"I don't know if it's anything. This guy sat by himself at the bar for maybe half an hour. He told me to make him the best drink on the menu. I did. He liked the drink but didn't seem like he wanted to chat, so I let him be. After another half hour, he ordered a second drink and told me he'd return shortly. Looked like he was heading to the restroom. A few minutes later, he returned and put a $100 bill on the bar. Said he'd gotten called away or something like that – and to keep the change. I saw him walk out. He left only a minute before things got crazy with the 911 scream."

"So, this guy was gone from his bar seat while the woman was in the Ladies room?"

"Yeah, I guess so."

"What did this guy look like?"

"Over six feet; well dressed in a black sports coat and slacks; black beard, and black-framed glasses."

"Anything else unusual. Marks on his skin or tattoos?"

"Nope."

"Any accent?"

"Perfect English, but definitely with a twinge of Spanish."

Sam handed him his card, "Thanks, call me if you remember anything else."

Rollins asked Manny, "Any cameras out front?"

"Two, but they're not working."

"Terrific," he scoffed.

He returned to the Ladies Room and asked a CSI, "Any idea what happened to her."

Dr. Michael Weintraub, a short, bespectacled man with a thin face and thinning gray hair, entered the restaurant. Sam said, "Hey Mike, hope you can tell me how she died. She was visiting from Columbia. Nothing popped out from our crime scene interviews. I'm driving over to the hotel where she was staying."

Dr. Weintraub glanced down at the body. "I'll do an autopsy and get back to you."

****

It took Sam only ten minutes to drive to the Washington Duke Inn & Golf Club Hotel, which overlooked the Duke Golf Course. As swanky as it got in Durham.

A dark-skinned Indian clerk with a nametag greeted him. Sam put his badge on the counter. "Sam Rollins, Durham Police Department. "Amir, I need to speak with the night manager."

The clerk was visibly trembling. "Yes sir, yes sir, I'll page Miss Gloria."

He'd met Gloria Lively, an attractive 30-something black woman once, but wondered if she'd remember.

She did. She shook his hand. "Sam, nice to see you again. What's up?"

"Gloria, can we talk somewhere private?"

"Follow me."

They walked down a hallway to the left. She used a keycard to enter a well-furnished small office.

"The manager's office, but I've got the master. Have a seat. Something to drink?"

"Water would be great."

She pulled two bottles out of the small frig. They sat down on opposite sides of a small round conference table.

"Now, what can I do for you?"

"You have, I should say, you had a guest staying here. Patricia Dias. She was found dead on the floor of the Ladies room at the Plum. I took a quick look, but the CSIs have no idea how she died. I need you to let me into her room."

She used her cell to call the front desk, "Amir, what room is Patricia Dias staying in?"

Amir said, "518."

She looked up at the tall detective on the way to the fifth floor. "I hope the Inn can be kept out of any bad press."

"No reason I can think of why the Inn would be involved," he half fibbed. It depended on how Miss Dias died.

Outside Room 518, he said, "Gloria, I also need to get into the safe."

"Hit 6991 and then pound twice to open it and the same number to close it."

"What's your cell?" He tapped it on his phone.

"Call you when I'm through."

****

Sam was tempted to look in the safe first but instead put the fancy duffle bag on the bed next to the TV. A couple of pairs of jeans, three shirts, two pairs of casual shoes, and underwear. He glanced through the dresser drawers. Nothing. In the bathroom, there were several toiletries and makeup items. Nothing stood out. Two dresses on hangars in the closet.

He pulled out one strap of $100 bills. Then, the other nine. He put them on the bed. $100K. The urge was strong to put all her belongings in the duffle bag with the cash, then leave the cash in his car before he entered police headquarters with the duffle bag. No one would be the wiser. He'd never knowingly taken one cent as a cop. The number of cops he knew that hadn't taken dirty money he could count on one hand. He would mull it over on the way to headquarters.

But he knew he couldn't do it. When he arrived at the station, he handed the duffel bag to the night supervisor and did a quick write-up on the evidence that only he had touched. He wondered what would happen to the money. Would it go directly downstairs and be locked up per protocol, or would some get diverted elsewhere? He didn't give a damn and left.

In his comfortable two-story colonial in one of Durham's better neighborhoods, he got a Molson from the frig and plopped down on his favorite living room chair to ponder the evening. From his pocket, he took out the card from the beautiful woman who'd identified herself only as Suzanne, the boy's aunt.

His reaction was, "Holy crap!"

She'd only introduced herself and the two others by first names. She was the famous Atlanta homicide detective who'd solved a string of cold-case murders that occurred over a century. He'd read a couple of articles about the books written about her. She'd been a superstar Atlanta cop --and she was a woman of color. Then something else struck him. On his iPhone, he Googled her. A couple of weeks ago, she'd found her husband dead on the floor inside their home. A healthy guy who died of a heart problem. A stretch, but could there be any relationship to what happened tonight?

He called and left a message, "Miss Delacroix, this is Sam Rollins. Let's meet at your convenience. I'd like your thoughts on the death of Patricia Dias."

****

After leaving the Plum restaurant in Durham, Javier Rubio tossed his fake beard and glasses in a bag in the trunk of his rental and drove to RDU. While sitting on the runway on Raoul's private jet, Rubio called him and gave an update. Raoul couldn't have been more pleased and promised a reward when he returned to Sinaloa. Rubio grinned. His hot girlfriend was going to do those extraordinary things he'd never experienced.

Menendez sent a Dark Web encrypted text message to schedule a meeting tomorrow, then poured another tequila and kicked back in his big leather office chair. He smiled at the gleaming little golden poison frogs on his desk and pondered where to use them next.

****

The Three met at 5:00 PM in their Dark Web video chatroom. Menendez filled them in. They learned that the assassin had missed Baldwin by a fraction on purpose. Then she was killed later with golden frog poison. Both Mary Jo and Michael were impressed.

Raoul laughed, "Bet there's smoke coming out of Delacroix's ears."

Mary Jo grinned, "Exactly what we'd hoped for. But we need to wait a few days before I tell her anonymously where and when you'll be in two weeks. She'll be suspicious, but regardless, her appetite to kill you is only escalating."

"Makes sense," Raoul told them. "You want me to go after other friends or family?"

She replied, "That would be overkill right now."

Michael commented, "Nice literal pun."

They all chuckled.

Chapter 23 – The Warrior

8 Years Ago, Birmingham, Alabama

It was a blustery, rainy, cold day in Birmingham when David Baldwin's middle school lacrosse team played in a big tournament that included three dozen teams. They now faced the top team in the South, Mountview from Birmingham. The Eagles were outsized and outmanned and should never have been invited to the tournament. David was a scrawny kid of 115 pounds and the second-string goalie who'd not been given a chance to play in any of the four games the previous day – despite his team getting pounded in each. Lacrosse Chairwoman Pamela Loncart had told her sleazebag coach to play David in the final round-robin game. The Eagles would get killed regardless. Hopefully, it would shut up his mom, who'd confronted her the prior evening. The Chairwoman decided to serve him up as cannon fodder. It was David versus Goliath. She had no doubt Goliath would win.

Amazingly, the Eagles were down only two goals after the first half. Then things got bizarre.

Before the horn went off for the second half, Sarah Baldwin watched her son standing alone in front of the goal he'd defend the rest of the game. With the wind howling and the rain pounding down, a man walked toward David out of nowhere. He was dressed like a Native American Indian. He had raven-black hair in braids and wore a headband with feathers, leather pants, and no shirt. He stood before her son and put his hands on David's shoulders. After a few seconds, her son pointed his lacrosse stick to the heavens and yelled, "We are Eagles!" Every Eaglewood player turned toward her son. In unison, their sticks rose to the sky. The Indian was gone. What in the world was that? Sarah wondered. The horn boomed to start the second half. When Eaglewood broke their huddle, the cheers from the burgeoning crowd were deafening – for the underdogs.

David and his Eagles played courageously and nearly upset the tournament favorites (if not for the opposing coach paying off a ref). The Baldwins wanted to return to Atlanta, the sooner, the better. They said a few goodbyes, got their cooler, and headed to the parking lot. Sarah couldn't resist asking her son, "David, you're going to think your mom's nuts, but as the second half was going to start, I saw a man, a Native American Indian it looked like, come up to you and put his hands on your shoulders, then vanish. Pretty crazy, huh?"

Her son smiled. He said, "Hosgeegehdoh."

"Say what?"

"In Seneca, it means, 'I am a warrior.' That's what he told me."

Sarah, who had Seneca blood going back generations — was too dumbfounded to say more. Indeed, David had battled like a true warrior – and like his biblical namesake.

****

Saturday – The Duke University Lacrosse Field, Durham, NC

The stands and sidelines were packed. Whereas that day long ago in Birmingham had been rainy and nasty, today, the sun shone brightly. David Baldwin shined the brightest of all. He was a warrior-possessed and stopped each of Carolina's twenty-six shots on goal— the final, Duke 11 Carolina 0. A Carolina lacrosse team had never been blanked, going back six decades.

After the game on the sideline in Durham, David, his eyes dripping with tears, told his mom and aunt, "I played for her."

Both women balled. They'd seen her photos and knew David had fallen in love – if only for a few hours -- two days before.

His mom said, "I saw him again before the game started."

He nodded.

"He said the same thing to you again, didn't he?"

The big-time lacrosse player sobbed. "Yeah, mom, he told me the same thing."

She hugged him tightly, "David, you were a warrior then, and you are now."

Suzanne looked perplexed by the comments. It wasn't until they walked to dinner that Sarah told the story to Suzanne. "Whacky, right? she asked.

Suzanne said, "Not at all. I've seen apparitions a few times: of the Atlanta twins who were murdered and -- most recently, Kip."

They both nodded that they and David had been privileged to experience an inscrutable dimension. Few were so fortunate.

****

Sunday morning, Durham, NC

On Saturday, Sam Rollins bought the two *Game of Twins* eBooks and, with fascination, speed read them – as well as a couple of dozen credible articles he could find about her. His reaction was wow! She'd returned his message and suggested they have brunch at the Inn on Sunday morning before she returned home. She'd heard it was great. He couldn't wait to see her again.

She was standing on the terrace when he arrived. "How about we eat out here? It's such a gorgeous day."

Another, wow! She was a beautiful, willowy spring flower. She wore an almost sheer white blouse with a wisp of a bra, a short, hot pink skirt, and matching heels. Spectacular long legs and long midnight black hair. Her face was one of an angel with perfect light mocha skin.

He shook her hand and said, "Suzanne, you look fantastic." She was fragrant like a spring flower as well.

She smiled and said, "You clean up good, too. Let's sit. They'll bring coffee."

He pulled out her chair and eased it back in.

He sat and bashfully admitted, "I'm sorta starstruck."

"Sam, before we talk shop, tell me a little about yourself. There's a lot about me, I know, online – some true and some not. I found almost nothing about you.

"Yeah, I don't have much of an online footprint."

"I did read that you were a basketball star in college."

"I played some ball at North Carolina Central, here in Durham, where I grew up."

"I peeked on Google. You dropped 20 on Duke."

"I did, but we couldn't compete with Duke, Carolina, NC State, and Wake. Serious basketball country."

"I love sports. My dad played tight end at Rutgers and was drafted in a late round but didn't go pro. Instead, he decided to become a policeman."

They sipped coffee, and she suggested they grab some food.

He made a point of following. Her hourglass figure was riveting. Nice brunch spread, and he was a bit surprised she piled her plate high with scrambled eggs, bacon, sausage, Danish, and fruit.

He commented at their table, "Hard to see where you put all that."

"I try to stay in shape, but I love to eat," she grinned.

"Sam, you've lived in Durham your whole life?"

"Yup, my mom and dad were both high school teachers. They've both passed."

"Mine, too. I don't see a ring. You're not married?"

"I was for fifteen years. My wife, Dana, died of breast cancer eight years ago."

He pulled out his wallet and handed her a photo.

"She's gorgeous."

"Yes, she was. A white girl, like her, being married to a Black man was harder on her than on me. I could kick the bejesus out of anyone who didn't like it, and I did more than a couple of times."

Suzanne chuckled, "Yeah, I'm the child of a Black father and a Chinese mother. No one fooled with my dad when it came to racial stuff. And hell, Atlanta's further South than Durham." Any kids?"

"No, Dana couldn't have kids. For some ridiculous reason, I didn't want to adopt. I regret that. She would've been a great mom."

"You may have gleaned from the Price books or online that I didn't give birth to my kids, but I never refer to my twins as stepdaughters. They are my daughters, my pride and joy – and even more precious now."

"I am jealous," he smiled.

The brunch was excellent. The plates cleared; they sipped coffee.

She looked him straight in the eyes, "Sam, when I first saw you Thursday night, I almost did a doubletake. You look a lot like my father. I've missed him every day for nearly twenty years."

"I read that he was one of Atlanta's top cops."

"Yes, and most likely would have become the first Black person to head the Atlanta Police Department until his cop buddy set him up to drown in Lake Lanier. Not everything that happened got into Bobby Price's books. John Carleton, the other Deputy Chief, and Dad's fishing buddy, was working with a Mexican cartel. If Dad weren't around, Carleton would get the top spot after the Chief resigned to run for mayor. He and his lackeys gave the narcos a pass to distribute and ship at will. Atlanta's drug trade flourished, and he was well compensated. With some persuasion -- I impaled a knife in the back of his hand – he admitted to me on a video call with his handlers who

Dad's murderer was and how he set Dad up. Carleton was toast and never saw the next day. But unfortunately, the Pacific cartel has only grown more prosperous and more powerful. It's headed by the man who had Patricia Dias murdered."

"Murdered, you're sure?"

"I'll get back to that."

"Fast forward, you read some about this bizarre, deadly *Game of Twins*. Pamela Loncart, Menendez's longtime, sicko witch DEA girlfriend—and I mean, literally, a witch-- escaped to Mexico after her brother and cousin tried to kill me in my condo. Instead, my old partner, Dusty, and I took them out. But two years later, Pamela had my twins kidnapped in front of their private school. When Dusty and I tried to exchange them for $8 million, she had him executed. Not part of Price's story, but with some friends' help, I kidnapped her twins, who were playing lacrosse under assumed names in Nashville. She was on every law enforcement's most-wanted list. But she was also a lacrosse nut; we hypothesized that her boys were in the U.S., where the best lacrosse is played. The most crucial help locating them came from David Baldwin, my nephew after I married Kip. The Loncart twins were his former lacrosse teammates. David identified the unique way they twirled their sticks among the hundreds of videos we collected. They were playing for separate private schools in Nashville."

"We traded the kidnapped boys for my girls on the Bonneville Salt Flats in Utah. Pamela and I agreed to fight to the death for our twins. Supposedly, with no weapons. But she'd cleverly attached a tiny vial with a sharp tip to her sunglasses. It got knocked off as we fought. I had no idea what was in it but was lucky enough to grab it and scrape it across her neck. She told me it was golden frog poison before she died. The most potent animal poison on the planet."

"Kip was murdered three weeks ago with the same type of poison that even the best pathologists couldn't identify unless they knew what they were looking for."

"How'd you find out this frog poison killed your husband?"

"Raoul Menendez made that clear. He had his guy leave a small golden frog figurine next to Kip's body after he pricked him with the poison. I knew better than to touch it with my bare hands. Turns out I was right. If I had, you and I wouldn't be talking now. Menendez was hoping for a double murder, but I think he's having more fun with me still vertical. The Fulton County M.E., a friend of ours, had it verified by an out-of-town pathologist specializing in rare animal poisons. He admitted that without a heads-up about the likely poison, it would have taken him a lot longer to identify it."

"She'd already documented the cause of death as an undetermined cardiac event. She understood how nutzo things could get if it were known a rare poison killed my husband. Law enforcement at multiple levels would screw it up and waste huge amounts of time and wick up the press so that I'd never be able to hunt Menendez myself. She didn't change her autopsy report. She knew it wasn't possible to connect the murderer to Raoul Menendez."

"I understand. Not possible with the dead girl either."

"No chance."

"I'm sure golden frog poison is what killed Patricia Dias. Those were the last words David heard before she died. Menendez sent her to kill him with a blowgun dart dipped in the poison. She put a dart past each ear from a long distance. The girl missed on purpose. She got cold feet and told David what was going on. Menendez offered her a lot of money to kill him and had paid her some.

"The money I found in her room safe, a down payment."

"That would be my guess. I gave David, who is a smart kid for his age, a couple of instructions. Stay out in public for a few hours until I could fly up on a friend's jet and get rid of her phone, which no doubt had a tracker. He did that. But in hindsight, I screwed up. Menendez had a backup on the ground watching his assassin to see what she'd do; he put a tracker on David's car. They went shopping and then out to eat. Apparently, the backup followed them into the Plum and killed her there with the poison – it only takes a couple drops on a needle or sharp object—death occurs in less than a minute.

Sam described what he'd heard from the bartender.

She said, "Yep, likely the killer, but even if you caught him on camera, you wouldn't find him. Besides, it was Menendez who put the order out. David took Patricia's death hard; she was a beautiful girl who'd decided *not* to kill him. For five hours, he was smitten. Whether Menendez had her killed because she failed in her mission – or to underline that he was coming after me and people I care about – I don't know. Maybe both."

"Now what?"

"Menendez must pay. I've got to take him off-the-board. Otherwise, he'll keep going after me, my family, my friends—hell, anyone I associate with. Besides, there's the Evil he will continue propagating as a zillionaire narco. He could send armies of sicarios to kill me and virtually anyone I know, but I think he's enamored with his golden frog poison iteration of the *Game*. Killing targets by poisoning them, one by one."

"It's only because of my involvement in this horrible *Game of Twins* that my husband was murdered; my dad was murdered; my cop partner was murdered; my twins were kidnapped; my nephew was almost murdered; and the girl from Columbia was murdered. It's all on me. All of it. And more bad stuff is coming if I don't deal with Menendez."

"That's a lot to put on one person, Suzanne. You're going to need help."

"I know."

"How will you get to Menendez?"

"I don't know yet, Sam. That was a nice breakfast," she said as she stood.

"Sounds like making Patricia's death a homicide investigation would be a waste of time."

"It would. Unless you were to tell your coroner exactly what to look for."

"Well, I won't do that, and I hate wasting time."

He winked at her," You've got my card, Suzanne. Stay safe."

She gave him a big hug and walked back inside. He couldn't help watching her.

****

Later, lying in bed, hands interlocked behind his head, Sam stared at his slowly swirling ceiling fan. He could only see Suzanne. Not since his wife had been alive had he interacted with a woman so intelligent and beautiful -- and passionate for justice. He thought she was a righteous, avenging angel of God but playing a dangerous game.

It wasn't like he was bored being a Durham detective, but after all these years, he needed something else. He decided that if she asked, he'd help her fry the biggest, baddest narco on the planet.

Chapter 24 – Suzanne the Assassin

A week later, Suzanne was taking a bath, trying to relax – racking her brain how she'd ever find Menendez, much less kill him. She'd explained the situation to her technology wizards, Arnie and Sheila, hoping they might have an idea. For the first time they'd worked for her, they were stumped. Short of asking the NSA to put 24-hour surveillance on his favorite mountain fortress and every jet, helicopter, and vehicle he traveled in – which was impossible – they weren't even sure that data would provide a satisfactory answer. The news had been depressing. She wondered if all her bravado about going after Menendez and taking him out was just her own yak.

While getting dressed in her bedroom, her phone dinged with the arrival of a new text. She thought she'd turned off her text notifications, but apparently not. An unusual sender indication was "Finding Menendez" and a link. She hoped the link sent wouldn't populate her phone with malware but couldn't resist clicking on it.

She clicked it. A scrambled voice said, "We know what Menendez, Pamela, and others have done to you and your loved ones. You know he won't stop killing with the golden frog poison. You've got one choice. Kill him. But first, you need to find him. What if we were to tell you when and where he'll be out of Mexico? On another continent."

Suzanne replied, "No doubt I'm listening to a scam Menendez set up."

The voice said, "No, and we've already done you a big favor."

"How so? She asked.

"We helped you get your twins back. Did you ever wonder why Pamela never learned about Lazlo Kianian's credit card receipt from Nashville where her twins were living? Or how the FBI agent who knew Kianian (and was being run by Pamela) disappeared? Or how the police pursuit car in Belle Meade ran into a tree so you could escape out of town? Or why Raoul's SUVs never went after you after you killed Pamela with her golden frog poison? We want to do another favor for you."

Suzanne nearly gasped. Not even Menendez could know those details. She'd long thought someone helped her get Pamela's twins kidnapped and exchanged with hers. A puzzle she'd put out of her mind.

The modulated voice sounded different, more high-pitched, "Suzanne, did you ever consider that others might have the same objective as you?"

"Eliminating Raoul?"

A pregnant pause.

"Why?"

"Pamela was always a bull in a China shop. Let's say that Raoul has become a loose cannon with whom we want to cut ties."

"You're another narco who wants to get rid of him?"

"No, but we've done business with him that we'd like to terminate. That would start with him."

"Whoever you are, you must have a ton of resources. Why not kill him on your own?"

The scrambled voice became more staccato, "Believe it or not, we think you deserve a shot at him, but more importantly, you'll be much more motivated than a professional assassin. Money makes the world go round. But revenge is even more powerful, and you're seeking it. No one hates him more than you. Getting a pro to take him out, we're not sure who could get it done better than you."

The voice continued, "Here's another way to look at this opportunity – it's your only good option before Menendez goes after you and others with his golden frog poison or whatever else. Not an easy task to take him out, we know. We want you to have the satisfaction of doing it. We'll provide whatever money, weapons, and materials you need – and the location where Menendez will be staying. Then it will be up to you. We have no reason to harm you. The DEA, FBI, Homeland, the President, and top politicos will be thrilled. The Mexican government is in bed with Menendez, but they'll make deals with whatever narcos succeed him. You'll be happy, and we'll be happy. We bet on you once, and we want to bet on you again."

Once more the disguised voice changed and was now slow and deep, "A couple more things to factor into your decision. First, after you kill Raoul, we'll provide you a bonus unlike you could imagine."

"So, I'm a paid assassin?"

"Only if you decide you want an amount in the eight figures. We prefer carrots to sticks, but here's a last consideration."

The voice paused, "Think of this not as a choice. Do you remember the beautiful girl who acted as the Loncart twins' Nashville housekeeper and security guard -- besides being their full-time fuckbunny."

"Yeah, I think her name was Lisbeth. I've not heard from her since. I assume Menendez wasn't impressed with her failure to guard the twins. I'd bet she's dead."

The now sing-song voice said, "Ah, but she's alive in Toronto; her getaway from Nashville she owes to us."

"So what?"

"Lisbeth Sanchez is now a successful private investigator. She's on a hefty retainer. Conveniently, you never mentioned publicly -- or to the cops -- that you'd kidnapped the Loncart boys to get yours back. And that wasn't in Price's book. She took enough photos of the boys and where they stayed and would be a credible witness. Besides, there was a camera hidden in the pool area. She was beaten up when you left her. We wouldn't want to turn her loose with that evidence and tell the world that the great Suzanne Delacroix is a kidnapper. Many might applaud, but not all, including the Nashville PD and the Atlanta PD – regarding yours and Deputy Chief Kianian's roles in multiple felonies."

"You're blackmailing me, too?"

Her question went unanswered. The scrambled voice changed again, "You've got some things to think over. In two days at 7:00 PM your time, I'll text you a link to a Dark Web chat room. The link will work one time only. We can discuss the details of your trip to Spain."

"Why Spain?"

"That's where Raoul Menendez will be."

****

Suzanne fetched a glass of Ramey Chardonnay and sat on her living room couch. Indeed, there was much to consider.

She called Arnie Friedlander, her go-to tech friend, and told him of the text and her scrambled conversation. She didn't know if she'd been talking to one or multiple people. Suzanne was far from being a techie, but she'd read about a few of the new Galaxy features. One that she thought might come in handy was the upgraded auto-record. It did; she'd recorded most of the scrambled conversation.

"Arnie, I'm not sure how this may be possible, but could you reverse engineer what I recorded and eliminate the scrambling?

He said, "Depends how sophisticated the app was they used. Sometimes easy, sometimes not. I'll see what I can do. Send it on."

"Also, in case I screw up, can you monitor and record my Dark Web communication on Thursday without them knowing?"

"Yeah, I'll figure that out. Let's talk on Thursday AM."

"Could you also determine where the communication originated?"

"Iffy, but I'll try."

Arnie Friedlander and his associate Sheila Cummings had been invaluable for several years, helping her solve murders. More than once, she'd offered to pay them a lot for their help, but they'd refused. One day, she'd promised herself that she'd do something special for them if she survived this latest iteration of the *Game of Twins*.

****

Two evenings later, she sat in Arnie's ultra-high-tech office in an old strip shopping center in Sandy Springs and gave the thumbs up. Arnie and Sheila were each glued to two large monitors.

She got the text on her Galaxy and clicked on the link. After several seconds that seemed like an eternity, she heard a garbled voice say, "Good evening, Suzanne. You've made up your mind about what we proposed two nights ago?"

"Yes, I'm going to Spain."

"Splendid."

"Where am I going, exactly?"

"Madrid. Have you ever been there?

"No."

"You'll like it. It's a big, beautiful, and festive city, especially during May's crème de la crème bullfights. Raoul could have been a great matador, but instead went into his family business."

"Selling drugs. No doubt more lucrative -- but more, or less dangerous than fighting bulls?"

"Good question. He would probably say less. I think he would have enjoyed the limelight of being a big-time matador. The best are like rock stars in Spain. But he's grown to thrive behind the scenes."

"Isn't he a narco rock star in Mexico? Making quick appearances in cities and towns across Sinaloa and throwing cash from one of his luxury SUVs?"

The answer, "Millions of hard-working Mexicans adore him."

"Right," Suzanne replied.

"He owns a large hacienda on the outskirts of Madrid – where he'll stay for a week."

"Security?"

"An estimated half dozen sicario bodyguards, besides the property staff. Rudimentary technical security."

"The address?"

"More when we talk again next week at 7:00 PM Monday."

****

Arnie and Sheila worked through the night with both files to come up with the best rendition of the authentic voice Suzanne was talking with. She was in bed at 6:30 AM when Arnie called.

"Sheila already went out for breakfast and Starbucks. You need to hear this. And yes, I may know where the contact originated.

Suzanne tossed off her jammies, took a one-minute shower, dressed in jeans and a top, pulled on her Nike's, ran a brush through her long hair, and bolted downstairs. Her Welsh Terrier Lilly followed, jumping shotgun into her Tesla. She did a typical 15–20-minute traffic drive in ten. She opened their door with her eye scan and rushed in.

Arnie and Sheila were sipping Starbucks and eating pastry when she blew into their conference room.

"Let me hear it."

Sheila explained, "We took your first clip and the one from last evening – here's the best rendition we came up with for the true voice. It was one, not multiple, and you were right about whose voice it was. We got several clips of her from YouTube."

If she hadn't eaten lunch with her a couple of weeks ago, she'd have had no clue who the female voice belonged to.

"Congresswoman Mary Jo Cogburn, no question."

"Yep."

"You all get a fix on where this conversation originated?"

Arnie said, "Not exactly, but our best guess is the Atlanta MSA."

Suzanne nodded without surprise.

Chapter 25 – The Man with the Midas Touch

Back home with a cappuccino in hand, Suzanne got an idea. She remembered hearing his name from Bobby Price – or her dad years ago -- but wasn't sure?

She called Price to see what he might know.

"Suzanne, how are you, my dear?"

"Bobby, I'd be lying if I said I was okay. Off the record, last week Raoul tried to kill David Baldwin in Durham with the same poison that killed Kip."

"Oh, my Lord. Is he okay?"

"He is. I wish it weren't so, but the *Game's* not over by a long shot. It's only getting nastier."

Bobby tried to be upbeat. "Hey, Netflix called me and reiterated they were interested in the *Game of Twins* story and wanted us to do the screenplay and maybe help produce it, but they understood if we needed more time to negotiate the deal. I told him we're interested but can't proceed now."

"Thanks for letting me know. Yeah, not a good time. I've got a question for you."

"Shoot."

"Thad Sutterland had a twin brother, right? Their births were celebrated by the sacrifice of the Brevard twins in 1973. What the hell happened to him?"

"Yes, his fraternal twin was born Jeremy Sutterland. He changed his name in college to Michael Abbott, a name from the Loncart-Sutterland family tree."

"Interesting. No doubt the family had a ton of money before the blow-up with Pamela and after Dusty and I killed Pamela's twin brother, Philip, and her cousin, Thad. Then what happened?"

"Apparently, the Feds took most of the Sutterlands' ill-gotten gains after Maddie and Franklin died on a South Pacific Island of some virus – and after Pamela disappeared. Kip Davies made sure that what rightfully belonged to Orville Johnston went into transforming his land into the wonderful park it is today in Woodstock and to other worthy causes

"Michael Abbott didn't get some of the family money?"

"As a college student, he made millions. He didn't need it. I didn't dive into his finances; much of what I know is hearsay, but apparently he was an early investor in Microsoft, Google, Apple, and other high-fliers."

"Wish I was. A Forest Gump thing?"

"Not hardly. This guy is a financial wunderkind. Mostly out of curiosity, I talked to a few of his old lacrosse buddies at Syracuse. Besides hitting the books hard and playing lacrosse, he made a ton of money for a few friends. They swore he was prescient. When investing, he knew what to do and when to do it. In college, he became known as the man with the Midas Touch. He was a multi-millionaire before his 21st birthday."

****

Four decades ago -- Atlanta

Unlike Pamela, Mary Jo Cogburn wasn't related to one of the original occult New England "name" families (Loncarts, Sutterlands, Hawthornes, Tillies, Abbotts, and others) going back to the 1600s. She was a recruit. Her nascent telepathic talents were discovered when she was eleven by Maddie Sutterland when Mary Jo attended an all-girls school outside of Atlanta. Through the grapevine, Maddie learned of a young girl who was never taught a card trick – and had never played cards – until she was goofing around with a few friends who wanted to teach her Hearts. She grabbed the cards and told each of the three others to pick a card, think about the card, and put it back in the deck. That day, she didn't miss guessing one card – or in any card trick contests after – and became a local legend. Maddie decided to visit her in person and discovered a lovely, delightful twig of a teen who was more than willing to tell Maddie her secret. It was simply, "They told me the card." Maddie smiled and asked her, "Tell me what I'm thinking." Without hesitation, she said, "I'll make a great witch."

Once they turned eighteen, Jeremy and his twin brother, Thad, became members of the Atlanta Tribe, the most powerful Coven on the planet, headed by their mom Maddie. The twins had a major falling out regarding their adopted cousin, Mary Jo. Jeremy pummeled his brother senselessly after he'd repeatedly raped and beaten her, and not for the first time. Maddie promised Thad would never touch her again. Jeremy promised Mary Jo the same thing.

Thad stayed in Atlanta and went to Georgia Tech, where he was a lacrosse stud and continued to abuse young ladies, including Suzanne Delacroix, when she attended Spellman. Jeremy matriculated to Syracuse, where he played lacrosse and was a 4.0 student in Business and Finance. Encouraged by his mom, Jeremy changed his name to Michael Abbott, effectively cutting off his once close ties to Thad.

On a visit home his sophomore year, he told his mother about a strange experience. He admitted to using weed, cocaine, meth, and other drugs, but he only liked mushrooms -- psilocybin. He couldn't control his hallucinogenic experiences but realized they sometimes enabled him to see the future – always about business and money. After a particularly vivid mushroom trip, he told her about a small Silicon Valley start-up company called Amazon that sold books online. In his fantastical trip, his mind wandered through a long, brightly lit, strobing multicolored tunnel until it stopped in 2018. A *Wall Street Journal* headline in front of him read: "Amazon Tops Trillion Dollar Market Cap."

Did he have the "sight," the ability to see the future? As far as his mother knew, no one in the Tribe had that power going back three centuries. But Maddie had her own premonition that her son Michael might become the most powerful witch in the Coven. She told her husband Franklin to give him $50,000 to invest in a young company – which he did, grudgingly. Michael showed the hockey-stick-escalating account to his mother. She told him to tell no one else – not even his father.

Michael regularly bought more Amazon stock until a few years later he owned $250 million worth. That story repeated itself with Apple, Google, Facebook, Netflix, and several dozen others, all with impressive results.

His stock and asset portfolio topped a half trillion dollars after the meltdown of 2008, which he knew in advance would decimate financial systems worldwide. He got out of most equities – other than shorting several billion dollars of stocks – and two years later was able to buy extensive real estate globally, most at a mere ten cents on the dollar. Off and on, he gave his dad a stock tip or financial advice. His son's golden touch floored Franklin. His father's friends were thrilled when Franklin would hold court in his vast, cherry-wood paneled study, smoking Montecristo cigars and drinking Thomas Hine cognac – where he would pass on a couple more of his son's invaluable tidbits.

After a couple of years of discovering his "sight," Michael learned that he no longer had to depend on psilocybin. Instead, he only had to focus his thoughts on a specific company to get an accurate sense of its future.

****

Present Day – Princeton, NJ

Ostensibly, Michael Abbott was a full Professor of Finance at Princeton, a five-figure-a-day consultant, an author, and an investor. He was *the* expert on global money laundering – while being the single biggest money launderer in the world. His contribution to the

Tribe was handling the Pacific Cartel's laundering at half market rate, with half of the profits going to the Tribe account controlled by Mary Jo. But it still gave Raoul a considerable advantage compared to what other cartels paid for cleansing their loot. Money laundering fascinated Michael so much that he authored a best-selling book, *Laundering the Big Bucks*. He had the perfect laboratory to test new approaches: the worldwide financial system was his oyster. His real-world strategies always remained a step ahead of his published expertise.

While Raoul Menendez's drug empire's contributions were impressive, that money now paled compared to what Michael was generating in his personal accounts – on six continents over the last few years. Abbott became the wealthiest person in the world -- worth more than the combined wealth of Bill Gates, Jeff Bezos, and Elon Musk. Only the Saudi family was close.

Besides his late mother, the only other person in the Tribe or anywhere else who knew about his "gift" and the magnitude of the money he was making was Mary Jo Cogburn. Maddie told her to keep that secret – and now she knew why. She had paved the way for her -- instead of Pamela -- to become the next Chief of the Atlanta Tribe and lead the coven to glory.

****

Bobby Price continued, "Abbott is Howard Hughes 2.0 or maybe 3.0 without the whacky persona. He's charming but politely refuses to be interviewed by any media. And he rarely appears in public and ruffles no one's feathers."

"That's a good trick. Congresswoman Mary Jo Cogburn, do you know anything interesting about her, even anecdotally?"

"Looking more and more like the Presidency is in her future. At least the Vegas oddsmakers think, so if not 2024, then in 2028."

"She's become a political superstar at a young age. How'd she do that?"

"Okay, here's one thing I've heard from more than a few folks in the know. She has impeccable judgment in her political decisions. Known to be one of Congress's most pleasant people, she's not against twisting arms, but only twists the right arm at the right time – and she twists hard."

"Like she can read minds?"

"Perhaps like Pamela Loncart could Umm, I don't know about that.. Bobby, I think Pamela and Mary Jo Cogburn were best buddies in their Atlanta Coven until someone helped me kill Pamela. And now want to pay me an eight-figure fee to kill Raoul Menendez."

"Never a dull moment in the *Game of Twins*," he smiled wryly on his end of the phone.

"I was thinking the same thing."

An uber-powerful politico and an uber-rich financial wizard were best buddies and business partners with the uber-drug kingpin. What could possibly go wrong with that?

PART III

Chapter 26 – Gary Redux

On her first visit to Gainesville, Dr Noah Kline had confirmed that the toxin from the biopsy slices of Kip's liver and heart – and on the frog figurine – was golden frog poison. Dr Jill Treece left the samples with Noah and took the rewrapped figurine back to Atlanta.

It had been an evening to remember for both – one that they needed and wanted for a long time. After a wonderful red snapper dinner and a bottle of wine, they barely made it into Noah's condo when they removed their clothes which littered the floor as he took her hand and led her to the bedroom. He had salt and pepper hair, a kind face, and a slender but well-toned physique. He was immediately in love with her shapely body, perfectly coiffed silver-white hair, and elegant face – but mainly her smarts and passion for work and play.

Two weeks later, Jill Treece made a second visit to Gainesville to visit him. Not to discuss business. They drove to the coast and boarded a big ship for a week's cruise in the Bahamas. They'd talked every day for two weeks; she'd teased him that she might tell the full golden frog poison story if things went well on the cruise. They got along swimmingly well.

****

Gary Popov had decided to morph into a well-behaved subordinate – making sure to stay in the good graces of Dr. Jill after she rescinded his suspension. He smiled a lot. He was polite. He gave her none of his typical, obnoxious yak about the cases he'd been working on. He didn't piss off other colleagues. And he continued to give her roses once a week. It couldn't hurt.

Gary walked into Jill Treece's admin's office and asked, "Julie, "Is the boss in? Her door's locked."

"Nope, she's on a cruise."

"Sweet! She deserves a vacation. By herself?"

"She has a friend who's a pathologist in Gainesville. Listen, Gary, I'll be late for lunch if I don't get going."

He handed her the roses. "Sure, sorry. They smell great. Why don't you enjoy them."

"Thanks. Gotta go."

****

He bet Dr. Jill was enjoying boinking her boyfriend a lot more than slicing dead people. She was an extraordinarily handsome woman at her age; he guessed she was a tiger in the sack. It piqued his infatuation with the bitch. Unlike others.

Loitering several steps down the hall, he had two options. He could enter Treece's office from the hallway or via her admin's office. Julie didn't appear to lock her door when she exited.

Indeed, it was unlocked. He looked both ways down the hallway and slipped in. He knew there was an adjoining door that was probably locked. An easy-peasy, old-time door lock With his pick kit, he was in Treece's office in fifteen seconds. He shut the adjoining door.

His squinty, yet eagle-like 20/15 eyesight scanned his boss's office. He'd been there a handful of times. Nice digs. About 350 square feet with floor-to-ceiling corner windows on the third floor. A good-sized traditional desk with only a blotter, pencil/pen holder, and monitor with no device attached. There was a generous conference table with six smartly upholstered chairs.

Gary walked to the back of her desk and perused her substantial book collection. A twenty-foot-long credenza was flanked by bookshelves with hundreds of books. One section was solely dedicated to Pathology and other medical references; another dedicated to popular nonfiction and fiction; and a big section of the serial killer classics: *The Jigsaw Man, Mindhunter, The Shrine of Jeffrey Dahmer, Zodiac: The Shocking True Story of America's most elusive Serial Killer, Ted Bundy: Conversations with a Killer*, among many others.

He pulled out the Zodiac story, chuckled, and told himself, "*They even caught you after a long string of kills. That's not happening to me. I've learned from you guys. Hell, you all didn't have to contend with phone and vehicle tracking and thousands of street cams constantly monitored by the cops. And all the other electronic stuff. Until someone opens my freezer, no one will know what I did. By then, I would have already disappeared. No one will find me. Hell, I'll need my own book section.*"

Turning back toward the desk, he heard a voice say, "*Yeah, but you're an investigator cop. A big advantage.*"

His head jerked back toward the shelves. No one was there.

He addressed the serial murderer's row and smiled, "*Yes, that is nice.*"

****

Gary wasn't sure what he was looking for. But hopefully, a secret of some kind.

He started with her calendar and thumbed back three weeks. Lots of in-house meetings. Outside meetings were always at expensive places for lunch or dinner, weekly massages (he wondered where), biweekly hair appointments, and others. His eyes caught "Kip's service," and "dinner with SD (he assumed Suzanne Delacroix). She'd drawn a red line extending seven days and wrote, "Noah CRUISE."

While technically not a CSI, Gary had more experience with crime scenes than most other veteran Atlanta CSIs. Clues could be stuck in books; a good place here because there were a thousand or more; or the two filing cabinets; or the coat closet. Nothing so far, but something was hidden here that had to do with Kip Davies.

He looked down at her big desk and snapped on gloves from his coat pocket. The front drawer wasn't locked. Mostly pens, pencils, rubber bands, swag from conferences, packs of Kleenex, lipsticks, makeup, and hairbrush, etc. He touched none of them.

He used his pick to open the top right-hand drawer. Hanging inside were personnel files. He snatched out his and put it on Treece's desk. His recent reprimand was there. It was hard to argue with what she wrote. He'd stepped over the line in letting out the unsubstantiated info about Delacroix and that she was a person-of-interest in her husband's death.

The bottom right drawer had parallel double-key locks. Probably needing two separate keys. He first tried the left-hand lock with a pick. It clicked, but the drawer wouldn't open. Then he tried the right lock; it clicked, but no dice. Then, he used two picks simultaneously. The drawer opened.

A fifth of Glenfiddich and two short glasses.

One file on the bottom.

A jewelry box on top of it.

He put the file and box on her desk.

The file first. After opening it, he could only smile. In it was a handwritten note to Dr. Jill Treece on letterhead of the University of Florida, Gainesville, Department of Pathology. "Jill, as you suspected, the frog figurine had golden frog poison on its surface, and the pathology samples also indicated the same poison."

Signed, "Noah."

He put the file down and opened the jewelry box. Inside was a small gold frog figurine wrapped in plastic. He wondered if the figurine still had poison on it. If so, he bet his gloves would offer enough protection. He took the tiny golden frog out of the wrapper and perused it up close.

He asked the frog, "How were you involved in all this, and why keep you a secret?"

Could Delacroix have murdered her husband using poison on the figurine?

Could the two bitches have conspired to cover it up?

Or was it something else?

He took a phone pic of the note and the figurine. He needed to do some research on the poison. He made a gut decision, which he usually didn't do. He placed the little golden frog reproduction back in the plastic and gently put it in his coat pocket. He shut the jewelry box. He put the file and empty jewelry box back in the bottom drawer.

Gary had discovered at least part of Dr. Jill's big secret.

But while trying to shut the drawer, he couldn't get both locks to re-engage. He tried for ten minutes. "Dammit," he muttered several times but had to get going. He had no idea how long Julie would take for lunch. He'd have to hope Treece thought she'd forgotten to shut her bottom drawer completely.

He opened the adjoining door to Julie's office and peeked in, then carefully cracked the door to her office. It automatically locked once he shut it. He left her main door open as he'd found it. Then Gary was gone.

****

Gary decided to take the rest of the day off. Before leaving the parking lot, he Googled "golden frog poison" on his phone. Indeed, deadly stuff. The deadliest.

On his twenty-minute drive from the Fulton County Coroner's office to home, he thought about the two bitches hiding a big secret.

He knew Treece lived in an immaculately kept ranch in the posh Brookwood Hills Atlanta neighborhood. He drove by a few times. He checked online. It was 2300 square feet. With a large yard and long winding driveway to the side garage. Appraised at $1,700,000. Nice digs, to say the least. He'd visited the best databases he could access to find a layout of the house and the type of security system she used. She had a decent system that protected all doors and windows, but one that didn't include video monitoring. He was surprised, but pleasantly so.

He'd been inside Delacroix's primo three-story condo the day her husband died. In a Northwest suburb near the ritzy Lovell School. It was 3400 square feet. Ground-level front garage At the end of a quiet cul-de-sac. Appraised at $2.4 million. Major league security system, apparently upgraded with new outdoor cameras. The couple times he drove by the same dark sedan was parked in front. No doubt security – perhaps due to the MAGA loons abusing her online? Go MAGA!

Neither woman fit his age sweet spot, but both with hot. What he was contemplating was fraught, to say the least. Degree of difficulty, 9-plus on a ten scale. "Gary, you're out of your freak'n mind," he told himself. But of course, he already knew that.

****

Once home, he grabbed a Coors Light from the frig, stretched on a new set of gloves, and placed the little frog on his kitchen table.

Typically, an ice-cold beer tamed his anxiety, but sometimes it started bubbling up regardless. The anger. The hatred. The fear. The anxiety. He had no control.

"Treece and Delacroix, you are lying bitches. Fuck both of you!" he screamed.

And lost it. He threw almost everything not nailed down against his kitchen walls.

While the tiny golden grog sat stoically watching like Jabba the Hutt.

Chapter 27 – Missing

The photo on his screen was that of a beautiful brunette with long black hair and crystal blue eyes staring back at him.

It happened again last night.

The latest missing woman was twenty-six-year-old Nelly Carlisle – last seen at Little Spirit cocktail bar sometime after midnight last night. Her roommate got worried when she didn't return home to her apartment in Buckhead by the next morning. She said that never happened to Nelly and that it seemed like her mobile was dead. She couldn't leave a message. The roommate was helpful in reporting Nelly missing. She provided her name, description, address, and mobile number, and she'd texted the photo in front of him.

Lazlo Kianian toggled to the photo of Amy Neyland, the cute brunette, who was last seen walking outside her condo building the evening she disappeared. Then the photo of Veronica Perkins, a tall blonde, last seen leaving Armond's, sometime after midnight the night she disappeared. Then back to Nelly Carlisle. *"Where are you all?* he asked.

Three disappearances of young, professional white women in less than five weeks – didn't bode well for the victims. Nor for the city of Atlanta. He didn't know what was happening but didn't want it to worsen. He was 99% sure these were forced abductions. But so far, they seemed random, or did the victims somehow know the person who took them? Maybe sex trafficking, but he knew the Eastern European thugs liked their girls much younger. Kidnapping for ransom? Nothing had been reported, and contrary to popular belief-- abductions for ransom were highly unusual in the U.S. Unfortunately, that left the wacko serial killers. Wonderful!

He read through the current Missing Persons information on the first woman. It wasn't much. Amy Neyland lived in a small condo complex in the trendy Old Fourth Ward; single, with no roommate;

well-liked by her colleagues at the small biweekly, *The Atlanta City Paper*, where she was an investigative reporter.

The time log that her apartment complex kept via the key fob that she needed to enter indicated she'd last entered at 6:33 PM that evening. The system didn't log exit times. The detectives had talked to a few tenants. None remembered seeing her that evening. She was caught on two interior cameras walking out at 7:36 PM. Wearing a short skirt and heels. She likely disappeared somewhere near her condo. Whoever abducted her waited in his car. Her car was parked in the lot behind the condo building. Her car keys were in her flat.

Lazlo did a double-take looking at the date on the Missing Persons report again.

The same day Kip Davies had been murdered in his home with golden frog poison.

Lazlo yelled, "Unfreaknbelievable!" Loud enough for his admin, Molly, to peek in his office, "Boss, you okay?"

"Don't know yet."

She knew it would be best to leave him alone.

Lazlo Kianian didn't believe in coincidences.

One person had created havoc in the press that evening a few weeks ago. One person promulgated the rumor that Suzanne was a person-of-interest in her husband's death. He'd even admitted it and was suspended for two weeks.

Laz was pissed for not making the connection earlier. It seemed perfect. Somehow the guy knew Amy and that she was a reporter; he called her and pitched a great story. She was hooked. He picked her up at her place. He was a cop and probably showed his badge and pointed out his interior light bar. She was doubly hooked.

This could be a strange one, though. It was a stretch, but he thought he already knew who abducted Amy – and probably the other two women. Now, he'd have to prove it, which wouldn't be easy. From the Missing Persons report: no help so far from her laptop or cloud data. And unfortunately, she didn't automatically back up her phone records. Her cell phone was no doubt destroyed.

Another seeming coincidence was that the nearest city CCTV cameras were more than a block away from Amy's last whereabouts – and at least a block away from the other two victims' last whereabouts as well. Likely the abductor knew about the cameras. Amy's building could only be accessed by a key fob.

Lazlo ran a quick DMV search from his laptop and called his favorite techie in the Digital Division. He asked, "Hey Greg, I need to run something by you."

"Whatta you need, Chief?"

"All APD and private vehicles used by cops have a GPS, right."

"Yep."

"So, the location of any car can be tracked, right? This may sound dumb but refresh my memory what the tracking info is used for."

"Lots of things at the operational level, like adjusting logistics: staffing and routes in a geography; responding to emergencies if the officer loses contact; finding a stolen police vehicle; providing evidence of a cop and his or her car's location in legal cases; and then there's real-time Big Brother monitoring like if a senior officer like yourself wants to check up on a specific cop and car and see that on a map."

"There's a module for that, isn't there? I've never used it."

"Yeah, it's called, "LocateX." I can show you, but basically, you enter the module, and your security clearance gives you immediate access after you type in a Badge #. And voila, that car appears on a Google map."

"Send me instructions."

"Sure."

"Is the tracking always on?"

"Yes but here's the rub. I doubt many cops know it, but you can open the main console and there's a small, unmarked knob. Turn it clockwise, and the GPS goes off. Counterclockwise, it's on again. It's not that hard."

Laz took a deep breath. "Greg, I'm not asking you to do this right now. But hypothetically, assuming the GPS was on, you could dig into your data and tell me where a specific car was on a specific date, time, and place?"

"Accessing archived car-level data is a big deal. Terabytes of data. Right now, we keep it, I think, for around a month, then it's gone. But the answer is, yes. It would take me a little time, but I could do it."

"Greg, I owe you big time. Thanks."

Lazlo Kianian wished he had more tech wisdom at his age but then had an epiphany.

He'd invite the fox into the henhouse.

Two hours later, he called Greg back with three dates, approximate times, and approximate locations – and a badge number. He wanted to know if the vehicle's GPS info was available.

He heard Greg, gulp, and barely mumble, "Okay, yes, Sir, but it could take a day or so."

Kianian said, "The sooner, the better. Keep track of your overtime hours; I'll pay you from my own pocket. Thanks a lot."

****

Later that afternoon Gary Popov got a forwarded email from Lazlo Kianian to attend an 8:00 AM meeting the next day of a group of APD detectives and investigators in Conference Room B. The subject: Recent disappearances of 3 women. The forward included a note from

Kianian. It read, "Gary, sorry I forgot to include you in the list. I'd like you to be part of our task force. Dr. Treece told me you have an incredible, analytical mind. I need a pro to help us break these cases. She said you're assigned full-time. Thx, Lazlo."

Upon reading the email, Gary was so excited that he immediately got hard. At home, he decided it was time to admire his work. In his basement, with protective gloves, he unlocked and opened the cryogenic freezer. He lifted his four girls, stiff as boards, out one by one. He stood them upright against the basement wall. They were so beautiful. He stroked himself. They could stay like this forever. He'd pondered necrophilia, but it didn't float his boat. At least right now.

****

Gary knew it was hypothesized that Richard Kuklinski was the most prolific serial killer ever in the United States -- some estimates were between 100 and 200 murders. No question Kuklinski killed a lot of guys -- most in his role as a Mafia hit man -- though he refused to kill women or children. But Gary thought it was an abomination for Kuklinksi to be called the "Iceman." The press latched onto the name when one supposed victim was stored, temporarily in a large industrial freezer, then thawed out to disguise the time of death. It was also rumored that Kuklinksi used an ice cream truck to stash another victim. Never substantiated. No, no. Gary believed *he* was the true Iceman. He had no clue what the media might call him one day. He hoped not Iceman II. But he trusted they would help cement his unique place in history.

Gary palmed his dick and decided to jack off on one of his special women. Today, Amy got that honor.

****

GOLDEN FROG POISON A GAME OF TWINS THRILLER

Chapter 28 - Ted Bundy

The following morning, notepad in hand, Gary arrived fifteen minutes early. Coffee and his favorite food, glazed Dunkin Donuts, were in abundance. Plenty of time to consume his half-dozen fair share, which he did before the introductions. He listened to Kianian's presentation about what was known so far about the three women's disappearances. Gary smiled; APD was so fucking pitiful.

Gary was vaguely familiar with a few of the detectives and investigators assigned to the new task force. No question that Kianian was bringing his big boys and girls to the rodeo. Kianian assigned him and two other investigators to dive deeper into any city or private CCTV cameras that may have picked that evening Amy Neyland disappeared.

Toward the end of the presentation, Gary began to hyperventilate. He didn't know why. Sitting in the back of the big room, he eased his way out the door and rushed to the Men's Room. He entered and locked the last stall. He puked up his Dunkin Donuts and most of his large coffee in the toilet. God, he hated to puke up anything ever. The last time he'd puked was when he was six. His mother forced him to eat the slimy canned peas, his only dinner. When he balked, she shoveled in a few bites and told him to swallow. He puked on her hand. She jerked him up from the table and slapped him so hard with the back of her hand that it knocked him down. She slapped him again when he tried to get up. But a few years later he got his revenge.

In the stall, he thought he heard a voice, *"So you wanna be a hotshot serial killer? Well, do ya punk?"* He had to get a grip.

He heard another guy come in and take a piss. Leave without washing his hands. What a dirtbag. When he was sure he was the only one in the Men's Room, he emerged from the stall jittery as hell. He turned on the faucet, washed and dried his hands, wiped off his mouth, and looked at himself in the mirror.

In the reflection, another guy stood next to him.

"Gary, I must say. I like your taste in babes. Hotties, for sure."

Gary started to turn but couldn't. He looked into the mirror. Ted Bundy was as handsome as Gary was ugly. A half foot taller than him, lots of long dark hair, good cheekbones, and a rakish, engaging smile.

Gary was mesmerized by his hero.

"Gary, I'm honored that you wrote your thesis about me and sorry I didn't tell you earlier. Of course, I know why you picked me. You're a smart guy like me and Dahmer. We're over 140 IQ. Ridgway, Rader, and the rest killed a lot of people but were pretty much morons. You're off to a heckuva start, my man; I'm impressed. I know about you annihilating your family back in the old country. That was awesome!"

Gary felt vertigo and thought he might puke again.

In the mirror, Ted broke up laughing, "Gary, you're giving 'cop killer' an entirely new meaning. Not sure why you didn't rape those young thangs or at least bite off a nipple or a pussy lip, but to each his own. Your high-tech, deep freeze is very cool, no pun intended."

Ted started to crack up at his own comment. "And much better than what Kuklinski did, and Dahmer tried."

Gary was teetering and sought to get his bearings.

"Couple words of advice from a guy who knows so you can live to kill many more hotties. The itch will get itchier, much itchier, faster, and faster. Coke, psilocybin, weed – they didn't help me slow it down. It was my downfall, and I got sloppy. It'll be hard, but dial it back while you can, then regroup."

Gary nodded and half-whined, "Ted, they're coming after me. All of them."

Bundy gave him another iconic smile, "What did you expect, Gary? You're making your mark, buddy. Enjoy. Don't be a pussy."

GOLDEN FROG POISON A GAME OF TWINS THRILLER

The restroom door swung open.

Gary stood stunned in front of the mirror as Lazlo Kianian entered. Bundy's reflection had vanished.

"Gary, you okay? You look a little green around the gills."

He was struck by the fact that Kianian had similar looks as Bundy but had blonde hair.

"I'm fine, Chief. Maybe ate one too many donuts."

Lazlo winked at him, "I appreciate you coming to the meeting on short notice. Everything's copacetic now with Dr. Treece?"

Gary gagged with new anxiety but swallowed without throwing up again. He managed to say, "Dr. Treece was more than fair. I apologize and know that I was way out of line. It won't happen again."

"Water under the bridge, no worries," Lazlo lied, then took a whiz.

When he was sure Gary was the guy, Lazlo wanted to disappear his body forever. Gary had abducted and likely killed multiple women in his city and fooled with the most important woman in his life. He would invoke Lazlo's Code. Jill had told him that Gary was exceptional at wheedling out critical information – even with his brusque analytical approach. Lazlo was sure that Gary could get played. He intended to do that.

****

Popov walked out as Kianian took his whiz. He was in desperate need of fresh air. At the elevator, he hit G.

Sliding into the elevator, Bundy was back, now in claustrophobic quarters.

The elevator wasn't moving.

"Gar, my boy, Can't tell you how jealous I am of you. Getting a seat at the big table investigating the babes you murdered. You'll go far."

Gary managed to ask, "Ted, are those CCTV tapes going show anything that points at me?"

With another devil-may-care smile, Bundy said, "Sorry, buddy, above my pay grade. Knock 'em dead. Make us boys proud!"

Gary had to choke back his reflux as he exited the elevator and ran into the sunlight. His only thought was, "*This serial killer shit can be a bitch.*"

****

Gary Popov often had violent dreams. Typically, the people in them were begging to be killed. There was no panic when he slaughtered them. But that wasn't his dream that evening. Instead, he was in an auditorium speaking to a large audience of cops dressed in blue. His first slide: "The Top Serial Killer of All Time."

The following slide: "Gary Popov."

The audience was silent. Gary realized he was standing naked. And like the Wicked Witch of the West, he dissolved off the stage, screaming.

****

Lazlo wasn't too surprised when Molly announced after lunch, "The Big Chief is here and would like a word."

He got up from his desk and stood by his small conference table as she entered.

He'd always worked well with Atlanta Chief of Police Deidra Yost. Before he took the job, Suzanne had told him that Deidra was from good, solid people and had worked her way up the ranks against all odds. Deidra was a full-bodied, black woman with a lovely face. She wore stylish clothes with high heels to add a few inches to her five-foot-two inches height. Soft-spoken and sharp, she wasn't a person to be trifled with. Many people thought she'd make a good mayor in two years. He did, too.

He shook her hand and pulled a chair back for her to sit. He knew he'd sound like a dope if he said something like, "To what do I owe the pleasure, Chief?" He was trying to process what he'd say to her. It was going to be tricky. He knew neither wanted these disappearances to blow up in their faces or APDs'.

She broke the ice, "Lazlo, I know you're friends with her. How's Suzanne doing?"

"I haven't talked to her for a few days; She's taking it a day at a time."

Deidra nodded, "Handling the loss of my Chauncey was, "Well, it was devastating."

Her husband, Chauncey was a successful businessman who had controlled a big chunk of the vendors at Hartsfield until he blew a left main a few years back.

Lazlo couldn't imagine how ballistic Deidra would go if she knew that Kip didn't die of natural causes but instead was murdered -- and that he and Suzanne and the County M.E. knew that --and that Suzanne's nephew was targeted for assassination in Durham. No reason to go there now.

He started with a half-truth, "Deidra, so far, we don't have dick. I convened a couple dozen of my best detectives and investigators this morning. We're on it."

Deidra nodded, "Off the record, do you have an inkling what happened to these women who are disappearing off our streets?"

He hesitated, then looked into her stunning green eyes and said, "I have an early theory, but that's all it is now. No solid evidence."

"Please keep me informed."

"I promise."

She stopped at his doorway, turned, and asked, "These women are dead, aren't they?"

Lazlo Kianian said, "Most likely."

"He'll kill again?"

Lazlo Kianian said, "Not if I have anything to say about it."

****

It was late in the day as he started to dial; her number popped up simultaneously.

"Suzy, great minds. I was calling you. How are you doing?"

"Up and down, Laz. It's hard. Worse than hard."

He couldn't imagine losing a spouse like she had. "Heard anything new from the bad guys?"

"Nope, but that doesn't necessarily surprise me."

"Menendez, you're going after him?"

"Yes."

"You got a plan?"

"Working on it, but listen, Laz, I don't want you to be part of it. You mean too much to me. You hear me? And you've got your own bad guys to catch."

"I hear you. Maybe dinner tomorrow night?

"Laz, look, let's get through this thing."

"Reluctantly, he said, "Okay. Suzy, but I may need your help. We've got a new serial killer roaming our streets. The press is only now putting together the disappearances of three attractive, single white women in the last five weeks. Flat out gone. And not from their homes. I'd like to be an optimist, but I think they were kidnapped and murdered."

He wasn't sure if she was listening or not. She said, "Laz, I'm flying to Durham tomorrow to check on David and Bernie and assure

Sarah and Tim they're okay. Go figure that David and Bernie, the former mafioso hit guy, are now best buds; David's lacrosse buddies think he's the coolest uncle ever in the history of the universe."

"Suzy, say hi to them for me. I know you've got a lot on your plate, but maybe on your flight, gnaw on this for me. The first woman of the three who disappeared, Amy Neyland, was an investigative reporter for a small paper. Here's the thing: she disappeared the same day Kip was murdered."

He waited for a response, then said, "You and I don't believe in coincidences."

"Almost never. See you when I get back."

Chapter 29 – The Objective

There was a vestige aroma of his cherrywood pipes; three handmade by his grandfather sat in a wooden holder on his desk. She'd allowed him to smoke indoors— only in his study with the door shut and air purifier on. He only smoked Lane-1 Pipe tobacco and always kept a tin in his top drawer. She smiled; it was there. She picked up one of the pipes, put it to her nose, and breathed in. Kip. Suzanne never admitted to him that although she hated the smell of cigarette smoke, the aroma of a pipe was as erotic as it got.

His impressive college, legal degrees, and other awards certificates hung on the far wall. But she knew his favorite was the one given by colleagues in his young thriving firm – after he broke off from the mega-firm where he and his dad had been the top criminal attorneys in the Southeast. It was a playful, ornate certificate in gold leaf and black print. Simply with the words, "Kip Davies, Attorney-at-Law, You Rock!" With a photo of the seven of them, Kip smiling in the middle. After returning from Madrid, she made a mental note to take them all to dinner. And make it a monthly invitation.

There were many photos of the beautiful blonde twins at various ages with their dad. And she and Kip on their wedding day – a photo of them kissing on a beautiful Atlanta day in Piedmont Park. Her favorite was one of the four taken on the edge of the spectacular Santa Barbara bluff overlooking the Pacific.

She might have another love one day, but Kip Davies would always be her truest. She sat in his comfy leather desk chair where he'd appeared after his death and had spoken to her. She took a deep breath and tried to conjure up his supernatural being. Couldn't do it. Deep down, she knew she had no such power but was always receptive to the supernatural.

She walked into her study two doors down. An unused bedroom that lacked the pizzazz of Kip's study. On the walls were a few photos from her past days: a gangly teenager playing hoops and golf; with her mom and dad in Atlanta and at Seaside; with her past APD colleagues. And a high-tech whiteboard she used periodically to organize thoughts about her Interpol consulting cases.

That evening, two of the photographs seemed to glow. Like they were backlit. A photo of her father in his dress blue Atlanta Police Department uniform hugging her and a photo of her standing with her longtime APD homicide partner, Dusty Rayfield, her arm draped over his shoulder, a half foot below hers.

There was something behind her. She jerked around and heard his unmistakable South Georgia twang. "Suzy."

There stood his apparition, a big grin on his pock-marked, round face, in his blue jeans, cowboy boots, white muscle shirt, and shiny bald head.

"Dusty."

With a smile, he said, "Suzy, short visit, but you gotta promise me."

"Promise what, Dusty?"

"That you'll trust yourself to make the right call. You were the best homicide detective APD ever had. And promise that you'll come back to your daughters and friends."

"I promise."

He nodded and disappeared.

****

She had to make the call. "Hey, Sam."

"Hi, Suzanne. How'd your chat go?"

"I learned a few things."

"Like?"

Mary Jo and Abbott are all in to get Menendez. I'm not 100% sure I'm not merely cannon fodder. They have nothing to lose if I fail; they'll get him one way or another if they want to. Obviously, I have a lot more to lose."

"You're thinking about not going to Madrid?"

After hesitating, she said, "Sam, I've thought about it all day. I'm going. Mary Jo was agreeable to anything I needed. Your list of weapons, etc. – no problem. There was one deal breaker. I told her I needed a current photo of Raoul Menendez. After a minute, a photo popped up on my screen. Interpol and every major law enforcement agency worldwide would love to have a clear photo of Mexico's top narco. He'd done a masterful job of staying out of the public eye and the ever-roaming eyes of spy satellites. I was shocked that Mary Jo provided it. Thank God I got a screenshot because the image disappeared in thirty seconds."

Sam said, "You keep saying "I" and not "we." It's your thing, but I'll be there to back you up."

She took a moment. "I already told you about some of the loved ones and friends whom I put in Harm's way. A couple who are no longer alive. I can't do that with you."

Scarcely able to breathe, she said, "Sam, you can't come with me."

He tried to digest what he'd heard. "You're sure about that?"

As painful as it was for him, Sam took the high road. "I understand, but Suzanne, I want you to know I have feelings for you."

"Sam, I know but I can't...it's all too raw. I'm sorry."

He waited for something positive but knew it wouldn't happen on this call or maybe ever.

"A couple of observations from an old guy, if you are open to them?"

"Always, and you're hardly old."

"A question. Are you seeking revenge or justice?"

"I guess both."

"Revenge can be righteous but also a slippery slope that clouds real intentions. Consider your main objective, Suzanne. Is it to kill Menendez or keep him from killing you and yours?"

"I don't see the difference."

"Maybe there is none but keep it in mind."

"I will. Thanks."

"Godspeed, Suzanne. Keep the faith and keep in touch if you can."

He hung up dispirited but knew that come hell or high water, he wouldn't change her mind. He would pray for her protection in a foreign land.

Suzanne sat and pondered what he'd meant about her fundamental objective.

****

Chapter 30 – James Bond

By the following morning, Suzanne had snapped out of her funk and got moving. Something Dusty reminded more a few times: "Move your spectacular ass. Never stop."

She managed to get Arnie Friedlander to carve out some time the next day. She'd always offered to pay his top consulting rate; he'd always refused. One way or another, she would compensate him when this was over. She'd forwarded the latest clip of her conversation with the "Voice,' AKA Mary Jo Cogburn, to see if they could glean anything else.

She arrived at noon, holding two of Bernie's famous pizzas. Sheila took them from her hands and said, "Awesome, we're both famished. Follow me. Something to drink?"

"A water, thanks."

Sheila gave her friend a double-boob squeeze. "You okay, Suzy?"

"Hang'n in."

"I'll fetch Arnie and drinks."

The generous conference room sported a half dozen six by 10-foot H.D. screens. All the screens were busy. A couple ran software analyses to block and strike back at the bad guys attacking a client's data and information technology systems. Two others were on TV channels. Another caught her eye: an overhead view of the majestic city of Madrid. It zoomed in on a bullfight at Las Ventas, the biggest bullfighting ring in Madrid. She'd be there in four days and wondered if there would be a play at Menendez in the crowd. It didn't seem likely.

Arnie and Sheila entered with drinks and laptops.

Arnie was upbeat. "You ready to rock and roll, Suzy?"

"Let's do it."

Sheila said, "We deciphered the clip you sent last night. The same voice you identified as Mary Jo Cogburn in most of it. But they got sloppy. There's a guy's unmodulated voice in the background whispering to her off and on. Perhaps Michael Abbott? Here are a few snippets that may or may not make sense to you. The whispers were only audible after amping up the background volume and eliminating the rest.

Suzanne listened:

"…weapons & equipment to her room, not locker..."

"... know if she checked in...."

".... bugs on bag and room..."

"...small investment..."

"...game of twins..."

"... no big deal..."

"...she could do it...

"...less than 20%..."

"...either way..."

"...both dead..."

Suzanne asked, "Can you replay those?"' Which Sheila did.

"No doubt Menendez wants me dead. Mary Jo and Abbott are enigmas to me, but I detect more than a bit of ambivalence. They'll provide support, but it's unclear what their grand scheme is.

Sheila chimed in, "Like you need more enemies."

Arnie pointed to one of the big screens.

A view from above, the beautiful, hilly terrain outside the city. Then, the screen zoomed into one palatial hilly estate. "That's where Menendez lives per the address you provided."

"Wow," Suzanne exclaimed, looking at the static photos.

"Google Earth satellite pics?"

He smiled, "Nope, the photos you're looking at are recent real-time images from a private satellite over a couple of minutes as it continued to orbit."

Suzanne was amazed at the detail. She could make out the type of cars in the driveway, both Mercedes and their license plate numbers.

"The photo of Menendez you provided is good. But it's doubtful he could be identified without a full view of his face. And he'd have to be there when the satellite is orbiting, which happens every ninety minutes. We can provide heat signatures of people in his hacienda at various times of the day to give you an idea of how many people are there and when and how that number changes. We've got the best facial recognition software but picking him out in a bullfight crowd would be nearly impossible, especially if he wears a hat. Maybe if we had our own drone. Kidding."

****

Sheila said, "I'm starving! Let's eat pizza."

With little conversation, the three demolished one pizza. Sheila said, "There's another one."

Suzanne said, "No Mas."

Arnie said, "I'll bet you're a James Bond fan. Do you remember Q, who came up with new gizmos for Bond?

"Q is one of my favorite characters in Bond movies."

"Sorry, no Aston Martin DB5."

"Darn," she laughed.

"You remember a few years ago, there was an issue with the GPS tracker I put in your emerald and diamond gold cross necklace.

Ancient tech stuff. I can't take credit, but I shopped for a few gadgets that could help you."

He walked around the conference table and said, "Suzy, give me your hand."

He had something tiny on the tip of his finger. He pushed it under her long, violet index nail.

"Not getting fresh; going to put this other one on the back of your earlobe, okay?"

She nodded. He put another super-small dot on the back of her ear and gently pressed it.

She chuckled, "Arnie, you're giving me a manicure and an ear massage?"

"You can use it as a two-way encrypted system without needing a phone. Think of this as a stealthy way to communicate – initiated by your fingernail. Only you can hear the communication. You can say a number or name. There is no record of the call, and only you can listen to the response. And we can give you a heads-up on anything we think you should know and vice versa.

"Nice."

"You can tap to direct what you want to see with your voice and view it virtually in front of you. No phone screen needed.

"No way."

"Okay, put on these sunglasses, tap your fingernail, and say, "I want to see a map of Metro Atlanta."

The map appeared in space about two feet from her eyes. She extended her arm through the holographic image. Or you could call up AI information on any topic you choose."

She tried it. "What are the cities in Spain that hold bullfights ranked by size of stadium?"

The list popped up.

"Amazing!"

Another practical use is locating surveillance bugs: mico-mini cameras, microphones, and GPS trackers. And you'll think of other uses, I'm sure."

"Plus, the glasses are also binoculars."

Sheila said, "I dubbed them "magic glasses." They have a binocular mode that you can activate and zoom with your voice or fingernail. Take this pair home with you and check it out."

"Thanks, guys, Sean Connery would be jealous."

Chapter 31 – The Bait

The shiny little golden frog had fascinated him since he'd absconded with it from Jill Treece's office drawer. He knew better than to touch it. As he stared at the figurine in plastic wrap, he smiled and said out loud, "Both bitches lied to me and need to pay. Don't you think?"

Gary Popov knew he'd be wading into deep, murky, dangerous waters. To go after both now would be nuts – even more nuts than he knew he certainly was. He got it that others like him wrestled with similar stuff. Could or should they murder people they knew – or only strangers? Drinking a longneck Coors at his kitchen table with the golden frog before him, he landed on his best course of action in the short term.

Delacroix lived in an affluent cluster-condo neighborhood in the Northside area of northwest Atlanta. Her building was at the end of a cul-de-sac-- making any surveillance difficult at best – even worse since it looked like she had ongoing 24/7 police or other protection. With binoculars, he could divine that from a hundred yards away. By all accounts, Delacroix had been a hard-ass, big-time homicide cop. She'd be heavily armed even if he found a way into her place. No, it would take something else and somewhere else to kidnap and kill her. He needed to focus on the best target.

****

Working on the Task Force was making Gary more paranoid than he already was. He understood that his personal car, his Nissan sedan – besides being outfitted with APD communications – also had a GPS tracker. He'd always been careful to turn off the tracker as he left work or home when he planned to surveil. He had no idea who might be interested in surveilling him but was taking no chances.

He was fighting not to get manic. He did the prep and injected a healthy hit of heroin, which he hadn't done in the last couple of years.

The rush was better than he remembered. Dr. Jill wasn't young but attractive and had a nice body. He imagined having fun with her alive before she entered his deep freeze. Then he drifted off.

****

The day after she returned from her much-needed vacation, Jill found herself back in the grind of office life. She made a pot of coffee, turned on her laptop, and sank into her desk chair, a mix of exhaustion and anticipation. She knew she'd pay the price for her time off, but the memories of the past week kept a smile on her face. She closed her eyes and was transported back to the beach in the Bahamas where she put her hand in Noah's. It was a week of pure bliss, a rare respite from the grief that had consumed her since her husband's death a decade ago.

As Jill settled into her office routine, a glimmer of unease flickered in her mind. Her right-hand desk drawer, the one with the double locks, was slightly ajar. A chill ran down her spine. She knew she couldn't have left it that way. Her heart raced as she reached for the jewelry box, only to gasp in shock. The golden frog, a precious memento from her vacation, was gone!

Jill's mind raced as she tried to make sense of the situation. No one else had duplicates of her desk keys; the only other copies were safely locked away in her home safe. Her admin, while trustworthy, didn't have access to her desk. She had considered installing cameras in her office, but the idea had remained just that -- an idea. The only cameras in the vicinity were down the long, dimly lit hallway, a good forty yards from her office door.

Jill's mind raced with questions. Who could have known about the golden frog, a rare and deadly creature, and its lethal poison? The thought of bugs and spy cameras crossed her mind, but she dismissed it as paranoia. She needed answers. With a determined stride, she descended the stairs and stepped outside, her heart pounding in her chest.

GOLDEN FROG POISON A GAME OF TWINS THRILLER

"Jill, how was your break from the chaos of our work?" Lazlo's voice was warm and familiar.

"Lazlo, it was a great vacation, but something's wrong. I need your help," Jill's voice quivered with a mix of fear and urgency, a stark contrast to her usual composed demeanor.

Itd didn't sound like the usual cool, calm, and collected Medical Examiner.

"What's wrong, Jill?"

"I know that Suzanne told you about the golden frog figurine and that I had it checked by a world-class animal poison pathologist. He kept the tissue samples. I brought the golden frog back to Atlanta in a small jewelry box that I locked in my desk drawer at work. It has a double lock. The drawer was cracked open. No possible way I left it like that. My admin doesn't have extra keys to the drawer -- only a key to my office that adjoins hers. As far as I know, only you, Noah, Suzanne, Menendez, and Menendez's assassin know anything about the golden frog and golden frog poison. Much less that I'd have it and where I kept it.

"Was there anything else in that drawer?"

"Yes, a short note from Dr. Kline confirming the poison on the figurine and tissue sample. Which, if either of those things got out, could land me in deep pooh-pooh."

"I get that, but I don't see why Menendez's thugs would want that information."

"Someone is fishing for information to discredit me and Suzanne. And he likely photographed the note."

A pregnant pause, then at the same instant, both said, "Gary Popov."

"Jill, this can't get out, okay? I'm running a task force trying to solve the recent disappearances of three women. You were on vacation, and I put Gary on the Task Force to help check out any relevant CCTV videotape. I think he kidnapped the three women and likely murdered them."

"What!"

"Yep, but I can't make a case of any kind."

After explaining where his initial suspicion came from, she remarked, "Oh my God!"

"Jill, I know you suspended Gary for a couple of weeks. He's been okay since?"

"Obsequious as hell before I left on vacation. Not like him."

"Let's suppose that Gary somehow got into your office while you were gone, broke into your desk drawer, and left with the golden frog figurine and a photo of the note. How pissed would he be at what he found?"

"Hard to imagine—and pissed at Suzanne, too."

"Jill, you and Suzy are beautiful women. Not exactly in his age wheelhouse so far as we know, but three disappearances of young attractive women do not necessarily make a pattern. Could Gary be a kidnapper and even a killer?"

Jill hesitated, then said, "Honestly, it wouldn't surprise me. And think about it -- a brilliant crime scene special investigator learning the nuances of serial killing on the job."

"I agree. He's obviously intelligent but always seemed a bit off. He uses his personal car for police business. It has GPS. I'm having that tracked, but the GPS can easily be turned off, and we've monitored that he's turned it off a few times. Sometimes at work and sometimes at home – or elsewhere. You're a runner, right? When do you usually run?"

"Varies, but typically around 7:00 PM, I run through the neighborhoods around my home but have no specific route. Pretty quiet around here and not much traffic."

"How long do you run?"

"About a half hour."

"I'm guessing that Gary has cruised by your place a few times and may have seen you running. I can have the traffic cam CCTV analyzed further, but few are nearby. I assume you carry your phone when you run."

"No. It's my time away from my iPhone, but I carry a Ruger Max .380."

"Good, but you should also carry a phone. Jill, this is an extraordinary situation. If it gets out internally what we're doing, Gary is likely to catch wind of it, especially since he's on the Task Force. We don't want to spook him. Only my tech guy and an undercover cop I trust implicitly are in on this. And I'm going to run it by Suzanne."

She smiled, "You want me to be bait for Gary, don't you?"

Before he could answer, she said, "I'm willing to do that."

****

Lazlo was surprised he hadn't heard back from Greg yet. So, he called him. "Greg, what's the scoop?"

"Sorry, Chief. I've run dozens of queries using your parameters and variations of them. No hits at all for that vehicle. Obviously, he'd turned off the GPS on the dates of the abductions. I dug deeper into when and where that usually happened. Typically, he turned it off near his office or home in the evening. I'll send you a map of the days and times when his GPS went dark. The past two weeks, he's been going dark more frequently."

"Excellent work. Thanks, Greg. And let me know your extra hours."

*****

Lazlo told Jill he'd be back in touch and run his plan by her. In the meantime, he told her not to run this evening. He'd have an undercover cop stay with her until she went to work in the morning as long as this investigation took.

He knew Suzy was working on her plans but called her anyway.

"Sorry, I know you've got a lot on your mind, but I need a few minutes to see what you think about my plan to catch Gary Popov, who I believe will go after Jill next."

She nearly shouted, "Whatever it is, you can't put Jill in Harm's Way, you got that, Laz? She's not going to be bait for Gary Popov."

"No, mam, I've got a plan to keep her safe 100%, I promise."

He explained but neglected to mention the details about the policewoman he was stationed to keep watch, who wouldn't be running with her.

"Okay, but how does that get you any closer to catching Gary?"

"I believe I've got enough Probable Cause that I can sell if I can get a few photos of Gary surveilling her neighborhood. I had an additional tracker put on his vehicle this morning. A reach, but I've got a chit to call in -- to a judge I know."

"You keep her safe, Laz, above all else."

She hung up. She needed to get back to her plan.

Chapter 32 - The Freezer Killer

Fulton County Superior Court Judge Sylvester Claxton owed Lazlo a favor. A chit Lazlo decided he'd try to cash in. A few years back, when he was in Narcotics for a short time, Lazlo disappeared something for the Judge whose niece he caught with a Meth 8-ball. He knew the Claxton name. After that, he got invited to Claxton's monthly poker game. Lazlo called Janice, the Judge's admin, to get on his calendar for a half hour tomorrow. Before she could ask, Lazlo said, "Janice, it's a personal matter—and important."

"Lemme check, Lazlo."

Janice buzzed into the Judge. She was back on the line in a minute. "How about 4:00 PM?"

"Perfect."

****

Lazlo loved the historic architecture in Atlanta. The Fulton County Courthouse, over a century old, in South Downtown, was on the National Register of Historic Places. Neoclassical/classical exterior, but he most loved the foyer with its thirty-foot ceiling and marble floors. He thought it majestic. It exuded law and justice.

The Judge's chambers were sartorially typical of an Atlanta Superior Court Judge with his seniority. Dark polished walnut paneling, an enormous mahogany desk, and a generous conference table. Maybe more square footage than Lazlo's apartment, and the eleven-foot ceiling height made it look even bigger. What made the Judge's chambers so different, though, was the art and mementos that hung on his walls. No verdant landscapes or horsey fox-hunting horseshit. Lazlo bet there wasn't anything like it in any other judge's chambers in the country. Instead, historical wooden lacrosse sticks and balls, lacrosse paintings, many with indigenous Americans, and photos dominated three walls.

The judge's chambers were a glorious tribute to a sport that Lazlo had enjoyed in high school and at Georgia Tech. He'd been in the Judge's chambers several times. Still, he was always mesmerized by the photos of NFL Hall of Fame running back Jim Brown, who was an All-American in football and lacrosse at Syracuse. And two photos, particularly one with Brown, his brawny arm around Sylvester Claxton, who didn't reach the athletic heights of Brown but was an honorable mention All-American. The other of Jim Brown, Sylvester Claxton, and his son, Dante, who was awarded a full Jim Brown-endowed lacrosse scholarship at Syracuse.

Judge Claxton, who friends like Lazlo called Sly, was out of his robes and in khakis, a button-down shirt, and pricey Italian loafers without socks. Fifteen years ago, when he became a Superior Court Judge, he was one of three black Superior Court judges in Atlanta. Now, there were fifteen out of thirty. Claxton deemed that progress.

The solid, smiling, six-foot black man strolled to the built-in bar behind his desk.

"A drink?"

"Yes, sir." Lazlo knew the Judge only drank top-shelf Scotch.

Lazlo pinched his forefinger and thumb to indicate only a couple of fingers. The Judge poured double that in his tumbler.

"Laz, I'm guessing your police investigations are keeping you busy."

"Yeah, no kidding. You've undoubtedly read about the recent disappearances of the three young women. I have a Task Force on it now. It's part of the story I'm going to tell you."

Standing, the Judge took a swig of Scotch, "I'm listening."

"Sly, a ways back, I did a favor, and you said I deserved one in kind. Never thought about it until now."

"The thing with my niece Val?"

"Yep."

"She's done well and hasn't had any more drug problems. She's an attorney and has a kid on the way."

"That's great."

They both took slow sips of their drinks. Lazlo sat while the Judge roamed around his chamber. Judge Claxton liked conversation, but when it might involve the law, he didn't beat around the bush a lot.

"So, you're calling in your marker in for what, Laz? I hope it's not something too illegal."

Kianian half grinned. "I'd like you to issue a search warrant."

"For what?"

"Lemme get to that in a couple of minutes. A bit of background. And Judge, this must all be off the record."

The Judge waved his hand okay. Then, he smiled like he was pulling his chain. "Umm, this already sounds like a part of a good crime novel."

Laz found it interesting that the Judge was a crime novel addict even though he dealt with the shit every day. Sly had told him that he'd write a thriller one day. Laz was sure it'd be a bestseller. He could tell he had the judge's attention.

"Sly, the punchline of the story, so far, is that I think there's a crime scene investigator who works for both me and the Fulton County Medical Examiner, Jill Treece-- who is abducting these girls, and God, I hope not, but maybe killing them. He's gotta be stopped before it happens again."

"And you know this how?"

"Judge, I'm going to leave out some stuff you don't want to know. You'll have to trust me on that. Maybe down the road, but first things first. This is more than a bit unusual. No one in the department knows I'm doing this."

Sly looked him in the eyes, "Okay."

Laz said, "I'm guessing you're not big on coincidences."

The Judge paused and continued strolling with an empty glass.

After a minute of cogitation swirling his Scotch, he said, "My favorite quote about coincidences is, "Coincidence is logical." Written by a guy named Johan Cruyff a long time ago."

Lazlo was struck by the truth in the quote. He'd never thought of coincidence that way.

"Judge, I missed one a few weeks ago. In hindsight, it seems very logical. I didn't realize the first part of the coincidence of the woman reporter disappearing on the same night that Kip Davies died."

The Judge's face was now quizzical, and he said, "Your story is getting more intriguing."

Lazlo thought, *"Boy, if he only knew the whole story."*

He continued. "The crime investigator who got into the Davies-Delacroix residence before Jill Treece got there acted like a major jackass when he was interviewing the recent widower. On arrival, Jill heard the tail-end of it and told him to leave the crime scene ASAP. He was undoubtedly pissed but then realized he had information that only a very few in Atlanta had that evening: that Kip Davies was dead. It hadn't been announced on any media. And there was no obvious cause of death. Neither Dr. Treece nor the APD would comment without Suzanne's okay."

"How is Suzanne doing? An amazing woman who has been nothing but helpful in contributing her time and money to black causes in the city."

"I talked to her a couple of days ago. She's tough, but it's been hard."

The Judge nodded gravely. "Sorry to interrupt."

"No problem. For the investigator, it was the perfect opportunity to con and kidnap a young reporter. I don't know how he knew her, but he did. He took her and, that evening made anonymous calls to the media with the salacious accusation that Suzanne Delacroix was a person of interest in her husband's death. The right-wing media had a heyday, and you might have seen other crap. The next day, Jill Treece made him fess up that he was the disinformation leak about Kip Davies' death and Suzanne's involvement. She suspended him for two weeks. Gary, that's his first name, I'm sure he was pissed at Jill and Suzanne. But he's had plenty of time to continue his next kidnappings."

"Lazlo, was Suzanne involved in her husband's death?"

There was no way to explain to the Judge all the stuff about golden frogs or the golden frog poison or Suzanne and Jill covering up the reason for Kip's murder, or, for God's sake, a Mexican drug cartel being involved. It was a sort of fib that he'd anticipated he'd have to make.

Lazlo said, "No."

The Judge stopped in front of his mahogany desk and sat. "So you have this theory about the investigator, Gary?"

The Judge poured another stiff one and held the bottle up. Lazlo declined.

"Do you have *anything* connecting this guy to the first girl or the others?"

Laz couldn't mention that he and Jill had come to the same conclusion about Gary after the golden frog disappeared from her office drawer.

"Not yet."

"No physical evidence?"

"Not so far."

"Not even electronic?"

"Judge, you know I work strictly by the book."

The Judge gave him a smirk and rolled his deep brown eyes.

Laz hoped he wasn't losing him. "But let's say the electronic stuff via APD communications showed nothing which it didn't."

"Lazlo, what the hell do you want to search, where, and why?"

"Not exactly sure. Somewhere, the three women are hopefully alive. If not that, their dead bodies and any other evidence that would tie Gary to the abductions of the young women. Maybe it's not a serial thing yet, but Atlanta women are disappearing. I could be wrong. I've accessed his house's building plan. It has a generous basement and a big garage for a single-story ranch. They could be in there – or not."

Laz took a breath and told the Judge what else he'd been doing to investigate, namely, he'd put Gary on the Task Force looking into the murders.

"You what?"

"I've got several officers looking at CCTV tape of the second and third abductions -- the City's and business's cameras around the locations where the women were last seen or known to have been. Hundreds of hours of video -- going out five miles from where they were last seen. Needle in a haystack to see any of them. But I hope it might make him nervous– he might come across some CCTV tape where he made a mistake in one of the abductions. With my top tech guy, we're monitoring the movements of his car. Even a cop's private vehicle is outfitted with an APD GPS tracker. But any surveilling of him has gotta be on the Q.T., or the jig is up. The problem is that if a cop has any basic tech knowledge, he can turn the GPS in his vehicle off and on any time he wants. We know Gary turned off his GPS on the evenings of the disappearances, but that proves nothing. He's been turning his GPS off and on a lot more lately. He's hunting."

"Sounds like a smart SOB."

"You got that right, Sly."

"I believe Gary's next target is Dr. Treece. I had another tracker put on his vehicle this morning, and I've already assigned one officer to Jill's location, mainly to protect her while she's not at work. I'm sure he knows where the cams are and avoids them, which I'm guessing he did in the other abductions."

"Laz, do you think he knows you're looking for him?

"Not 100% sure; I don't think so, but I think he's now beyond paranoid and super-cautious."

The Judge walked about his chambers with his Scotch. Then he stopped as he viewed his vibrant city from the window. "Laz, I hate to overstate the obvious, but you don't have diddlysquat, do you?"

It didn't hit him like a ton of bricks – but maybe a half-ton. He said, "No, Judge. Not yet."

"Laz, I want to help you get this prick, but the ask is too big."

Lazlo Kianian had a suspicion that's what Sly would say.

The Judge turned and said, "Tell you what. I'll have Janice draft a warrant that will give you carte blanche: home, car, phone, computer, whatever else he owns, the works. Give her the guy's info. It will be ready to go for an electronic signature. Just one single shred of good evidence. That's all I ask.

On the way out, Judge Claxton hugged him. "Laz, you got this."

He left without a search warrant but was buoyed by the Judge's words. The hunt was on. And now Lazlo was the hunter.

****

Lazlo knew he would lose the battle if he didn't allow Dr. Jill Treece to do her evening jog. They both understood that if Gary had been surveilling her at all, he'd probably shut his thing down if he'd thought there was anything suspicious about her recent actions. If all Lazlo got was new tracking information that Gary was surveilling, he knew that wouldn't be enough for the Judge.

Bypassing his own bureaucratic crap, Lazlo approved twelve hours per day of APD security for Jill using one of his top cops, Azir Mella. A slender, attractive, Middle Eastern woman who perhaps weighed 110 pounds. Azir was intelligent and always dependable.

Jill Treece typically jogged a half hour through her safe, hoity-toity Brookhaven Atlanta neighborhood from 7:00 PM to 7:30 PM. The protocol that Lazlo approved was a custom app that his tech guy set up -- on Jill's, Azir's, and his phones; if, in any way, shape, or form, Jill or Azir encountered Gary, they only needed to double-click their screen. An emergency alert would go to all. Jill was to get the hell out of Dodge and run anywhere except on the road she'd been jogging. Azir would fetch her within a couple of minutes.

That evening, as she'd done the past week, Azir paced in Dr. Treece's gorgeous living room, waiting for her to finish her run as she monitored her jogging on Google Maps. The kind doctor often brought home a delicious take-out for them both, and her wine collection was divine (she allowed herself one glass). She liked her a lot. Though the idea of being responsible for her – but not being allowed to protect her on her runs – gnawed at her. She rarely chewed gum, but tonight, she was chomping fiercely on two sticks of Juicy Fruit.

Then she saw something strange on her notebook and phone maps; about six blocks away, Jill had stopped. Maybe saying hi to a neighbor? Then, her Alert was triggered. Azir's phone shrilled and lit up with a pulsing red circle. Immediately, she ran to the garage to put up the god-awful-slow automatic garage door. In her car, she put on her earpiece. The first thing she heard was her boss, who'd also been alerted. "Azir, you got this?"

"On my way to her location."

GOLDEN FROG POISON A GAME OF TWINS THRILLER

****

For the Fulton County Medical Examiner, death was a daily way of life she'd tried to get used to. But not a day like today when she had to do an autopsy on a young child. After seeing the hideous marks on the four-year-old's body, she was 100% sure the poor girl had been brutalized her whole short life. Dozens of contusions, burn marks, and many broken half-healed bones. She was sure this girl would have become a beautiful young woman. She scanned the arrest file and was aghast that more than a dozen domestic complaints had been treated as rubbish. She made a note to have Lazlo Kianian kick some ass.

God almighty, how could people do this to one another? It was hard to squash her own violent eye-for-an-eye thoughts when she saw this mayhem. That evening, she tried but couldn't get the girl's bruised and battered dead body from her mind. She jogged almost in a stupor on her quiet neighborhood streets; her Nikes were the only sounds, pounding the pavement louder than usual. There was some sidewalk on her run, but not a lot. Typically, she ran down the right edge of the street.

She only noticed the white van slow and stop when it was adjacent to her. The right window rolled down. She heard an unmistakable voice.

"Dr. Treece, how you are doing this fine evening?"

She knew the make and model of Gary's sedan. The van didn't compute.

She leaned toward the passenger window and hesitated momentarily before double-tapping her phone. She was too late, though, to run away. Gary grinned and tased her in the face. In pain and shock, she dropped motionless to the pavement. Gary knew this was risky but had seen no one on that stretch of the dark, suburban street. It took him less than twenty seconds to run to the other side of the van, pick her up, and shove her in the passenger side. She'd dropped her iPhone. He grabbed it, and after weaving in and out a few blocks at a reasonable speed, he pitched it with his left hand over the hood of his van into a thick hedge on the right. Treece was out cold, but to make sure, he grabbed his bottle of chloroform and sprayed her in the face, then pulled a blanket over her. He knew there was a danger of killing her when tasing her face, but she seemed to be breathing. And heck, if she croaked, she croaked. He'd put her on ice, regardless.

****

At APD Headquarters, Lazlo watched Jill's location icon, which appeared to speed up but then stopped again. But knew he needed to let Azir, who was closest to the scene, pay attention to her Google map.

"Heading toward her...just a couple blocks away."

In less than a minute, she said, "Lazlo, I'm at her location, but I don't see her or Gary's car."

He said, "I'll get back to you in a minute."

He looked at Gary's GPS location, which showed that he was home. *The new tracker indicated the same. What the fuck!*

Lazlo took a few deep breaths and walked to the far side of his office. Then, he shouted out loud, "He's in a different vehicle. Not his sedan. Jesus, Laz, how could you be so stupid?"

As he raced to his Mustang in the APD garage, these things needed to happen. First, he called Judge Sly, who, thank God, picked up. "Judge, I hope that Jill Treece sending a distress message that Gary had kidnapped her – is enough. She's now in mortal danger, of that, I've no doubt. Please email me the signed Search Warrant. Thx, Laz."

Lazlo Kianian hung up before the Judge could ask him any questions.

"*Jesus,*" the Judge told himself as he did the online signature and sent it. "*Why don't we have more law enforcement pros like Kianian protecting our Atlantans?*" Then smiled, "*Lazlo is on the job tonight.*"

GOLDEN FROG POISON A GAME OF TWINS THRILLER

****

Did Lazlo know where Gary was heading? He'd bet his reputation on it.

Next, Lazlo gave Azir an order she'd not expected. "Haul your ass to Gary's home address. I'll text it to you. Blue light it all the way. I may need backup. Go! If you make it before me, ease off when you're close."

Lazlo knew what kind of cop she was – and, more importantly, tonight, what kind of driver she was.

****

Azir Mella's family emigrated to the U.S. from Syria two decades ago. Her family struggled but eventually found their place as esteemed mechanics who also loved racing. Two of her brothers worked for professional drivers. Their sister was not taken seriously, but they let her watch and sometimes ride shotgun while test-driving. For her, the experience of riding in a car moving at more than 150 miles per hour was thrilling. She graduated Summa Cum Laude from Georgia Tech in Mechanical Engineering but became a cop since no one took her seriously as an auto engineer. Her dream had always been to drive NASCAR. Now, her boss was giving her a chance at something even more important – to save Jill Treece's life and maybe others.

Azir drove a royal blue Camaro 1SS, not the most expensive of so-called muscle cars, but she deemed it the best and fastest. 455 Horsepower. Zero to sixty in less than four seconds. It could hit 175 miles per hour. In the right hands, like hers, it became a rocket ship.

She put Gary's address into the APD GPS that mimicked Google's. Nice that it wasn't high traffic time. Estimated trip time was 35 minutes. From 400 to 285West, then into Mapleton, an Atlanta suburb she'd never seen. She hit 140 miles per hour on both interstates. She did it in seventeen minutes without causing any accidents on her way.

****

Lazlo wasn't there yet. She parked a block away from Popov's place. Mostly one-story houses. Not the big burbs but not a bad-looking area. A couple of minutes later, a white van passed her and headed up his driveway. The garage door opened automatically. She caught a glimpse of a black sedan before the door shut. She called Lazlo. "I'm here. A white van pulled into his garage next to the Nissan."

Laz said, "Okay, do you have binoculars? I don't."

"I do."

"See if you can spy any cameras pointed toward his front yard and sidewalk."

She got out of her car and scanned for a minute. "None that I can see."

He found that curious, but it allowed him to use a measured entrance without leading with the search warrant.

"Azir, I hope not, but this could quickly become a clusterfuck once I get inside Gary's house. No doubt he's a violent psycho. Stay hidden outside but near the door once I enter. "If I double tap my phone or you hear any gunshots, come in hot, but try not to kill him. I want to get Gary alive so we can find Jill Treece and the others. I'm going to knock on his door first and see if he opens it -- under the guise of talking about the Task Force and giving him more responsibility for reviewing the CCTV tapes. I'll use the search warrant if necessary to enter."

"Lazlo, but if you need the warrant, why not let me go in with you?"

"Just be there if I need you. Call me now, and I'll leave the line open so you can listen in."

"Got it."

Lazlo Kianian knew that Azir was a great cop, but he wasn't putting her young life in extra jeopardy tonight. This was between Gary Popov and him.

****

After shutting the garage door seven minutes earlier, Gary slung Jill Treece over his shoulder and carried her from the van into his kitchen. The taser and chloroform had done their job. He schlepped her to his bedroom and was glad she wasn't dead – yet. He removed her Nikes and pulled off her short athletic shorts and panties, then her tight top and sports bra. He marveled at the shape his boss was in at her age. He'd not fucked any other women he'd kidnapped while they were alive, but his dick got hard as he fondled her.

Gary almost freaked out when he heard a knock on his front door. It made every hair on his hairy neck and shoulders shoot to attention. No one ever knocked on his door. Other than solicitors that he simply ignored after checking them out via his front door peephole. He'd thought about security cameras but never saw the need. No reason for anyone to fool with Gary Popov, and certainly not in his home. If they did, he'd kill them.

He had an outdoor intercom. He was stunned by the voice, "Hey Gary, I just wanted to talk about the Task Force and how you could play a bigger role. And do it outside of work."

Gary wasn't big on firearms but knew how to use them. His Glock17 was in his top bedroom dresser drawer. He slotted a clip into it. He stuffed it in the back of his pants. He shut the bedroom door and ran to his basement door to ensure it was closed and locked.

Gary knew he had no choice. A minute later, he opened the front door and said, "Chief Kianian, this is a surprise. Come on in."

Gary was more stoutly built than Kianian had realized up close. Biceps bulging from his Polo. Thick neck. And that strange Eastern European Southern twang.

"Sorry to intrude, Gary."

"No problem, Chief. Could I get you something to drink?"

"Long day. Yeah, I could use a cold beer."

Gary managed a smile. "Back in a jiff."

But Lazlo followed him into the kitchen. And there on his kitchen table sat something Gary had forgotten to put away.

"Interesting piece," Lazlo remarked. "Is that a frog?"

Their eyes locked in.

Gary yanked the Glock from his pants and aimed it at Lazlo's head.

"Gary, you know you're fucked. I even have a search warrant on my phone. Where are Jill and the others?"

Listening in, Azir had already tiptoed to the entrance to the kitchen. As Gary stood and zeroed in on Lazlo's forehead. She dropped to the linoleum. Her Glock 19 sprayed bullets under the table, across his kneecaps and lower legs.

****

The aftermath.

Jill Treece went through a tough couple of weeks, winding her way out of the fog caused by the taser to her head. But she was doing much better and was expected to recover 100%. Her recovery was made easier when Dr. Kline took a leave of absence to care for this woman he'd fallen in love with.

After Azir put Gary down -- saving Lazlo's life – he'd told Gary, "Tell me where Jill and the other women are. You've got exactly ten seconds."

Gary groaned in pain but said nothing. Lazlo didn't care; he took a page from Dirty Harry. He stood on one of Gary's mangled kneecaps until he answered. That took all of five seconds.

Jill wasn't in great shape but was alive in his bedroom.

Lazlo got the key to Gary's freezer, opened it, and saw the bodies stacked on one another. No murder scene had ever impacted him more.

The story was on the front page of the *Atlanta Journal and Constitution*, on every local news channel, and on the big cable networks. Popov got anointed the "Freezer Killer," which probably made him happy until he'd likely be executed. Georgia continued to do them.

Lazlo did his best to give the credit for saving his and Jill Treece's life to Azir Mella. In one national interview, he mentioned her driving skills in getting to Popov's place so quickly. Within an hour, she'd already gotten calls from the heads of two heavy-hitter NASCAR driving teams – who were impressed and recognized her last name.

Lazlo Kianian hated to lose her, but maybe she'd get to follow her dream. And that was okay by him.

****

Then came the call he dreaded. Not from the press.

"How's it going, hotshot?"

Suzanne's tone wasn't friendly.

"Thought she wasn't going to be the bait, Laz. But that's what she was, wasn't it, asshole?"

He replied, "Yes," but dared not offer any excuses. He knew deep down he'd gotten lucky catching Gary Popov and not getting anyone else killed.

"Laz, if Jill had gotten killed, I'd cut your nuts off myself."

He didn't doubt that. Holding his phone, he nodded silently.

"Gotta go to Spain."

She hung up before he could tell her to be safe.

PART IV

Chapter 33 – Spain

Starting this chapter, the author thought it might be helpful to review the story of golden frog poison for the reader. Here we go:

-In the prequel, *Game of Twins – The Special Agent*, a key character is murdered with the poison several decades prior.

-In the previous *Game of Twins* book, *Game of Twins- Kidnapped*, bad girl Pamela Loncart tries to murder Suzanne Delacroix with the poison, but it backfires. Suzanne scratches her with the ampoule, not knowing what's in it. Only with Pamela's dying breaths, Suzanne discovers it was golden frog poison.

In this book, *Golden Frog Poison*:

-The Golden Frog figurine is designed by a Sinaloa goldsmith per the request of Raoul Menendez, the most powerful narco in Mexico and the South American continent. Menendez commissions several solid gold frog figurines and purchases a significant amount of the deadly Golden Frog poison. He'd not known poison could be a hundred times more expensive than gold, but it mattered not.

-Menendez tasks one of his sicarios to deliver the golden frog, now covered with golden frog poison, to the address of Kip Davies and Suzanne Delacroix in Atlanta. The sicario/courier uses a pen to pop Kip Davies on his wrist with the deadly poison.

-Suzanne arrives home from playing golf only to find her husband dead on the foyer floor with a small golden frog near his body; she immediately knows who had him killed, how, and why.

-She suspects the little figurine is covered with Golden Frog poison. With gloves, she places it in a small jewelry box and buries the box in a sugar container in her kitchen.

-After the death of her husband, the autopsy is inconclusive, indicating a natural cause of death – likely cardiac, but two weeks later, Suzanne confides in Fulton County Medical Examiner Jill

Treece, a family friend – that she found the golden frog figurine next to Kip.

-Jill contacts a pathologist in Florida who is an expert in animal poisons. She takes a pathology sample from Kip Davies and the figurine to Gainesville. Noah Kline, the pathologist, confirms that golden frog poison killed Kip Davies, and the little figurine has the deadly poison on it.

-Jill returns the figurine to Atlanta and puts it in her double-locked desk drawer.

-Serial killer Gary Popov, Treece's top CSI, had suspected there was something fishy about how Kip Davies got killed; while Jill is on vacation, he breaks into her desk drawer at work. He reads the note written by Dr. Kline and takes the golden frog figurine. And becomes incensed.

-He takes it home and puts the cellophane-wrapped figurine in the middle of his kitchen table as he thinks about his next kidnapping victim.

-Raoul Menendez is just getting warmed up trying to kill others who are close to Suzanne. He hires a Columbian girl known to be Columbia's best jungle hunting guide. She kills game with a blowgun. She's paid $100k to fly to Durham, N.C., to kill Suzanne's nephew, David. A one million dollar bonus is promised when the deed is done.

-Intentionally, she misses from 70 yards away with two golden frog poison darts. She confesses to David why she is there. They hit it off, but Menendez has a sicario following her. She and David go out for a fancy dinner in Durham. Menendez's guy kills her in the restaurant's ladies' room – with a pen, its tip covered with Golden Frog poison. She dies.

-Suzanne gets on a private plane after David tells her what happened earlier with the poison that kills Patricia Dias, who he'd already fallen in love with.

-Suzanne shows up at the murder scene and meets a top Durham detective. But it's a couple of days later before she admits to him that she knows golden frog poison killed the girl. She explains the situation. He understands and tells her he won't investigate the death as a murder.

-Serial killer, Gary Popov continues his Atlanta killing spree. Jill Treece agrees to be bait for Lazlo Kianian to catch Gary. But she is kidnapped. Lazlo figures out where Gary is – at home, despite the GPS tracking on his car. Gary has forgotten the poison golden frog figurine is on his kitchen table. Lazlo is about to be shot but is saved by a young cop.

Back to the story…and you haven't yet heard the last of golden frog poison.

****

Raoul Menendez was excited to return to the beautiful city he wished he could visit more often. Madrid was the third largest city in Europe behind London and Berlin, but it seemed almost quaint compared to Mexico City and its 20 million people.

Nearly three decades ago, he'd fought bulls in Mexico's largest arena, Plaza del Toros, in Madrid. After his father demanded he retire from bullfighting at the ripe old age of twenty, he purchased a large estate in Madrid. He encouraged Raoul to enjoy bullfighting as a spectator whenever he wanted to.

Raoul let nostalgia transport him back to his last corrida (AKA bullfight) in Mexico City. The packed crowd of 40,000 cheered and clapped loudly as he appeared in the bullring. He bowed in four directions, then waved to the throngs his montera, his chartreuse velvet hat decorated with gold embroidery and tassel.

Being of money, his traje de luces, his costume, was heads above other young bullfighters that day. Bright white with embroidery spun of real gold and hundreds of ruby red sequins; fringes decorated with silver tassels. It made him feel invincible – like Superman.

He'd been told that the bull he'd fight weighed more than a ton: an all-white Spanish Fighting Bull – bred solely to be nasty. He and his comrades watched the massive animal with horns the size of which he'd never seen, in the next-door pen. His immense ivory-colored horns jerked up and down and side to side. He was bred to be a warrior.

Trumpets sounded as the first part of the bullfight began. He watched as skilled picadors tried several times to close in on the bull with their lances. The bull was not only fast but also quick and ornery, head and horns down, diving at one and then the other. Finally, one of the picadors got close enough to lance the bull's neck. He pawed the sand with his hooves, snorted angrily, and went after one galloping picador who barely escaped into the bullpen area. The second picador rode a few circles around the bull and made a move to harpoon the bull's neck in a series of quick jabs. As the bull swung around, he grazed the picador and knocked him off his horse. As he got up, the bull charged. He dodged and rolled on the sand as the other picador and two other riders distracted the animal. A near miss.

The trumpets blared again to usher in the next phase, hopefully weakening the big bull more.

****

Next, two more riders, banderilleros, went after the bull on horseback to soften him up. The white bull was going crazy, snorting, and kicking. They stabbed the bull's neck with lances and sharp decorative banderilla sticks, leaving a dozen impaled in the pissed-off animal. Raoul noticed that the lance and stick pokes were causing the bull to lower his head, but the bull looked revved up and ready to rumble.

Trumpets again announced the third stanza of the bullfight.

Raoul appeared on foot with his red cape backed by a stick, the muleta, enticing the monster white bull to attack. Back and forth and side to side, backward and forward, he teased the bull that had yet to lose much of his gusto. He sashayed with the muleta gracefully, yet athletically, trying to tire him more. The long horns were frightening, but he focused on the bull's red eyes, where he saw some panic. He firmly controlled the 2400-pound monster who followed the cape as Raoul teased it and let the bull pass him several times with only inches to spare.

He was getting closer to the final act of this deadly game, the Tercio de Muerte. He skillfully extracted his sword from behind his cape as he enraged the tiring bull. He moved closer until he had a good angle. Then the estocada. He drove his long, straight sword between the bull's shoulder blades and into his heart. The blow was fatal. The bull collapsed on the sand. The final trust was ten times better than any orgasm that Raoul had ever experienced. Thousands of people cheered; it was deafening. Proudly, he strode around the arena, often bowing. He spied a young boy in the first row and handed him his hat. The crowd went nuts.

He'd read Hemingway's *The Sun Also Rises* at least a dozen times. Like Hemingway, Raoul understood the thrill of the bullfight as the ultimate male act – but unlike the famous novelist – he understood it as a matador.

****

Raoul thought his last bull was his most admirable foe. After he'd impaled it with his sword, he solemnly watched the dead animal dragged through the sand and out of view. He asked a Mexico City specialty butcher to slice up the animal and put the prime pieces on ice. His dad agreed to get them to Sinaloa tomorrow. Raoul thought it only appropriate for him, his family, and others in his town to eat this rarest beef delicacy from a brave bull killed in the ring.

He knew the humongous bull was playing in a rigged game and had no chance against a top matador like him. If any matador failed after three attempts to bring a bull down, he'd be slaughtered anyway; that said, he'd once seen another matador mauled and killed by a bull. They were dangerous as hell and should never be underestimated. But walking around a killer bull, keeping the bull's focus on his movements and not him -- inches from certain death in a bullring was unlike any rush he'd ever experienced.

He was saddened knowing he conquered his last bull. After that, his father sent his son to America to soak up as much learning as possible. He knew that knowledge would serve him better than bullfighting when he joined the family business, the largest illegal drug operation in Mexico. He intended to make it the biggest on the planet.

****

He loved Madrid when the historic city came alive with vibrant sounds, vivid colors, succulent aromas, and tastes – especially during the annual bullfights during the mid-May San Isidro festival at the Plaza de Toros de Madrid, AKA Las Ventas. Madrid had its faults but wasn't the mega discombobulated, foul, dirty, crime-ridden mess like Mexico City.

After a good night's sleep, a leisurely breakfast, and a swim in his pool, his anticipation grew on the short ride to Las Ventas -- accompanied by two of his sicarios, to watch the bullfights at the beautiful arena. They arrived at 4:45 PM, about an hour before the bullfights started. He had season seats in the barrera sombra section, only three rows from the sandy "ruedo" surface where the nitty gritty bullfighting would happen – in a circular sixty-meter diameter field, compared to a rectangular field of 100 by 40 yards – as in American football, which he loved more than traditional football that Americans called soccer.

Per information from Mary Jo Cogburn, Delacroix was to land in Madrid shortly, but he would not let her arrival sour his afternoon at the bullfights. He'd sent one of his half dozen sicarios to confirm that she'd landed, picked up her luggage, and arrived at her hotel.

******

The matador in the first bullfight was outstanding: graceful, stylish, athletic, and patient – egging on the bull to charge his seductive crimson cape (though all bulls are colorblind), smoothly, sashaying from side to side and back and forth, the movement of the bull, not its color, beckoning him. Then forward, only inches away. Seeing the sword drive into the bull's vertebrae between his shoulder blades almost made him hard. There was something violent and intensely sexual about the hunt and the sword kill. God, he missed it and missed driving into his beloved Pamela, whom Suzanne Delacroix killed.

Two corridas later, he got the text and smiled. Delacroix might have a chance at him, but not a good one. He would avenge the death of the love of his life. Delacroix would be dead within the week.

****

Suzanne flew nonstop from Atlanta to Madrid on Delta. A nine-hour flight. She practiced her rusty Spanish by quietly whispering her words as directed by a Spanish app – thankful that she was in an empty row. She watched *Top Gun Maverick*, then dozed off.

Suzanne didn't know how much Raoul might know about her location in Madrid but assumed the worst: that Mary Jo had told him where she was staying and when. Mary Jo was pulling all the strings; Suzanne had little doubt about that. Did she also tell him about the weapons she promised to provide?

As described on the websites she'd visited, getting around Madrid by car could be painful. Walking, riding a train, or grabbing a cab or Uber could get her around, but assuming Mary Jo came through with the items she promised, a rental car would be the best place to put them. And it would be much more convenient when visiting Raoul's place – and needing a getaway vehicle. She rented a Herz Audi under a bogus identity.

She'd economically packed a few sets of clothes in one bag. She could always buy more if needed. And she had her small computer bag. Neither contained anything that an airport scanner could detect. The tiny gizmos, one under her right index nail and the other attached to the back of her left ear lobe got through fine.

****

Getting to her hotel in the middle of Madrid at 6:30 PM wasn't the nightmare she'd anticipated. The professionally dressed, clean-shaven valet greeted her with a smile, "Hola, Senorita."

He pointed to her trunk to get her luggage, but she begged off with gracias and politeness, not right now.

She'd exchanged three thousand dollars for various denominations of euros before leaving, and she could always get more on her VISA card. She was too tired to attempt her basic Spanish and asked the valet if he understood English. He told her he did. She told him to return the car to the same spot in front of the hotel in fifteen minutes. 20 euros now and 40 more in fifteen minutes.

"Gracias, Yes, Senorita." He thought it strange that she didn't want her luggage taken to her room.

With a slight Spanish accent, the pretty front desk agent said, "Ah, Miss Delacroix, Hola, yes, we already have you checked in to one of our suites on the top floor. Your stay is prepaid, and you have five hundred euros in credit on your account. You have no luggage?"

"I'll have it brought up later, thank you."

"Very well, here are two room keys. Elevators are to your right. Let me know if you need anything."

"I will. Gracias."

She walked toward the elevators, then turned and scanned the lobby. Two middle-aged women were chatting on an oversized couch. One man was reading his newspaper, but she couldn't see his face. Nothing suspicious caught her eye.

On her way up to the eighth floor, she wondered how Mary Jo could get her bag of goodies to the room. But decided not to worry about it. She reminded herself that if the bag wasn't there, she'd drive back to the airport to catch the next flight to Atlanta.

The room was ritzy -- decorated in lush mauve, red, bronze, gold, and yellow colors, and designer furniture. In the bedroom were two king beds. Two giant planters held tall plants she didn't know. The view of downtown Madrid was spectacular, but she was only interested in what was on one of the king beds. The large, rectangular brown canvas duffel bag was about 4 feet long by 2 ½ feet by 2 feet.

She smiled but knew she needed to check for something else: She hadn't tried it yet, but all she had to do was put her "magic glasses" on and tap her fingernail 3 times. A holographic screen appeared. The surveillance dot mapped the presence of hidden cameras, microphones, and GPS trackers via the radio frequencies emitted by transmitters used in the devices.

Sure enough, slowly trolling her hotel room, she found one in less than thirty seconds. A mini cam recessed in the top of the wooden door frame, then another perched on the top of a tall lamp pointed at the main living area. There had to be one in the bedroom. Yep, at the edge of a big mirror, pointing at the bed where the duffel bag sat. Then another. A GPS tracker was somewhere in the duffel bag. She wanted to pull out all the weapons and examine them but could do that later.

On top of the bag was a short calligraphic note that simply said, "Enjoy Madrid, Suzanne." The bag didn't have locks. Instead, across the top zipper were several swirls of what appeared to be wax. Suzanne smiled. It was secured old style, like few still did with letters and packages, to deter those who might be curious.

She broke the wax seal, located a GPS tracker inside the duffel bag lining, and cut it out with the knife in the bag. She found two locks and keys and secured the duffel bag. She'd leave the other bugs, but this one had to go. On her way out with the duffel bag, she dropped it in the sink garbage disposal and turned it on.

GOLDEN FROG POISON A GAME OF TWINS THRILLER

The question was, who was watching? Minimally, Mary Jo and Michael; Raoul and others?

****

Via Michael Abbott's tech guy, Mary Jo could see Suzanne in the lavish hotel room via the three cams. She saw her break the seal, open the bag, and cut out the GPS tracker. When the tracker went offline in the hotel room, no doubt she killed it. More than 4000 miles away in Washington, D.C., Georgia Congresswoman Mary Jo Cogburn knew that she left her room with the duffel bag. She couldn't be happier. The *Game* was growing on her. This was too much fun!

****

Suzanne hoped a little cat-and-mouse would aggravate Raoul.

She carried the duffle bag downstairs without glancing at the registration desk. The man with the newspaper was gone. She walked out to the circular drive. The parking attendant was there standing by her rental. He grabbed for the duffel bag in her hand. "Here, Senorita, let me take that for you."

"Thanks, I got it. The car key, please."

He handed her the key. She handed him two 40 Euro banknotes. She popped the trunk and put her duffel bag in with her other piece of luggage and computer bag.

"Gracias again."

He looked confused but also happy to get a good tip.

Before leaving, she put on her magic glasses -- for her virtual screen to guide her to her next destination in Madrid. With a voice that was no doubt more accurate than Siri. Regardless of what she found in her hotel room, she'd decided before leaving Atlanta that once she had the weapons in hand she would move to another hotel, swanky but smaller and only a mile from Las Ventas.

She registered under the name Mia Zuang, her mother's maiden name and her Homeland friend's first name. Her credentials were impeccable: an Amex Card, VISA card, U.S. Driver's license, and U.S. passport. Arnie had a lot of contacts. No doubt, some from the Dark Web, a world she didn't know and didn't want to know.

She asked the front desk clerk if any packages had arrived for her. She grinned when the matronly woman handed her a shoe-box-sized package.

"Gracias."

She tipped the valet 20 Euros to transport her one clothing bag and duffel bag from registration to her top floor room. She handled the package and computer bag. Upon entry, she kicked her off her heels. Another fantastic view, this one overlooking a vast plaza. She could take a stroll tomorrow morning and buy a couple of outfits. After all, a girl needed to look her best when stalking a top narco.

She was most excited about the package that Arnie had sent her. She used the large knife in the duffel bag to open the package. The two tasers were each in a package of several plastic pieces, including batteries, chargers, and instructions to pop them together. Nice. She'd put the two 3D-printer-created tasers together later. Also, there was a pricey-looking gold pen in a plastic covering, a small dart gun, and three golden frog poison-tipped darts. The instructions said that the dart gun, which looked like a toy gun, could shoot accurately up to twenty feet; the darts could shoot through light clothing. Handle with care.

Cool, she thought. Arnie was amazing. He'd provided more than she'd requested.

The other "toys" were carefully wrapped in foam inside the duffel bag to eliminate any jangling sound. She pulled them out individually: She'd winnowed down Sam's list, but the bag included enough weapons to make her dangerous.

-Automatic pistol and a dozen clips – Sig Sauer P365 with a silencer

-A long combat knife SOG Seal Pup Elite

-A utility belt

-A small, high-powered flashlight

-A Faxon Firearms FX5500 Ultralight: A compact A.R. style long gun with a dozen high-capacity clips

-A half dozen Flashbang grenades

-A light Kevlar vest that would protect against most handgun rounds or shotgun pellets

-A half dozen zip ties

She was impressed. Everything was as ordered. Whether she'd use any or all the weapons in Madrid -- worst case, she had them if needed for offense or defense.

She put her armaments back into the duffel bag and collapsed on the bed. She fell fast asleep with her clothes on.

The dream was disturbing. She was in the first hotel room with nothing on; the guns and equipment were in full view on the bed. There was a banging on her door. And someone yelling, *"Room service."* She didn't bother getting dressed. At the door stood Raoul Menendez. He said, *"They're coming to get us both. He shut the door and slid a clip into his Glock.*

Another knock on the door. "Suzanne, it's me and Michael. We just want to talk."

Menendez shook his head as she began to answer. Gunfire blew the door lock away. They stepped in.

She thought, what will become of my twins when I'm dead?

Sweat dripped off her brow and between her breasts. She dropped her clothes on the floor and climbed into the hot shower.

Mary Jo had booked her original room and provided the weapons she'd asked for – but also planted bugs to surveil her. Were Mary Jo and Michael playing both sides of the street? Duh! It was a deadly game again – that she was in the middle of. One spawned by the original *Game of Twins*. And like that game, one where the rules continued to morph.

Chapter 34 – Las Ventas

Day 2 in Madrid

Each of his six hand-picked sicarios from Sinaloa had multiple photos of Suzanne Delacroix on their phones. Her pictures were easy to find on the Internet, and they were impressed by the exotic milf. Rumor was they'd all get at least one turn with her before the Patron killed her on the recently placed slab of black granite on the lowest level of the hacienda. Raoul's sicario Joaquin had confirmed that Delacroix arrived at the hotel at 6:30 PM the previous day. Raoul got the text and texted back to return to his hacienda. "We'll deal with her tomorrow. Gotta go. The second corrida is starting."

The previous evening, he'd ordered two of his sicarios to be at her hotel at 7:30 AM the next day. They were to monitor her movements in and out of the hotel – but not engage in any way. Engaging Delacroix was his department.

Alvaro was stationed in the lobby, and Pablo was outdoors with a good view of the main entrance. But nearly four hours later, neither had seen her. Alvaro, who spoke the best English and was blonde, walked up to the best-looking front desk clerk and turned on his charm. He glanced at her nameplate and said, "Sophia, I love that name. Could you please help me? I have a business colleague staying here, but I can't reach her by cell phone. Could you please ring her room for me? Her name is Suzanne Delacroix. My name is Fredo Lonco.

Though it wasn't strictly kosher to indicate if a person was staying at the hotel, she had difficulty ignoring his smile and handsome body. She called. After several rings, Sophia said, "I'm sorry, Senor, there is no answer."

"Sophia, I'm worried about Senorita Delacroix. How about you or one of your valets accompany me to her room? I just want to see if she's okay. I will pay you and your bellboy 60 euros each for your trouble."

She hesitated but nodded okay and summoned one of the bellhops. She told him to let Mr. Lonco into room 801 while accompanying him. It was a strange request, but the valet nodded. Mr. Lonco put 120 Euros in 20 denominations on the front, and they walked to the elevator.

It was one of the two penthouse suites that overlooked downtown Madrid that had been reserved for Suzanne Delacroix. Alvaro strolled through each of the rooms. He looked in the closets and dresser drawers. The bathroom was pristine. Nothing. No luggage or clothing. It looked like no one had slept in the bed. After ten minutes, he'd seen enough. He thanked the valet and joined his colleague Pablo outside.

"Anything?"

"The parking attendant said he remembered her. A tall, beautiful dark-haired woman. Hard to forget. She left her car – sounds like a rental – with him for only about twenty minutes. She told him she was leaving her luggage in the trunk for now. When she returned, she was carrying a duffel bag; she insisted on putting it in the back seat herself. He thought it strange, but she tipped him an additional 40 Euros. And she left."

"Is there a camera or cameras that would catch the type of car and license?" Alvaro asked his colleague.

"Yes, there're two." He pointed to them above the front entrance. "Security monitors those and others on all floors of the hotel. I'm way ahead of you. Already asked security for footage from 6:30 to 7:30 PM yesterday. The Security guy initially refused, but I slid him 100 Euros and said he'd get another 100 Euros when he showed me that piece of the tape, which clearly showed Delacroix as the valet described. License plate number 2640ZJY."

"Good work, "Alvaro told him.

They walked out to the cobblestone sidewalk in front of the hotel fountain and called Menendez at his hacienda. The Patron said, "I doubt the car information will be helpful, but at least we've got it. Hell, she could easily switch rentals or not even use one. So, she left with her luggage and a duffel bag she got from her room?"

"Si, Patron"

"I can only guess what was in the bag. I'll find out, though. No doubt she's staying somewhere else in the city, but there are hundreds of hotels, inns, B&Bs, and Airbnb rentals." His voice trailed off. "Okay, come back to the hacienda and drive around the area – maybe we'll get lucky and see her car."

"Si, Patron."

Menendez hung up and thought to himself. There was no choice other than to spot her in person one way or another. He doubted she'd try some ridiculous disguise. He emailed an encrypted meeting request to Mary Jo Cogburn.

Three minutes later, she responded, "Raoul, darling, how are the gory bullfights? You having fun?"

He didn't answer but instead said, "You wouldn't know, by chance, where Suzanne Delacroix is, would you?"

Mary Jo tried not to giggle. "Raoul, you mean you already lost the beautiful statuesque Blasian? I even gave you her arrival time and hotel."

He almost replied, "Fuck you, bitch" but held off. "She's not staying at the hotel you indicated."

She wondered if he'd continue that lie.

"She did check in but has neither stayed in the room nor checked out. She only picked up a duffel bag. We're trying to…"

Mary Jo interrupted, " She's in the wind, Raoul. She's good. Exceptional. She knows where you live and that you love bullfighting."

Sarcastically, she added, "But I'm sure you have your top sicarios in Madrid to help you find one woman."

Menendez snarled, "The duffel bag. What was in it?"

"Just a few toys she requested to help level the playing field a bit."

"You're enjoying the *Game*, aren't you, Mary Jo?" he chided.

"I've always enjoyed *Game of Twins*," she mocked back.

"How does she even know what I look like?"

"I described you as incredibly handsome, over six feet, with jet-black hair, strong build, and a stud by any measure, in your late-40s."

"You also provided photos, didn't you, Mary Jo?"

"Gotta go, Raoul, good luck."

That was a yes. Suzanne knew what he looked like. That was fine. She would soon see a lot more of him up close and personal.

****

Suzanne didn't set her alarm and was shocked it was 9:00 AM local time. She'd eaten no dinner last night after her nap and was ravenous. She threw open the curtains. It was going to be a beautiful day in Madrid. Blue skies with a few puffy clouds. After a luxurious shower, she dressed and checked to see if the duffel bag was locked. She put it in the closet and headed to the hotel's main floor. She asked the front desk clerk if she could recommend a good breakfast place.

"Ah, no reason to go far for that, Senorita Delacroix. There's none better in Madrid than ours. And you can dine outdoors."

"Perfecta."

She was directed toward the entrance to the outdoor café where a distinguished white-haired maître 'd asked how many would be dining.

"Only me."

Lots of well-heeled folks in the cafe, smiling, chatting, and eating. Pleasant guitar music from a nearby café wafted in. People walking by were obviously enjoying themselves. There was only one table available where he seated her. "Coffee or tea or something else?"

She smiled and put on her sunglasses. "Gracias, maybe water and an espresso."

"Right away."

Her hotel in the historic district of Madrid was about a mile from the bullfights—with good train access. She'd need to figure out how she'd get reasonably close to Las Ventas in her rental car.

The waiter was back promptly with her drinks and a menu.

"What do you recommend, Mateo?"

"How hungry are you Senorita?"

"Starved. I didn't get a chance to eat dinner last night."

"Okay, why don't I order one of my favorites that combines the best of our items, and take it from there? Do you eat meat and dairy?"

She gave a thumbs up.

The people watching was awesome; a faint voice in her head said, *"Could someone be watching you?* The food arrived.

"OMG," she exclaimed after taking one bite of her golden-brown Tortilla Española, an omelet like none other with thinly sliced Iberian Ham (Jamón Ibérico).

The waiter left her to enjoy every bite which she did.

She was notoriously a fast eater but tried to pace herself.

When her plate was clean, the waiter approached and said, "Ah, I see you didn't like it." Then smiled mischievously.

"Terrible," she announced. Then laughed. It was excelente!"

"Okay, I will bring you another favorite of mine."

She started to protest but nodded okay.

Mateo reappeared in a few minutes with a cup of hot chocolate and three churros, deep-fried dough pastries crispy on the outside and soft on the inside.

"They taste best when you dip them in the hot chocolate."

After dipping it, he watched while she took a bite of the first churro. He wished he saw that kind of pleasure on his wife's face when he was inside of her. And fantasized about something else.

****

After breakfast, Suzanne walked onto the plaza adjacent to her hotel and searched for a spot where she could do some solitary thinking. The burgeoning San Isidro festival crowd strolled and chattered in the plaza. Still, it was a peaceful place to think – as she always found in her busy local Starbucks in Atlanta. She sat on an empty bench in the middle of Madrid.

She'd seen Arnie's encrypted email to her late Madrid time but had yet to open it. With some trepidation, she did. Via two satellite firms who owed Arnie favors, she saw heat images from Raoul Menendez's estate on the eastern outskirts of Madrid. Clocked at 10:00 AM Madrid time. She counted seven figures, two stationary and the others walking around. Only a few images, but it didn't look like a small army was camped there; she saw that as good news.

But, she had to have a come-to-Jesus meeting with herself on the park bench. She wasn't a freak'n superspy like those played by Jennifer Garner, Matt Damon, Tom Cruise, Keanu Reeves, or others. So, how in the world did she think she could get to Raoul Menendez in or around his place? Even with the weapons she'd been provided. Without getting killed herself. Then maybe worse, getting people important to her killed after they got her.

She conjured up limited scenarios to kill Menendez. When he was coming in or out of his well-fortified hacienda. The problem with that was he'd likely be in a bulletproof vehicle. With at least one bodyguard inside and maybe others outside, too. She could shoot but wasn't an expert sniper. The other two options were attacking Menendez before he entered Las Ventas to watch one of his bullfights – or as he left. Also, fraught choices, but, barring an epiphany, she had no others.

Instead of touring Menendez's posh Madrid neighborhood in her rental, she decided to do her reconnaissance on Las Ventas -- and put all her eggs in one basket.

There was a train station a block from her hotel. The trip to Las Ventas took less than three minutes. Today, she'd walk. She'd looked at dozens of photos and YouTube videos of Spain's most famous bullfighting arena. In person, it was a majestic, century-old, large red brick building, in what she read was the Mozarabic, Moorish, and Spanish style, with intricate, distinctive, tall horseshoe arches, and windows, inlaid ceramic art, plaques of famous matadors. All perfectly placed. She'd never seen anything like it.

The crowd assembled four hours before the first bullfight, which started late afternoon. Suzanne found bullfighting repulsive and barbaric. She remembered her first reaction to the spectacle described vividly by Hemingway in *The Sun Also Rises* as the ultimate, over-testosteroned, macho crap and certainly not a fair fight. It was no surprise that Raoul Menendez had been a matador in his younger years. Too bad a bull hadn't gored him to death back then.

She was concentrating on the Las Ventas bullfighting arena and had done much of her homework online. She was 99% sure that Menendez would attend the bullfights that week and 90% sure that his primo seats would be in one of the barrera sombra sections with the best seats in the late afternoon shade and were nearest the bloody bullfight action. She bought three seats in different rows on the opposite, sunny side of the arena for the next two days to get a good sight angle of narco murderer Raoul Menendez -- to pick him out in the crowd.

She brightened at the realization that she still had the significant advantage of surprise. Raoul knew that she was somewhere in Madrid and wanted to kill him. But he didn't know how she would attack – or the weapons she'd use. He didn't know where she'd attack him from. And he didn't know when she'd attack. Really, he didn't know jack.

****

They connected by encrypted video at least once a week – but more often lately, with the situation they'd orchestrated in Madrid heating up – to discuss the next scenarios.

For years, they'd both traded valuable information with one another. Michael Abbott often got a "heads-up" premonition about significant market events or specific companies. It didn't happen daily or even monthly, but when it did and when he concentrated on the big-hitter stocks, his results beat other Wall Street investors by a ton. His "sight" had made him hundreds of millions of dollars since college. The last several years, coupled with Mary Jo's political connections, the millions kept hockey-sticking. Mostly for him, but also for Mary Jo and the Atlanta Coven that she presided over – and for Raoul and his Pacific drug cartel.

The cartel provided the early, critical seed money for their worldwide venture, but the cartel had become a multi-million per year cash cow that had outlived its usefulness. Mary Jo and Michael, who had successfully nixed Pamela from the mix with Suzanne's help, now agreed it was time for Menendez himself to go.

It was Mary Jo's idea. What better way to do that than to put two archenemies in the same Madrid arena? *Game of Twins* in Spain. Much better and more fun than a Las Ventas bullfight!

The two narcissist voyeurs wanted to see who would survive and who would die this next round, but anyone standing would be put down, regardless. Like a bull that survived a skilled matador, the magnificent animal would be slaughtered as soon as he left the ring.

Then they would move on to something that would become so much bigger and more important.

Their contact tonight was different. Much different.

It was a special evening in her Buckhead penthouse, where she'd hosted Suzanne Delacroix a few weeks ago. Michael flew into Hartsfield on his Challenger 500, one of his dozen private jets.

They'd not met in person since they were teenage lovers. Jeremy Sutterland, now Michael Abbott, was part of the Sutterland witch progeny, and she was the girl with exceptional occult skills adopted into his secretive Atlanta family. After his limo ride from Hartsfield, Michael was ushered in and given private elevator access to the penthouse.

Mary Jo was dolled up in a two-thousand-dollar skintight short black dress with a plunging neckline. The two childhood friends and lovers stood face-to-face, in the flesh, for the first time in nearly three decades. Michael was a handsome 48-year-old: rangy, fit, six feet tall – with a full head of short brown hair perfectly coiffed, pleasant versus sharp facial angles like his twin brother had, and a friendly smile. Dressed in a limestone linen silk jacket, complementary slacks, a Brioni shirt, and Santoni loafers.

Their eyes locked.

"You dress up hot for a financial guy," Mary Jo said. They kissed and began shedding their pricey garb.

She took his hand and led him to the panoramic window overlooking Atlanta. She braced herself against the window. From behind, Michael took care of the rest. Their pent-up desire exploded high over Atlanta.

TOM RANSEEN

****

Now dressed in silk bathrobes, felt they were on the cusp of moving ahead with their plan. They noshed a smorgasbord of southern-style foods and sipped wine. After eating and drinking more champagne, they sat next to one another on the tiger skin sofa, the tiger head propped against the far end.

"This is the real thing?"

She smiled as if he needed to ask.

Michael asked, "Mary Jo, do you really think Delacroix has a chance to kill Menendez?"

She kidded, "You mean that you can't predict it?"

"Only finances, my dear, you know that."

She smiled, paused, and said, "Not likely, with all the advantages he has. We've told him when she gets to Madrid and where she's staying. We provided the weapons she asked for, but I don't think they'll make any difference – and, in fact, might get her killed sooner than later. When Raoul kills her, *The Three* must celebrate!"

Cuddling on the tiger skin, she told Michael a soccer mom story.

"Hell, I only made it to a few games a year. My husband oversaw all that. He didn't coach but helped. Last year of middle school, my older girl played on a mediocre team that wasn't rated high enough to be seeded. In the first round, in the year-end tournament, they had to play a team that was predicted to win it all in our district, and maybe even the state and go to the Nationals."

She paused, "Then, out of the blue, using none of my own occult powers, my daughter got that killer look. You remember that from when we were young?"

"I do. And I'm still surprised you didn't kill Thad. You're point being?"

"My daughter kicked the winning goal that year in the Georgia state championship game. They didn't win the Nationals. But never underestimate the underdog with that killer look. Especially one like Suzanne Delacroix, who continues to amaze."

"If she's that good, maybe we can recruit her instead of kill her?"

"Not in a million years. She doesn't roll that way."

They both slunk back into the tiger skin. Michael asked, "So, who are we helping or hurting more at this point?"

"I'll guess we'll have to see, my love. But does it make a difference in the end? I just love the *Game* we're playing with them. Now, fuck me again."

Chapter 35 - The Bullfights

Day 3 in Madrid

Suzanne had made all the preparations she could. The first bullfight started at 6:00 PM. It was a warm, sunny afternoon when it all got started.

She needed to see Menendez in the arena before she executed her plan. His seat location was an educated guess at best. Then she needed to know how many sicarios were acting as bodyguards in and out of Las Ventas—who might be on the prowl for her.

Immediately, she understood why her seats on the sunny side of the arena were less expensive. It was freak'n hot, even wearing a stylish hat. She had one task in mind, but the pageantry of the arena was hard to ignore: the brilliant colors worn by the men on foot and horses, the choreography of their movements, the fanfare of Spanish music, the roars and cheers of the raucous 23,000 fans, and the authoritative yet friendly announcement of each bullfight. What struck her most, though, was how quiet the arena got as the matador went for the kill. She looked away. The crowd exploded in applause.

Using her binocular sunglasses, she spent an hour trying to locate Menendez across the arena in the shaded section during the first two bullfights. She hoped she'd not messed up and made a poor assumption about where he'd be seated. Before the third bullfight began, she switched seats to a lower row in the same section. And tried to stay positive.

It wasn't until the end of the third bullfight that he stood up after the latest kill. She saw the face she'd never forget from the photo Mary Jo had sent her. The face of the man who had her Kip murdered with golden frog poison.

It looked like he had only one sicario seated next to him. She knew there would be others outside the arena to provide more security when he left. She hoped it would only be one or two plus a driver. She'd seen enough inside the arena. Now, her focus was on the outside of Las Ventas. Plenty of light in Madrid in mid-May until 9:00 PM. It was still quite warm. She took a few swigs of water on the way out but resisted taking her hat off and pouring the bottle over her head.

Her rental car was parked in an alley three blocks away. She hoped it would be there when she returned. Regardless, she needed to locate where Raoul's ride would be parked. No way he'd taken public transportation. No doubt an expensive sedan. No doubt, it was closer than her car to Las Ventas. Some of the crowd had started to filter out. She could hear the announcer say that the fourth corrido (bullfight) would begin in ten minutes.

She had her two plastic, yet robust, tasers, the toy-looking dart gun and poison darts, and the golden poison pen in her handbag that also held snacks, waters, her I.D., money, and a fake Madrid police I.D. She wished she also had the Glock in the trunk of her rental, but it would waste too much time to retrieve it now. She wished she had any ground support, but there was no time for a pity party.

****

Outside Las Ventas, she saw another sicario – dressed identically as the guy who was sitting next to Raoul: dark hair, shades, black silk shirt, black jeans, gold belt buckle, gold jewelry. This one, though, had a pistol tucked in the back of his jeans—which he probably couldn't have gotten through security.

She followed the outside sicario to an empty gate he was trolling. From behind him, she said, "Hey, could you tell me where Raoul is?"

He spun around. The shock told all. She told him, "Move forward as I say, or you're dead."

She pointed the way. "Let's go tinkle in the little boys' room."

Inside the restroom, she checked the stalls. No one. In thick Spanish, he spit out, "You're a fucking dead bitch."

"What did you say?"

She tased him in the face, then his balls. He screamed and dropped to the floor. She took his phone and dragged him into a stall. Then zip-tied his hands and feet and shut the stall.

One down.

She headed back toward the gate nearest Raoul's seats but didn't get far.

She felt a gun in the small of her back.

"Miss Delacroix, the Patron would like a word."

She turned her head a fraction. A blonde sicario. She'd not been paying enough attention. She went with her best weapon. Her body was honed by Krav Magda training over three decades. She dropped to the cobblestones and sliced his legs from under him. He fell, hit his head, and got up woozily.

"She asked, "Would you like to live or die?" He laughed, got up, and walked into a direct kick into his balls. He dropped again.

"I guess you want to die. She pressed the pen into his neck and quickly withdrew it. There was now a crowd gathering, watching the outdoor spectacle.

She held up her fake credentials and announced, "Sorry, Policia…a major drug dealer. As he lay on the brick, she frisked him for his wallet and phone. Then disappeared into the gathering crowd. The sicario's phone dinged in her hand.

"Leaving now, meet at the car." It was Menendez.

She raced back toward the outer part of the plaza surrounding Las Ventas. Directly perpendicular to his arena seats. She ran toward Menendez, who was twenty meters from his ride. Then she yelled, "Stop, or you're a dead Patron."

He stopped. She continued walking toward him, pointing her dart gun at his head. "Wanna guess what's in the little dart this little gun shoots, asshole?"

Raoul Menendez and Suzanne Delacroix faced each other for the first time. She saw genuine fear.

" Walk to your car and tell the driver to get out, or I'll kill you and him."

He nodded and told him. The sicario driver got. She tossed him two zip ties.

"Tie Menendez's hands and feet now, or you die."

He hesitated.

"Do it!" Menendez told him.

He complied. "Now, put him in the trunk and shut it."

The sicario looked at his Patron who nodded.

With Menendez in the trunk, she tased the driver's head, left him on the ground, and got in the driver's seat.

****

Chapter 36 - A Deal With the Devil

She located her car with her handy virtual map. It was only a couple of minutes away. In the cobblestone alley, she jerked Menendez out of her trunk. Zip-tied, he stumbled and fell; she stood over him.

"Is this the way you thought it would go down, Raoul? Dying in an alley in Madrid?"

The fear was there.

She raised her lethal plastic gun and ordered him, "Kneel on the ground and face me. Just you and me now. You know what this puny gun shoots, don't you?"

She backhanded him across his face as hard as possible. He toppled over and banged his head on the stones.

"Get back on your knees. Ready to die, Raoul?"

His fear was ten on the Richter Scale. He was sure she'd pull the golden frog poison trigger.

It kept reverberating around her brain: what Sam Rollins had asked her, "Are you seeking revenge or justice? Revenge can be righteous but also a slippery slope – and can cloud real intentions. Consider your main objective, Suzanne – is it to kill Menendez or keep him from killing you and yours?"

In his whole life, the only panic attacks Raoul Menendez had ever experienced were about being incarcerated. If it came to that, he'd kill himself.

"You're going to turn me in -- to the authorities?"

"Besides the U.S. and Mexico, Interpol has a hefty reward on your head, Menendez. Serious money for your hide would also mean serious justice for many."

The fear in his eyes intensified.

She took a deep breath. It almost made her sick to say it. "We're going to be partners."

His eyes flickered with astonishment. "Whatever money you want. Just give me an account number. It can be there in a couple of minutes."

"I don't want your stinking drug money. Sit down."

His butt found the cobblestone as she stood over him in the Madrid alley. Suzanne said, "I'm going to tell a story, the true story about who got your Pamela killed. Your Pamela kidnapped my twins from Atlanta and took them back to Sinaloa. You were salivating at the idea of torturing and raping them before killing them the sicko *Game of Twins* way."

He said nothing.

"I decided the only way to get them back was to kidnap Pamela's twin boys who were playing lacrosse in Nashville, Tennessee, anonymously, on two different teams. You knew where both boys were, didn't you? But didn't really care."

"Si."

"You've read the non-fiction novel by Bobby Price about me rescuing my twins in Utah but were curious about that part of the story?"

He nodded.

Then, shock and awe.

"Listen up, asshole. No possible way I could have gotten away with kidnapping her twins and driven them to Salt Lake City without a lot of help, which, frankly, I didn't fully understand until recently. On the sands of the Great Salt Lake, yes, I scratched your dear Pamela with a vial that fell from her hands after she pulled it from her sunglasses. I had no idea what it was. I was only trying to get my twins back safe and sound. That support I got was always curious to me. I never spoke of it in public. I got our twins back home safe and sound. That was enough for me and Kip."

She took a breath.

"That help was from Mary Jo Cogburn."

It sent a shiver down Raoul's spine. He'd known about Pamela's and Mary Jo's *Game of Twins* rivalry but shot back,

"How the fuck do you know that?"

"Well, not all *Game of Twins* escapades were included in Bobby Price's book, but I can also tell you the last words your Pamela said to me were. "Mary Jo."

"What?"

"Take a listen to this. A conversation I had with Congresswoman Mary Jo Cogburn in her Buckhead condo a couple weeks after you had my husband killed."

She pressed the button behind her ear and let him listen. He sat silent for a minute, nodding his head.

"What's their game, Cogburn and Abbott?"

Without hesitation, Menendez said, "They want to control everything, politically and financially, worldwide. Every. Fucking. Thing."

This time, Suzanne was taken aback.

"Do you think they could do it?"

"Not impossible."

"So, your mega-business becomes a dinky fish in a world where a trillion bucks is a rounding error, and you are, at best, a lowly third wheel."

"That's becoming clearer."

"Do you not get that you're already as expendable as I am? They've been jerking both our chains in Madrid -- and no doubt before. We're both targets. If I kill you, they could care less. If you kill me, they could care less. They'll send someone else. We're both targets in their *Game*. How do we and our families – and I know you have two sets of twins without a mom -- and our friends and colleagues survive and live to enjoy more days?"

She stopped briefly, then continued. "Step One is that we need a lifelong truce. Neither of us will ever go after each other, or family, or friends. And that includes any of your cartel boys coming after any of us."

The narco asked her, "Do you have a knife?"

"Pardon?"

"It's part of my Mexican culture and *Game of Twins*. Pamela and I did this three decades ago. A blood pact."

Suzanne Delacroix extracted the long knife from the duffel bag in the trunk.

"Cut the zip ties off my feet and my hands."

Why she did that, she was never sure. He stood.

"Give me the knife."

She did.

He slashed his left palm with the knife. His blood dripped to the cobblestones below.

She then offered the knife to her. She remembered the Clint Eastwood scene from *Outlaw Josey Wales*. She reciprocated, her blood staining the cobblestones.

He looked deep into her amber eyes. "We both need to seal this pledge of no harm to us and any of ours."

They pressed their bloody palms together.

He looked to the heavens and saw his long-deceased bruja smile.

Suzanne looked skyward as well and saw her dear Kip smiling.

******

That same evening at Raoul Menendez's palatial estate in Madrid, Suzanne asked him, "You got an idea about what should happen next? The narco grinned and said, "Si, Senorita, Suzanne."

After sending Mary Jo and Michael a few AI-doctored-up photos of Suzanne Delacroix naked and covered with blood on a slab of stone – part of prior *Game of Twins* gruesome murders, he sent them an encrypted message. *The Three* needed to celebrate getting rid of Delacroix. "I'd love to invite you to my place in Sinaloa but understand that the logistics aren't ideal and that it might not be advisable, especially with the mystery of Delacroix's disappearance. How about we party in our own locations? Maybe you two could meet somewhere. I will send you a bottle of the best Anejo tequila that has ever touched a human's tongue. We'll toast online and drink."

Mary Jo figured it was the least they could do. "Sounds good, Raoul. Send it to my place in Atlanta. Michael will be there, too."

Two days later, Abbot flew from New Jersey on his favorite private jet after Mary Jo messaged him that the tequila had arrived. Hell, if he could get laid again like the last time in Atlanta, he'd drink rotgut whatever, but he loved fine tequila. Mary Jo looked ravishing in a silky red and black Asian evening outfit. He stepped into her condo and immediately locked his lips on hers. She felt him grow.

"Easy Tiger, let's have some fine tequila first."

They walked into her mammoth great room overlooking Atlanta. She opened the package that included the tequila and two shot glasses. Sparkling crystal with a golden sheen. She connected to their encrypted link and clicked it. Raoul was beaming. An identical bottle of tequila and a golden shot glass were sitting on his desk in Sinaloa.

Mary Jo picked one up and said, "These shot glasses are spectacular."

Watching and listening online, Raoul said, "I'll send you a dozen more. Wait until you taste the tequila. It's divine. Go ahead and open your bottle. Pour, and we'll drink together."

Michael opened the bottle and poured their shots. Raoul toasted, "My friends, I am thankful for you helping me make millions of dollars that I hope will become trillions. I toast to our future success."

Raoul threw back his shot.

Mary Jo and Michael smiled and did the same.

TOM RANSEEN

Epilogue

Two weeks later

The headlines had hardly died down about the strange deaths of House Representative Mary Jo Cogburn, who many had predicted might run for President, and Howard Hughs-like mega financer Michael Abbott. Republican nutcases immediately blamed Democrats for another ridiculous deep-state conspiracy. There was no reaction from the very secretive financial network that Abbott controlled.

The two were found dead in Cogburn's Buckhead penthouse condo. After two weeks of investigation, Fulton County Medical Examiner Jill Treece determined the cause of death for both was poison from a rare golden frog species found only in the jungles of Columbia. Asked by reporters if it could have been a joint suicide or a murder by a third party, she said, "Either is possible. But I'm not sure we'll ever know."

****

When Suzanne Delacroix arrived back in Atlanta, she literally kissed the tarmac at Hartsfield. Still, she knew she'd have some serious "splaining" to do about her extended, incommunicado "vacation" in Spain, mainly to her twin daughters. What she related to them was private, and she hoped it always would be. She fessed up to them on Zoom.

"Goddammit, mom. How could you let the asshole who killed Dad get away? And you know what he did with us. He is the Devil!" In unison, Saville and Sarah screamed at her.

She tried to explain it rationally, but the twins weren't buying any of it. She could only hope that someday they would – when they realized they could both be dead – along with many others if she hadn't done what she did.

Suzanne had little doubt that what she had told them would haunt her for the rest of her life. But sitting in Kip's study, he appeared again as an apparition standing in front of his desk. "My love, you made tough decisions, but believe me, you saved the twins, yourself, and more people than you could ever imagine." His apparition smiled, "Give yourself a freak'n break." And he was gone.

******

Seaside, Florida had been her favorite place since she was a teenager. Now, she was lost with no clue where to go. She still owned a small beach house at Seaside that she'd often rented out the last few years. Thank goodness, it was empty. She packed a few things. Her dog, Lilly, her only true comfort, rode shotgun.

When she arrived and parked at her place, she and Lilly ran toward the surf that always gave her joy and some peace. The sunset was beyond spectacular in wavy hues of blue and orange. God painting the sky with his best stuff. She sat on her screen porch after frolicking in the surf with Lilly. She stared at her phone for a while. She made the call.

Lazlo Kianian answered on the first ring.

Sobbing, she said, "Laz, Will you come down to Seaside and take care of me?"

"Yes, mam, I'm on my way."

The End

Author bio

Tom Ranseen is a longtime Nashville, TN business guy who now writes crime thrillers. His *Game of Twins* series includes *Game of Twins, Game of Twins – Kidnapped, Golden Frog Poison – Game of Twins,* and *Game of Twins – The Secret Agent* – and he's working on the 5th in his series. He loves that his two grown kids live in the Nashville area, and he spends a lot of time with his Airedale Terrier, Keri. As a Duke graduate, he's a fanatic college basketball fan.

The books are all available online at your favorite online bookseller as eBooks and paperbacks. The "anchor" book, Game of Twins is also available as an audiobook. Go to www.gameoftwins.com for more information.

www.ingramcontent.com/pod-product-compliance
Lightning Source LLC
Chambersburg PA
CBHW072150070526
44585CB00015B/1077